THE R

TURKISH
PHRASEBOOK

Compiled by
LEXUS

www.roughguides.com

Credits

Turkish Phrasebook

Compiled by Lexus
with Memduha Tee
Lexus series editor: Sally Davies
Layout: Ankur Guha and Anita Singh
Picture research: Scott Stickland

Rough Guides Reference

Director: Andrew Lockett
Editors: Kate Berens, Tom Cabot,
Tracy Hopkins, Matthew Milton,
Joe Staines

Publishing information

First edition published in 1996.
This updated edition published October 2011 by
Rough Guides Ltd, 80 Strand, London, WC2R 0RL
Email: mail@roughguides.com

Distributed by the Penguin Group:
Penguin Books Ltd, 80 Strand, London, WC2R 0RL
Penguin Group (USA), 375 Hudson Street, NY 10014, USA
Penguin Group (Australia), 250 Camberwell Road, Camberwell, Victoria 3124,
Australia
Penguin Group (New Zealand), Cnr Rosedale and Airborne Roads, Albany,
Auckland, New Zealand

Rough Guides is represented in Canada by Tourmaline Editions Inc., 662 King
Street West, Suite 304, Toronto, Ontario, M5V 1M7

Printed in Singapore by Toppan Security Printing Pte. Ltd.
The publishers and author have done their best to ensure the accuracy and
currency of all information in *The Rough Guide Turkish Phrasebook*; however,
they can accept no responsibility for any loss or inconvenience sustained by
any reader as a result of its information or advice.

A catalogue record for this book is available from the British Library.

978-1-84836-740-1

1 3 5 7 9 8 6 4 2

CONTENTS

How to use this book

The Rough Guide Turkish Phrasebook is a highly practical introduction to the contemporary language. It gets straight to the point in every situation you might encounter: in bars and shops, on trains and buses, in hotels and banks, on holiday or on business. Laid out in clear A–Z style with easy-to-find, colour-coded sections, it uses key words to take you directly to the phrase you need – so if you want some help booking a room, just look up "room" in the dictionary section.

The phrasebook starts off with **Basics**, where we list some essential phrases, including words for numbers, dates and telling the time, and give guidance on pronunciation, along with a short section on the different regional accents you might come across. Then, to get you started in two-way communication, the Scenarios section offers dialogues in key situations such as renting a car, asking directions or booking a taxi, and includes words and phrases for when something goes wrong, from getting a flat tyre or asking to move apartments to more serious emergencies. You can listen to these and download them for free from **www.roughguides.com/phrasebooks** for use on your computer, MP3 player or smartphone.

Forming the main part of the guide is a double dictionary, first English–Turkish, which gives you the essential words you'll need plus easy-to-use phonetic transliterations wherever pronunciation might be a problem. Then, in the Turkish–English dictionary, we've given not just the phrases you'll be likely to hear (starting with a selection of slang and colloquialisms) but also many of the signs, labels and

instructions you'll come across in print or in public places. Scattered throughout the sections are travel tips direct from the authors of the Rough Guides guidebook series.

Finally, there's an extensive **Menu reader**. Consisting of separate food and drink sections, each starting with a list of essential terms, it's indispensable whether you're eating out, stopping for a quick drink or looking around a local food market.

İyi yolculuklar!
Have a good trip!

BASICS

Pronunciation

In this phrasebook, the Turkish has been written in a system of imitated pronunciation so that it can be read as though it were English, bearing in mind the notes on pronunciation given below:

a	as in far
ay	as in may
e/eh	as in get
ew	as in few
g	always hard as in goat
H	a harsh 'ch' as in the Scottish way of pronouncing loch
ī	'i' as in might
J	's' as in measure
o	as in hot
oh	'o' as in open
s	always 's' as in dress (never 'z')
uh	'u' as in but
y	as in yes

Letters given in bold type indicate the part of the word to be stressed (although the stress is not heavy). In most cases, the stress is on the end of a word.

As i and u are always pronounced 'ee' and 'oo' in Turkish, pronunciation has not been given for words containing these letters unless they present other problems for the learner.

Turkish pronunciation

a	as in far
â	as in Latin
ay	'i' as in might
c	'j' as in jelly
ç	'ch' as in chat
e	as in 'get'

ey	'ay' as in m**ay**
g	always hard as in '**g**oat'
ğ	generally silent, but lengthens the preceding vowel
h	sometimes pronounced 'h' as in **h**en; occasionally pronounced 'ch' as in the Scottish pronunciation of lo**ch**
ı	'u' as in b**u**t
i	ee' as in 'n**ee**d'
j	s' as in 'mea**s**ure'
o	as in 'h**o**t'; sometimes 'o' as in **o**pen (usually when followed by ğ)
ö	'ur' as in b**ur**n (like German 'ö')
öy	'uh-i' run together quickly as one sound
s	's' as in dre**s**s (never 'z')
ş	'sh' as in **sh**ape
u	'u' as in p**u**ll, transcribed as 'oo' in the pronunciation
ü	'ew' as in f**ew** (like French 'u' and German 'ü')

When e occurs at the end of a Turkish word, it is always pronounced, for example bile (**already**) is pronounced beel**eh**.

Abbreviations

adj	adjective
fam	familiar
pl	plural
pol	polite
sing	singular

The Turkish alphabet

The Turkish-English section and Menu Reader are in Turkish alphabetical order which is as follows:

a, b, c, ç, d, e, f, g, ğ, h, ı, i, j, k, l, m, n, o, ö, p, r, s, ş, t, u, ü, v, y, z

Basic phrases

yes evet

no hayır hī-**uhr**

OK tamam

please lütfen lew**tf**en

thank you teşekkür ederim teshekk**ewr**

thanks teşekkürler teshekk**ewr**ler

don't mention it bir şey değil shay deh-**eel**

yes, please (evet) lütfen lew**tf**en

no thank you hayır, teşekkür ederim hī-**uhr** teshekk**ewr**

hello merhaba

good morning günaydın gewnī**duh**n

good evening iyi akşamlar akshamlar

good night iyi geceler gejeler

goodbye (general use) hoşça kalın hosh-cha kal**uh**n

(said by person leaving) Allahaısmarladık alaha-uhsmarladuhk

(said to person leaving) güle güle gewleh

hi! merhaba!

see you! görüşürüz! gurewshewrewz

see you later görüşmek üzere gurewshmek ewzereh

how are you?/how do you do? nasılsınız? nasuhl-suhn**uh**z

I'm fine, thanks iyiyim, teşekkür ederim teshekk**ewr**

nice to meet you memnun oldum

excuse me (to get past) pardon

(to get attention) affed**e**rsiniz

(to say sorry) özür dilerim urz**ewr**

(I'm) sorry özür dilerim urz**ewr**

sorry?/pardon (me)? (didn't understand/hear) ef**e**ndim?

what? ne? neh

what did you say? ne dediniz?

I see/I understand anlıyorum anl**uh**-yoroom

I don't understand anlamıyorum anlamuh-yoroom

do you speak English? İngilizce biliyor musunuz? eengeele**e**zjeh

I don't speak Turkish Türkçe bilmiyorum tewrkcheh

could you speak more slowly? lütfen daha yavaş konuşur musunuz? lew**tf**en – yavash konooshoor

could you repeat that? tekrarlar mısınız? muhsuhn**uh**z

please write it down lütfen yazar mısınız? lew**tf**en – muhsuhn**uh**z

I'd like... ...istiyorum

can I have...? bana-...-verebilir misiniz?

how much is it? kaça? kacha

(at) what time? kaçta? kachta

cheers! (toast) şerefe! sheref**eh**

where is/are the...? ...nerede?
ne**r**ede**h**

Dates

The formation of dates is similar to English, except that, both in speech and writing, only cardinal numbers are used (e.g. 1 November, not **1st November**) and years are also referred to by simple cardinal numbers (e.g. the year 1996 is referred to not as '**nineteen ninety-six**' but 'one thousand nine hundred and ninety-six'):

1 January 1 Ocak (Bir Ocak)
beer oj**a**k

10 April 1996 10 Nisan 1996
(On Nisan bin dokuz yüz doksan altı) on neesan been dok**oo**z yewz doks**a**n alt**uh**

Friday, 1 September 1 Eylül, Cuma (Bir Eylül, Cuma) beer aylew**l** joom**a**

Days

Sunday paz**a**r

Monday paz**a**rtesi

Tuesday salı sal**uh**

Wednesday çarşamba
charsham**ba**

Thursday perşembe pershemb**eh**

Friday cuma joom**a**

Saturday cumartesi joom**a**rtesee

Months

January ocak oj**a**k

February şubat shoob**a**t

March mart

April nis**a**n

May mayıs mī-**uhs**

June hazir**a**n

July temm**u**z

August ağustos a-oost**o**s

September eylül aylew**l**

October ek**i**m

November kasım kas**uh**m

December aralık aral**uh**k

Note: capital letters are used for days and months only when writing a specific date.

Time

what time is it? saat kaç? sa-**a**t kach

(it's) one o'clock saat bir

(it's) two o'clock saat iki

(it's) ten o'clock saat on

five past one biri beş geçiyor besh gechee-y**o**r

ten past two ikiyi on geçiyor

quarter past one biri çeyrek geçiyor chayr**e**k

quarter past two ikiyi çeyrek geçiyor

half past one bir buçuk booch**oo**k

half past ten on buçuk

twenty to ten ona yirmi var

quarter to one bire çeyrek var beereh chayrek

quarter to ten ona çeyrek var

at quarter to ten ona çeyrek kala

at quarter past one biri çeyrek geçe gecheh

at eight o'clock (saat) sekizde sa-at sekeezdeh

at half past four (saat) dört buçukta durt boochookta

2 a.m. gece iki gejeh

2 p.m. öğledensonra iki ur-ledensonra

6 a.m. sabah altı sabaH altuh

6 p.m. akşam altı aksham

10 a.m. sabah on sabaH

10 p.m. gece on gejeh

18.00 on sekiz

14.30 on dört otuz durt

noon öğle urleh

at noon öğleyin urlayeen

midnight gece yarısı gejeh yaruhsuh

hour saat sa-at

minute dakika

two minutes iki dakika

second saniye sanee-yeh

quarter of an hour çeyrek saat chayrek sa-at

half an hour yarım saat yaruhm

three quarters of an hour kırk beş dakika kuhrk besh, üç çeyrek saat ewch chayrek sa-at

Numbers

0 sıfır suhfuhr

1 bir

2 iki

3 üç ewch

4 dört durt

5 beş besh

6 altı altuh

7 yedi

8 sekiz

9 dokuz

10 on

11 on bir

12 on iki

13 on üç ewch

14 on dört durt

15 on beş besh

16 on altı altuh

17 on yedi

18 on sekiz

19 on dokuz

20 yirmi

21 yirmi bir

22 yirmi iki

30 otuz

31 otuz bir

32 otuz iki

33 otuz üç ewch

40 kırk kuhrk

50 elli

60 altmış altmuhsh

70 yetmiş yetmeesh

80 seksen

90 doksan

100 yüz yewz
101 yüz bir
102 yüz iki
200 iki yüz
300 üç yüz ewch
500 beş yüz besh
1,000 bin
2,000 iki bin
3,000 üç bin ewch
5,000 beş bin besh
10,000 on bin
1,000,000 bir milyon
1,000,000,000 bir milyar

Ordinals

1st birinci beereenjee
2nd ikinci eekeenjee
3rd üçüncü ewchewnjew
4th dördüncü durdewnjew
5th beşinci besheenjee
6th altıncı altuhnjuh
7th yedinci yedeenjee
8th sekizinci sekeezeenjee
9th dokuzuncu dokoozoonjoo
10th onuncu onoonjoo

Regional accents

Istanbul Turkish (İstanbul Türkçesi) is regarded as the standard form of modern Turkish and is the predominant form used in the

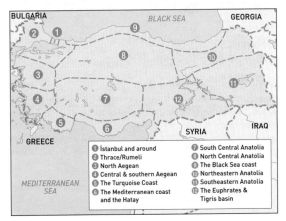

BULGARIA
BLACK SEA
GEORGIA

SYRIA
IRAQ

GREECE

MEDITERRANEAN
SEA

❶ İstanbul and around
❷ Thrace/Rumeli
❸ North Aegean
❹ Central & southern Aegean
❺ The Turquoise Coast
❻ The Mediterranean coast and the Hatay
❼ South Central Anatolia
❽ North Central Anatolia
❾ The Black Sea coast
❿ Northeastern Anatolia
⓫ Southeastern Anatolia
⓬ The Euphrates & Tigris basin

mass media, signage and in formal correspondence. It is always comprehensible to locals regardless of the region they live in.

With the exception of the Kurdish community in the southeast of the country, Turkey does not have any very large minority communities. Although minorities preserve their respective languages

			WESTERN DIALECTS	
		Istanbul Turkish	Thrace / Rumeli Edirne Tekirdağ Kırklareli	Aegean İzmir Aydın Manisa
k becomes g	koyun	ko-yoon	go-yoon	ko-yoon
p becomes b	piliç	peeleech	peeleech	peeleech
t becomes d	taş	tash	tash	tash
k becomes h or is omitted	akşam	aksham	a-sham	aksham
m becomes n	şimdi	sheemdee	sheemdee	sheemdee
ö becomes ü (ew)	börek	bur-rek	bewrek	bur-rek
ü becomes ö (ur) or u	hükümet	hewkewmet	(h)ewkewmet	hewkewmet
i becomes e	şehir	sheh-heer	sheh-heer	sheh-heer
a becomes e	şeftali	sheftalee	sheftalee	sheftalee
e becomes a	elektrik	elektreek	al-antreek	elektreek
e becomes a as in 'hat'	elma	elma	elma	elma
o becomes u or ı (uh)	doctor	doktor	doktor	doktor

(Kurdish, Arabic, Bosnian, Armenian, Lazuri etc) almost all locals can speak Turkish as well. So you will not have problems communicating using the pronunciation given in this book.

There are also local variations in pronunciation between the regions, as the following chart shows.

		EASTERN DIALECTS		
Aegean Hinterland Denizli Muğla Kütahya	**Black Sea** Samsun Trabzon Rize	**Central Anatolia** Ankara Kayseri Konya Niğde	**Southern Anatolia** Adana Şanlı Urfa Gazi Antep	**Eastern Anatolia** Erzurum Kars Van Diyarbakır
go-yoon	ko-yoon	go-yoon	go-yoon	go-yoon
beeleech	peeleech	beeleech	peeleech	beeleech
dash	taj	dash	dash	dash
a-sham	a-sham	a<H>sham	a<H>sham	a-sham
sheenjee	sheenjeek	sheendee	sheemdik	sheendee
bur-rek	bur-rek	bur-rek	bur-reh	bur-reh
hur-kewmet	hoogoomet	hurkurmet	hurkewmat	hurkewmat
sheh-er	sheh-her	sheh-her	sheh-her	shuh-eer
shefdalee	shefdalee	sheftelee	sheftelee	sheftelee
alak-treek	elet-treek	alet-treek	elet-treek	eleh-treeh
alma	ahlma	alma	ahlma	alma
toktoor	tohtor	tohtoor	tohtuhr	dohtoor

SCENARIOS

Download these scenarios as MP3s from
www.roughguides.com/phrasebooks

1. Accommodation

▶ Is there an inexpensive hotel you can recommend?
Pahalı olmayan bir otel önerebilir misiniz?
pahaluh olmī-an beer otel urnerebeeleer meeseeneez

▶▶ I'm sorry, they all seem to be fully booked.
Üzgünüm, hepsi dolu görünüyor.
ewzgewnewm hepsee doloo gurewnewyor

▶ Can you give me the name of a good middle-range hotel?
Bana orta sınıf iyi bir otel adı verebilir misiniz?
bana orta suhnuhf eeyee beer otel aduh verebeeleer meeseeneez

▶▶ Let me have a look; do you want to be in the centre?
Bir bakayım; merkezde mi olmak istersiniz?
beer bakī-uhm merkezdeh mee olmak eesterseeneez

▶ If possible.
Mümkünse.
mewmkewnseh

▶▶ Do you mind being a little way out of town?
Şehrin biraz dışında olmanızda bir mahzur var mı?
shehreen beeraz duhshuhnda olmanuhzda beer mahzoor var muh

▶ Not too far out.
Fazla dışında değil ama.
fazla duhshuhnda deh-eel ama

▶ Where is it on the map?
Haritada yeri neresi?
hareetada yeree neresee

▶ Can you write the name and address down?
İsim ve adresi yazar mısınız?
eeseem veh adresee yazar muhsuhnuhz

▶ I'm looking for a room in a private house.
Aile yanında bir oda arıyorum.
a-eeleh yanuhnda beer oda aruhyoroom

2. Banks

bank account	banka hesabı	banka hesab**uh**
to change money	para bozdurmak	para bozdurmak
cheque	çek	chek
to deposit	para yatırmak	para yatuhrmak
euro	avro	avro
pin number	şifre	sheefr**eh**
pound	sterlin	sterl**een**
to withdraw	para çekmek	para chekmek

▶ Can you change this into YTL?
Bunu Yeni Türk Lirası'na değiştirebilir misiniz?
boon**oo** yen**ee** tewrk leerasuhn**a** deh-eeshteerebeel**eer** meeseen**eez**

▶▶ How would you like the money?
Parayı nasıl istersiniz?
pari-**uh** nasuhl eesterseen**eez**

▶ Small notes. ▶ Big notes.
Küçük banknot. Büyük banknot.
kewch**ewk** bankn**ot** bewy**ewk** bankn**ot**

▶ Do you have information in English about opening an account?
Sizde hesap açılmasıyla ilgili İngilizce bilgi bulunur mu?
seezd**eh** hesap achuhlmasuhyl**a** eelgeel**ee** eengeel**eez**jeh beelg**ee** booloon**oor** moo

▶▶ Yes, what sort of account do you want?
Evet, nasıl bir hesap açtırmak istiyorsunuz?
evet nasuhl beer hesap achtuhrmak eesteeyorsoon**ooz**

▶ I'd like a current account.
Cari hesap açtırmak istiyorum.
jar**ee** hesap achtuhrmak eest**ee**yoroom

▶▶ Your passport, please.
Pasaportunuz lütfen.
pasaportoon**ooz** l**ew**tfen

▶ Can I use this card to draw some cash?
Bu kartla para çekebilir miyim?
boo kartla para chekebeel**eer** mee**yee**m

▶▶ You have to go to the cashier's desk.
Kasaya gitmeniz gerek.
kasi-**a** geetmen**eez** gerek

► I want to transfer this to my account at Akbank.
Bunu Akbank'daki hesabıma havale etmek istiyorum.
boonoo akbank dakee hesabuhma havaleh etmek eesteeyoroom

>> OK, but we'll have to charge you for the phonecall.
Tamam, ama telefon ücretini sizden alırız.
tamam ama telefon ewjreteenee seezden aluhruhz

3. Booking a room

shower	duş	doosh
telephone in the room	telefon odada	telefon odada
payphone in the lobby	umumi telefon	oomoomee telefon

► Do you have any rooms?
Boş odanız var mı?
bosh odanuhz var muh

▶▶ For how many people?
Kaç kişilik?
kach keesheel**eek**

▶ For one/for two.
Bir kişilik/iki kişilik.
beer keesheel**eek**/eekee keesheel**eek**

▶▶ Yes, we have rooms free.
Evet, boş odamız var.
evet bosh odam**uh**z var

▶ For how many nights?
Kaç gece için?
kach gej**eh** eech**ee**n

▶▶ Just for one night.
Yalnızca bir gece için.
yalnuhzj**a** beer gej**eh** eech**ee**n

▶ How much is it?
Ücreti nedir?
ewjret**ee** n**e**deer

▶▶ 90 YTL with bathroom and 70 YTL without bathroom.
Banyolu 90 Yeni Türk Lirası, banyosuz 70 Yeni Türk Lirası.
banyoloo doksan yen**ee** tewrk leeras**uh** banyosooz yetm**ee**sh yen**ee**
tewrk leeras**uh**

▶ Does that include breakfast?
Buna kahvaltı dahil mi?
boon**a** kaнvalt**uh** daнeel mee

▶ Can I see a room with bathroom?
Banyolu odayı görebilir miyim?
banyoloo odī-**uh** gurebeel**ee**r meey**ee**m

▶ OK, I'll take it.
Tamam, tutuyorum.
tam**a**m toot**oo**yoroom

▶ When do I have to check out?
Odayı ne zaman boşaltmam gerekiyor?
odī-**uh** neh zaman boshaltmam gerekeey**o**r

▶ Is there anywhere I can leave luggage?
Bavullarımı bırakabileceğim bir yer var mı?
bavoollaruhm**uh** buhrakabeelejeh-**ee**m beer yer var muh

4. Car hire

automatic	otomatik (vites)	otomateek (veetes)
full tank	tam depo	tam depo
manual	düz (vites)	dewz (veetes)
rented car	kiralık otomobil	keeraluhk otomobeel

▶ I'd like to rent a car.
Bir otomobil kiralamak istiyorum.
beer otomobeel keeralamak eesteeyoroom

> ▶▶ For how long?
> Ne kadar süre için?
> neh kadar sewreh eecheen

▶ Two days.
İki gün.
eekee gewn

▶ I'll take the...
...'yi alayım
...yee alī-uhm

▶ Is that with unlimited mileage?
Sınırsız kilometrede kullanım hakkı var mı?
suhnuhrsuhz keelometredeh koollanuhm hakkuh var muh

> ▶▶ It is.
> Evet.
> evet

> ▶▶ Can I see your driving licence, please?
> Ehliyetinizi görebilir miyim lütfen?
> ehleeyeteeneezee gurebeeleer meeyeem lewtfen

> ▶▶ And your passport.
> Ve pasaportunuzu.
> veh pasaportoonoozoo

▶ Is insurance included?
Sigorta dahil mi?
seegorta daHeel mee

> ▶▶ Yes, but you have to pay the first 100 YTL.
> Evet, ama ilk 100 Yeni Türk Lirasını sizin ödemeniz lazım.
> evet ama eelk yewz yenee tewrk leerasuhnuh seezeen urdemeneez lazuhm

> ▶▶ Can you leave a deposit of 100 YTL?
> 100 Yeni Türk Lirası depozit bırakabilir misiniz?
> yewz yenee tewrk leerasuh depozeet buhrakabeeleer meeseeneez

▶ And if this office is closed, where do I leave the keys?
Bu büro kapalıysa, anahtarları nereye bırakabilirim?
boo bewro kapaluhysa anaHtarlaruh nerayeh buhrakabeeleereem

▶▶ You drop them in that box.
Şu kutuya atarsınız.
shoo kootooya atarsuhnuhz

5. Car problems

brakes	fren	fren
to break down	bozulmak	bozoolmak
clutch	debriyaj	debree-yaJ
diesel	dizel	deezel
flat battery	boşalmış akü	boshalmuhsh akew
flat tyre	patlak lastik	patlak lasteek
petrol	benzin	benzeen

▶ Excuse me, where is the nearest petrol station?
Affedersiniz, en yakındaki benzinci nerede?
affederseeneez en yakuhndakee benzeenjee neredeh

▶▶ In the next town, about 5km away.
İlerideki kasabada, beş kilometre kadar mesafede.
eelereedekee kasabada besh keelometreh kadar mesafedeh

▶ The car has broken down.
Otomobil bozuldu.
otomobeel bozooldoo

▶▶ Can you tell me what happened?
Ne olduğunu anlatır mısınız?
neh oldoo-oonoo anlatuhr muhsuhnuhz

▶ I've got a flat tyre.
Lastik patladı.
lasteek patladuh

▶ I think the battery is flat.
Sanırım akü boşaldı.
sanuhruhm akew boshalduh

▶▶ Can you tell me exactly where you are?
Tam olarak nerede olduğunuzu tarif eder misiniz?
tam olarak neredeh oldoo-oonoozoo tareef eder meeseeneez

▶ I'm about 2km outside of Gebze on the D-100.
D-Yüz karayolunda, Gebze mevkiine yaklaşık iki kilometre
mesafedeyim.
de**h**-yewz kara-iolo**o**nd**a** g**e**b-zeh mevkee-een**eh** yaklash**uh**k eek**eh** keelometr**eh**
mesafeday**ee**m

▶▶ What type of car? What colour?
Arabanın modeli ne? Ne renk?
araban**uh**n model**ee** neh, neh renk

▶ Can you send a tow truck?
Çekici gönderebilir misiniz?
chekeej**ee** gurnderebeel**ee**r meeseen**ee**z

6. Children

baby	bebek	bebek
boy	oğlan	oh-lan
child	çocuk	choj**ook**
children	çocuklar	chojookl**ar**
cot	bebek karyolası	bebek karyolas**uh**
formula	bebek maması	bebek mamas**uh**
girl	kız	k**uh**z
highchair	mama sandalyesi	m**a**ma sandalyes**ee**
nappies (diapers)	bebek bezi	bebek bez**ee**

▶ We need a babysitter for tomorrow evening.
Yarın akşam için bir bakıcıya ihtiyacımız var.
y**a**ruhn aksh**a**m eech**ee**n beer bakuhjuhy**a** eeнteeyajuhm**uh**z var

▶▶ For what time?
Saat kaç için?
sa-**a**t kach eech**ee**n

▶ From 7.30 to 11.00.
Yedi buçuktan on bire kadar.
yed**ee** boochookt**a**n **o**nbereh kadar

▶▶ How many children? How old are they?
Kaç çocuk için? Kaç yaşındalar?
kach choj**ook** eech**ee**n, kach yashuhndalar

▶ Two children, aged four and eighteen months.
Dört yaşında ve on sekiz aylık iki çocuk için.
durt yashuhnd**a** veh **o**nsekeez il**uh**k eek**ee** choj**ook** eech**ee**n

▶ Where can I change the baby?
Bebeğin altını nerede değiştirebilirim?
bebeh-**een** altuhn**uh n**eredeh deh-**ees**hteerebeeleer**eem**

▶ Could you please warm this bottle for me?
Biberonu ılıtabilir misiniz lütfen?
beeberon**oo** uhluhtabeel**eer** meeseen**eez** l**ew**tfen

▶ Can you give us a child's portion?
Çocuk porsiyonu alabilir miyiz?
choj**ook** porseeyon**oo** alabeel**eer** meey**eez**

▶ We need two child seats.
İki çocuk koltuğu gerekiyor.
eek**ee** choj**ook** koltoo-**oo** gerekeey**or**

▶ Is there a discount for children?
Çocuklar için indirim yapıyor musunuz?
choj**ook**lar eech**een** eendeer**eem** yapuhy**or** moosoon**ooz**

7. Communications: Internet

▶ Is there somewhere I can check my emails?
E-postalarımı nerede kontrol edebilirim?
eh-postalaruhm**uh n**eredeh kontr**ol** edebeeleer**eem**

▶ Do you have Wi-Fi?
Wifi bağlantınız var mı?
wi-f**ī** ba-lantuhn**uh**z var muh

▶ Is there an Internet café around here?
Buralarda internet cafe var mı?
booralarda eentern**et** kaf**eh** var muh

▶▶ Yes, there's one in the shopping centre.
Evet, alışveriş merkezinde bir tane var.
evet aluhshver**ee**sh merkezeend**eh** beer tan**eh** var

@, at sign	at işareti	et eesharet**ee**
computer	bilgisayar	beelgeesi-**ar**
email	e-posta	**eh**-posta
Internet	internet	**een**ternet
keyboard	klavye	klav-y**eh**
mouse	fare	far**eh**

▶▶ Do you want fifteen minutes, thirty minutes or one hour?
On beş dakika mı, yarım saat mi, bir saat mi istersiniz?
onbesh dakeeka muh yaruhm sa-at mee beer sa-at mee eesterseeneez

▶ Thirty minutes please. Can you help me log on?
Yarım saat lütfen. Girmem için yardımcı olabilir misiniz?
yaruhm sa-at lewtfen, geermem eecheen yarduhmjuh olabeeleer meeseeneez

▶▶ OK, here's your password.
Tamam, bu şifreniz.
tamam boo sheefreneez

▶ Can you change this to an English keyboard?
Klavyeyi İngilizce'ye çevirebilir misiniz?
klav-yeh-yee eengeeleezjeh-yeh cheveerebeeleer meeseeneez

▶ I'll take another quarter of an hour.
On beş dakikalık süre daha alabilir miyim?
on besh dakeekaluhk sewreh daha alabeeleer meeyeem

▶ Is there a printer I can use?
Kullanabileceğim bir yazıcı var mı?
koollanabeelejeh-eem beer yazuhjuh var muh

8. Communications: phones

mobile phone (cell phone)	cep telefonu	jep telefonoo
payphone	ankesörlü telefon	ankehsurlew telefon
phone call	telefon	telefon
phone card	telefon kartı	telefonkartuh
phone charger	şarj aleti	sharj aletee
SIM card	SIM kart	seem kart

▶ Can I call abroad from here?
Yurtdışını arayabilir miyim?
yoortduhshuhnuh ari-abeeleer meeyeem

▶ How do I get an outside line?
Dışarıya nasıl hat alabilirim?
duhsharuhya nasuhl hat alabeeleereem

▶ What's the code to call the UK/US from here?
Buradan İngiltere'yi/Amerika'yı aramak için kod numarası kaç?
booradan eengeeltereh-yee/amereeka-yuh aramak eecheen kod noomarasuh kach

▶ Hello, can I speak to Mehmet?
Alo, Mehmet ile görüşebilir miyim?
alo mehmet eel**eh** gurewshebeel**eer** meey**eem**

> ▶▶ Yes, that's me speaking.
> **Buyrun, benim.**
> boo-ir**oon** ben**eem**

▶ Do you have a charger for this?
Bu telefonun şarj aleti var mı?
boo telefon**oon** shar**J** alet**ee** var muh

▶ Can I buy a SIM card for this phone?
Bu telefona bir SIM kart alabilir miyim?
boo telefon**a** beer seem kart alabeel**eer** meey**eem**

zero	sıfır	su**h**fuhr
one	bir	beer
two	iki	eek**ee**
three	üç	ewch
four	dört	durt
five	beş	besh
six	altı	alt**uh**
seven	yedi	yed**ee**
eight	sekiz	sek**eez**
nine	dokuz	dok**ooz**

9. Directions

straight ahead	dosdoğru ileride	dosdo-**roo** eelereed**eh**
past the...	...'i geçince	...**ee** gech**een**jeh
back	geride	gereed**eh**
just after	hemen sonra	hemen sonra
further	ileride	eelereed**eh**
opposite	karşı	karsh**uh**
in front of	önünde	urnewnd**eh**
on the right	sağda	sa-d**a**
turn off	sapın	sap**uhn**
street	sokak	sok**ak**
on the left	solda	sold**a**
next	bir sonraki	beer sonrak**ee**
over there	şurada	sh**oo**rada
near	yakın	yak**uhn**

▶ Hi, I'm looking for Bülten Sokak.
Selam, Bülten Sokak'ı arıyorum.
selam bewl**ten** sok**ak**'**uh** ar**uh**yoroom

> ▶▶ Sorry, never heard of it.
> **Üzgünüm, hiç işitmedim.**
> ewzg**ew**newm heech eesh**eet**medeem

▶ Hi, can you tell me where Bülten Sokak is?
Selam, Bülten Sokak nerede söyler misiniz?
selam bewl**ten** sok**ak** neredeh suh-iler meeseen**eez**

>> I'm a stranger here too.
Ben de buranın yabancısıyım.
ben deh **boo**ranuhn yabanjuhs**uh**yuhm

▶ Hi, Bülten Sokak, do you know where it is?
Selam, Bülten Sokak'ın nerede olduğunu biliyor musunuz?
selam bewlten sokak**uh**n neredeh oldoo-oon**oo** beeleey**or** moosoon**oo**z

>> Left at the second traffic lights.
İkinci ışıktan sonra solda.
eekeenj**ee** uhsh**uh**ktan s**o**nra solda

▶ Where?
Nerede?
n**e**redeh

▶ Which direction?
Ne yönde?
neh yurnd**eh**

>> Around the corner.
Köşeyi dönünce.
kurshay**ee** durn**ew**njeh.

>> Then it's the first street on the right.
Sonra sağdaki ilk sokak.
s**o**nra sa-dak**ee** eelk sokak

10. Emergencies

accident	kaza	kaz**a**
ambulance	ambülans	ambewlan**s**
consul	konsolos	konsol**o**s
embassy	elçilik	elcheele**ek**
fire brigade	itfaiye	eetfa-eey**eh**
police	polis	pole**e**s

▶ Help!
İmdat!
eemd**a**t

▶ Can you help me?
Bana yardım edebilir misiniz?
ban**a** yard**uh**m edebeel**ee**r meeseen**ee**z

▶ Please come with me! It's really very urgent.
Lütfen benimle gelin! Gerçekten çok acil.
lewtfen beneemleh geleen, gerchekten chok ajeel

▶ I've lost my keys.
Anahtarlarımı kaybettim.
anaHtarlaruhmuh kibetteem

▶ My car is not working.
Arabam çalışmıyor.
arabam chaluhshmuhyor

▶ My purse has been stolen.
Cüzdanım çalındı.
jewzdanuhm chaluhnduh

▶ I've been mugged.
Saldırıya uğradım.
salduhruhya oo-raduhm

▶▶ What's your name?
Adınız ne?
aduhnuhz neh

▶▶ I need to see your passport.
Pasaportunuzu görebilir miyim?
pasaportoonoozoo gurebeeleer meeyeem

▶ I'm sorry, all my papers have been stolen.
Maalesef, bütün kağıtlarım çalındı.
ma-alesef bewtewn ka-uhtlaruhm chaluhnduh

11. Friends

▶ Hi, how're you doing?
Selam, nasılsın?
selam nasuhlsuhn

▶▶ OK, and you?
İyidir, ya sen?
eeyeedeer ya sen

▶ Yeah, fine.
Ya evet, çok iyi.
ya evet chok eeyee

▶ Not bad.
Fena değil.
fena deh-eel

▶ Do you know Mark?
Mark'ı tanıyor musun?
markuh tanuhyor moosoon

▶ And this is Hannah.
Bu da Hannah.
boo da hannah

   ▶▶ Yeah, we know each other.
   Ya evet, tanışıyoruz.
   ya evet tanuhshuhyorooz

▶ Where do you know each other from?
Nereden tanışıyorsunuz?
nereden tanuhshuhyor-soonooz

   ▶▶ We met at Emre's place.
   Emre'de tanışmıştık.
   emredeh tanuhsh-muhshtuhk

▶ That was some party, eh?
Ne partiydi di mi?
neh parteeydee dee mee

   ▶▶ The best.
   Eşsiz.
   eshseez

▶ Are you guys coming for a beer?
Bira içmeye gelen var mı?
beera eechmayeh gelen var muh

▶▶ Cool, let's go.
Cool, hadi gidelim.
kool hadee geedeleem

▶▶ No, I'm meeting Aylin.
Olmaz, ben Aylin'le buluşacağım.
olmaz ben îleenleh boolooshaja-uhm

▶ See you at Emre's place tonight.
Akşama Emre'de görüşürüz.
akshama emredeh gurewshewrewz

▶▶ See you.
Görüşmek üzere.
gurewshmek ewzereh

12. Health

antibiotics	antibiyotik	anteebeeyoteek
antiseptic ointment	antiseptik merhem	anteesepteek merhem
cystitis	sistit	seesteet
dentist	dişçi	deeshchee
diarrhoea	ishal	ees-hal
doctor	doktor	doktor
hospital	hastane	hastaneh
ill	hasta	hasta
medicine	ilaç	eelach
painkillers	ağrı kesiciler	a-ruh keseejeeler
pharmacy	eczane	ejzaneh
to prescribe	ilaç yazmak	eelach yazmak
thrush	pamukçuk	pamookchook

▶ I'm not feeling very well.
Kendimi pek iyi hissetmiyorum.
kendeemee pek eeyee heessetmeeyoroom

▶ Can you get a doctor?
Doktor çağırabilir misiniz?
doktor cha-uhrabeeleer meeseeneez

▶ Where does it hurt?
Nereniz ağrıyor?
nereneez a-ruhyor

▶▶ It hurts here.
Buram ağrıyor.
booram a-ruhyor

▶ Is the pain constant?
Ağrı devamlı mı?
a-ruh devamluh muh

▶▶ It's not a constant pain.
Devamlı bir ağrı değil.
devamluh beer a-ruh deh-eel

▶ Can I make an appointment?
Randevu alabilir miyim?
randevoo alabeeleer meeyeem

▶ Can you give me something for...?
...için bir şey verebilir misiniz?
...eecheen beer shay verebeeleer meeseeneez

▶ Yes, I have insurance.
Evet, sigortam var.
evet seegortam var

13. Hotels

maid	kat görevlisi	kat gurevleesee
manager	müdür	mewdewr
room service	oda servisi	oda serveesee

▶ Hello, we've booked a double room in the name of Cameron.
Merhaba, Cameron adına iki kişilik bir oda ayırtmıştık.
merhaba kameron aduhna eekee keesheeleek beer oda ī-uhrtmuhshtuhk

▶▶ That was for four nights, wasn't it?
Dört gecelikti değil mi?
durt gejeleektee deh-eel mee

▶ Yes, we're leaving on Saturday.
Evet, cumartesi günü ayrılıyoruz.
evet joomartesee gewnew īruhluhyorooz

▶▶ Can I see your passport please?
Pasaportunuzu alabilir miyim?
pasaportoonoozoo alabeeleer meeyeem

▶▶ There you are, room 321 on the third floor.
Buyrun, üçüncü katta üç yüz yirmi bir numaralı oda.
boo-iroon ewchewnjew katta ewch yewz yeermee beer noomaraluh oda

▶ I can't get this keycard to work.
Kart anahtar çalışmıyor.
kart anaHtar chaluhshmuhyor

▶▶ Sorry, I need to reactivate it.
Özür dilerim, yeniden etkinleştirmem gerekiyor.
urzewr deelereem yeneeden etkeenleshteermem gerekeeyor

▶ What time is breakfast?
Kahvaltı saat kaçta?
kaHvaltuh sa-at kachta

▶ There aren't any towels in my room.
Odamda havlu yok.
odamda havloo yok

▶ My flight isn't until this evening, can I keep the room a bit longer?
Uçağım akşama. Odayı biraz daha geç boşaltabilir miyim?
oocha-uhm akshama, odî-yuh beeraz daha gech boshaltabeeleer meeyeem

▶ Can I settle up? Is this card ok?
Hesabı ödeyebilir miyim? Bu kart geçerli mi?
hesabuh urdayebeeleer meeyeem, boo kart gecherlee mee

14. Language difficulties

a few words	birkaç kelime	beerkach keleemeh
interpreter	tercüman	terjewman
to translate	tercüme etmek	terjewmeh etmek

▶▶ Your credit card has been refused.
Kredi kartınız kabul edilmedi.
kredee kartuhnuhz kabool edeelmedee

▶ What, I don't understand; do you speak English?
Nasıl, anlamadım; İngilizce biliyor musunuz?
nasuhl anlamaduhm eengeeleezjeh beeleeyor moosoonooz

▶▶ This isn't valid.
Bu geçerli değil.
boo gecherlee deh-eel

▶ Could you say that again?
Tekrar söyler misiniz?
tekrar suh-iler meeseeneez

▶ Slowly.
Yavaş yavaş.
yavash yavash

▶ I understand very little Turkish.
Çok az Türkçe anlıyorum.
chok az tewrkcheh anluhyoroom

▶ I speak Turkish very badly.
Türkçem çok kötü.
tewrkchem chok kurtew

▶▶ You can't use this card to pay.
Bu kartla ödeme yapamazsınız.
boo kartla urdemeh yapamazsuhnuhz

▶▶ Do you understand?
Anlıyor musunuz?
anluhyor moosoonooz

▶ Sorry, no.
Üzgünüm ama hayır.
ewzgewnewm ama hī-uhr

▶ Is there someone who speaks English?
İngilizce bilen birisi var mı burada?
eengeeleezjeh beelen beereesee var muh boorada

▶ Oh, now I understand.
Ha, şimdi anladım.
ha sheemdee anladuhm

▶ Is that ok now?
Şimdi tamam mı?
sheemdee tamam muh

15. Meeting people

▶ Hello.
Merhaba.
merhaba

▶▶ Hello, my name's Aylin.
Merhaba, ben Aylin.
merhaba ben īleen

▶ Graham, from England, Thirsk.
Ben, İngiltere Thirsk'den Graham.
ben eengeeltereh thirskden graham

▶▶ Don't know that, where is it?
Hiç duymadım, nerede o?
heech dooymaduhm neredeh o

▶ Not far from York, in the North; and you?
Kuzeyde, York'a yakın; ya siz?
koozaydeh yorka yakuhn ya seez

▶▶ I'm from Ankara; here by yourself?
Ben Ankara'lıyım; burada yalnız mısınız?
ben ankaraluhyuhm boorada yalnuhz muhsuhnuhz

▶ No, I'm with my wife and two kids.
Hayır, eşim ve iki çocuğumla beraberim.
hī-uhr esheem veh eekee chojoo-oomla berabereem

▶ What do you do?
Ne iş yapıyorsunuz?
neh eesh yapuhyorsoonooz

▶▶ I'm in computers.
Bilgisayar işindeyim.
beelgeesi-ar eesheendayeem

▶ Me too.
Ben de.
ben deh

▶ Here's my wife now.
İşte eşim de geldi.
eeshteh esheem deh geldee

▶▶ Nice to meet you.
Tanıştığımıza memnun oldum.
tanuhshtuh-uhmuhza memnoon oldoom

16. Nightlife

▶ What's a good club for…?
… için nereyi önerirsiniz?
… eecheen neray-ee urnereerseeneez

dancing	dans	
electro	elektro	
folk	halk müziği	halkmewzee-ee
hip-hop	hip-hop	heep-hop
jazz	caz	jaz
rock	rock	

▶▶ There's going to be a great gig at Parkorman tomorrow night.

Parkormanda mekanında yarın akşam harika bir program var.
parkormanda mekanuhnda yaruhn aksham hareeka beer program var

▶ Where can I hear some local music?
Nerede yerli müzik dinleyebilirim?
neredeh yerlee mewzeek deenlay-ebeeleereem

▶ Can you write down the names of the best bars around here?
Buralardaki en iyi barların adlarını yazar mısınız?
booralardakee en eeyee barlaruhn adlaruhnuh yazar muhsuhnuhz

▶▶ That depends what you're looking for.
Ne tür bir şey istediğinize bağlı.
neh tewr beer shay eestedee-eeneezeh ba-luh

▶ The place where the locals go.
Buralıların gittiği türden bir yer.
booraluhlaruhn geettee-ee tewrden beer yer

▶ A place for a quiet drink.
Bir içki içecek sakin bir yer.
beer eechkee eechejek sakeen beer yer

▶▶ The casino across the bay is very good.
Körfezin karşısındaki casino çok iyidir.
kurfezeen karshuhsuhndakee kaseeno chok eeyeedeer

▶ I suppose they have a dress code.
Herhalde kıyafet zorunluluğu vardır.
herhaldeh kuh-yafet zoroonlooloo-oo varduhr

▶▶ You can wear what you like.
İstediğinizi giyebilirsiniz.
eestedee-eeneezee gee-yebeeleerseeneez

▶ What time does it close?
Kaçta kapanıyor?
kachta kapanuhyor

17. Post offices

▶ What time does the post office close?
Postane saat kaçta kapanıyor?
postaneh sa-at kachta kapanuhyor

airmail	uçak postası	oochak postasuh
post card	kartpostal	kartpostal
post office	postane	postaneh
stamp	pul	pool

▶▶ Five o'clock weekdays.
Hafta içi saat beşte.
hafta eechee sa-at beshteh

▶ Is the post office open on Saturdays?
Postane cumartesi günleri açık mı?
postaneh joomartesee gewnleree achuhk muh

▶▶ Until midday.
Öğlene kadar.
ur-leneh kadar

▶ I'd like to send this registered to England.
Bunu taahhütlü olarak İngiltere'ye göndermek istiyorum.
boonoo ta-a-hewtlew olarak eengeeltereyeh gurndermek eesteeyoroom

▶▶ Certainly, that will cost 10 YTL.
Tabii, 10 Yeni Türk Lirası ediyor.
tabee-ee on yenee tewrk leerasuh edeeyor

▶ And also two stamps for England, please.
Bir de İngiltere için iki adet pul, lütfen.
beer deh eengeeltereh eecheen eekee adet pool lewtfen

MEKTUP	letters
PAKET	parcels
YURTDIŞI	international
YURTİÇİ	domestic

▶ Do you have some airmail stickers?
Yapışkan uçak postası etiketiniz var mı?
yapuhshkan oochak postasuh eteeketeeneez var muh

▶ Do you have any mail for me?
Bana posta var mı?
bana posta var muh

18. Restaurants

▶ Can we have a non-smoking table?
Sigara içilmeyen bölümde bir masa verebilir misiniz?
seegara eecheelmayen burlewmdeh beer masa verebeeleer meeseeneez

bill	hesap	hesap
menu	yemek listesi	yemek leestesee
table	masa	masa

▶ There are two of us.
İki kişiyiz.
eekee keesheeyeez

▶ There are four of us.
Dört kişiyiz.
durt keesheeyeez

▶ What's this?
Bu nedir?
boo nedeer

▶▶ It's a type of fish.
Bir tür balık.
beer tewr baluhk

▶▶ It's a local speciality.
Yörenin özel yemeği.
yureneen urzel yemeh-ee

▶▶ Come inside and I'll show you.
Buyrun girin de size göstereyim.
boo-iroon geereen deh seezeh gursterayeem

▶ We would like two of these, one of these, and one of those.
Bunlardan iki, bunlardan bir, şunlardan da bir tane istiyoruz.
boonlardan eekee boonlardan beer shoonlardan da beer taneh eesteeyorooz

▶▶ And to drink?
Ya içmek için?
ya eechmek eecheen

▶ Red wine.
Kırmızı şarap.
kuhrmuhzuh sharap

▶ White wine.
Beyaz şarap.
bayaz sharap

▶ A beer and two orange juices.
Bir bira ve iki portakal suyu.
beer beera veh eekee portakal sooyoo

▶ Some more bread please.
Biraz daha ekmek lütfen.
beeraz daha ekmek lewtfen

▶▶ How was your meal?
Yemeğiniz nasıldı?
yemeh-eeneez nasuhlduh

▶ Excellent, very nice!
Mükemmel, çok güzeldi.
mewkemmel chok gewzeldee

▶▶ Anything else?
Başka bir şey?
bashka beer shay

▶ Just the bill thanks.
Sadece hesap, teşekkürler.
sadejeh hesap teshekkewrler

19. Self-catering accommodation

air-conditioning	klima	kleema
apartment	daire	da-eereh
cooker	ocak	ojak
fridge	buzdolabı	boozdolabuh
heating	ısıtma	uhsuhtma
hot water	sıcak su	suhjak soo
lightbulb	ampul	ampool
toilet	tuvalet	toovalet

▶ The toilet's broken, can you get someone to fix it?
Tuvalet bozuk, onarmak için birini gönderebilir misiniz?
toovalet bozook onarmak eecheen beereenee gurnderebeeleer meeseeneez

▶ There's no hot water.
Sıcak su yok.
suhjak soo yok

▶ Can you show me how the air-conditioning works?
Klimanın nasıl çalıştığını gösterebilir misiniz?
kleemanuhn nasuhl chaluhshtuh-uhnuh gursterebeeleer meeseeneez

▶▶ What apartment are you in?
Hangi dairedesiniz?
hangee da-eeredeseeneez

▶ We're in number five.
Beş numaradayız.
besh noomaradî-uhz

▶ Can you move us to a quieter apartment?
Bizi daha sessiz bir daireye geçirebilir misiniz?
beezee daha sesseez beer da-eerayeh gecheerebeeleer meeseeneez

▶ Is there a supermarket nearby?
Yakında süpermarket var mı?
yakuhnda sewpermarket var muh

▶▶ Have you enjoyed your stay?
Ziyaretinizden memnun kaldınız mı?
zeeyareteeneezden memnoon kalduhnuhz muh

▶ Brilliant holiday, thanks!
Harika bir tatildi, teşekkürler!
hareeka beer tateeldee teshekkewrler

20. Shopping

▶▶ Can I help you?
Yardımcı olabilir miyim?
yarduhmjuh olabeeleer meeyeem

▶ Can I just have a look around?
Şöyle bir bakabilir miyim?
shuh-ileh beer bakabeeleer meeyeem

▶ Yes, I'm looking for…
Evet, …arıyorum.
evet …aruhyoroom

▶ How much is this?
Bu kaça?
boo kacha

▶▶ Thirty-two YTL.
Otuziki Yeni Türk Lirası.
otoozeekee yenee tewrk leerasuh

▶ OK, I think I'll have to leave it; it's a little too expensive for me.
Peki, kalsın o zaman; benim için biraz fazla pahalı.
pekee kalsuhn o zaman beneem eecheen beeraz fazla pahaluh

▶▶ How about this?
Ya bu nasıl?
ya boo nasuhl

▶ Can I pay by credit card?
Kredi kartıyla ödeyebilir miyim?
kredee kartuhyla urdayebeeleer meeyeem

AÇIK	open
DEĞİŞTİRMEK	exchange
İNDİRİMLİ SATIŞ	sale
KAPALI	closed

▶ It's too big.
Fazla büyük.
fazla bewyewk

▶ It's too small.
Fazla küçük.
fazla kewchewk

▶ It's for my son – he's about this high.
Oğlum için – aşağı yukarı şu boyda.
o-loom eecheen asha-uh yookaruh shoo boyda

▶▶ Will there be anything else?
Başka bir şey ister miydiniz?
bashka beer shay eester meeydeeneez

▶ That's all thanks.
A hepsi bu, teşekkürler.
hepsee boo teshekkewrler

▶ Make it twenty YTL and I'll take it.
Yirmi Yeni Türk Lirası yapın da alayım.
yeermee yenee tewrk leerasuh yapuhn da alī-uhm

▶ Fine, I'll take it.
Pekala, alıyorum.
pekala aluhyoroom

21. Shopping for clothes

to alter	düzeltmek	dewzeltmek
bigger	daha büyük	daha bewyewk
just right	tam	tam
smaller	daha küçük	daha kewchewk
to try on	denemek	denemek

▶▶ Can I help you?
Yardımcı olabilir miyim?
yarduhmjuh olabeeleer meeyeem

▶ No thanks, I'm just looking.
Hayır, teşekkürler. Sadece bakıyorum.
ha-yuhr teshekkewrler, sadejeh bakuhyoroom

▶▶ Do you want to try that on?
Denemek ister misiniz?
denemek eester meeseeneez

▶ Yes, and I'll try this one too.
Evet, ayrıca bunu da deneyeyim.
evet, īruhja boonoo da den-ayayeem

▶ Do you have it in a bigger size?
Bunun daha büyük bedeni var mı?
boonoon daha bewyewk bedenee var muh

▶ Do you have it in a different colour?
Bunun başka rengi var mı?
boonoon bashka rengee var muh

▶▶ That looks good on you.
Size yakıştı.
seezeh yakuhshtuh

▶ Can you shorten this?
Bunu kısaltabilir misiniz?
boon**oo** kuhsaltabeel**eer** meeseen**eez**

▶▶ Sure, it'll be ready on Friday, after 12.00.
Elbette, cuma günü on ikiden itibaren hazır olur.
elbetteh jooma gewn**ew** **o**neekeeden eeteebaren hazu**h**r oloor

22. Sightseeing

art gallery	sanat galerisi	san**a**t galeree**see**
bus tour	otobüsle tur	otob**ew**sleh toor
city centre	şehir merkezi	shehe**er** merkez**ee**
closed	kapalı	kapalu**h**
guide	rehber	rehber
museum	müze	mewz**eh**
open	açık	achu**h**k

▶ I'm interested in seeing the old town.
Eski şehri görmek isterim.
eski**ee** shehr**ee** gurm**ek** eester**eem**

▶ Are there guided tours?
Rehberli turlar var mı?
rehberl**ee** toorlar var muh

▶▶ I'm sorry, it's fully booked.
Üzgünüm, tamamen dolu.
ewzg**ew**newm tamamen dol**oo**

▶ How much would you charge to drive us around for four hours?
Bizi otomobille dört saat gezdirmek için ne alırsınız?
beez**ee** otomob**ee**lleh durt sa-**a**t gezdeermek eeche**en** neh alu**h**rsuhnuhz

▶ Can we book tickets for the concert here?
Konser için biletleri buradan ayırtabilir miyiz?
konser eeche**en** beeletler**ee** b**oo**radan ī-uhrtabeel**eer** meey**ee**z

▶▶ Yes, in what name?   ▶▶ Which credit card?
Evet, isim ne olacak?   **Hangi kredi kartı?**
evet eese**em** neh olajak   hange**e** kredee kartu**h**

▶ Where do we get the tickets?
Biletleri nereden alacağız?
beeletler**ee** nereden alaja-**uh**z

▶▶ Just pick them up at the entrance.
Girişte istemeniz yeterli.
geereeshteh eestemeneez yeterlee

▶ Is it open on Sundays?
Pazarları açık mı?
pazarlaruh achuhk muh

▶ How much is it to get in?
Giriş ne kadar?
geereesh neh kadar

▶ Are there reductions for groups of six?
Altı kişilik gruplar için indirim var mı?
altuh keesheeleek grooplar eecheen eendeereem var muh

▶ That was really impressive!
Gerçekten çok etkileyiciydi!
gerchekten chok etkeelayee-jeeydee

23. Taxis

▶ Can you get us a taxi?
Bize bir taksi çağırır mısınız?
beezeh beer taksee cha-uhruhr muhsuhnuhz

▶▶ For now? Where are you going?
Hemen gitmek için mi? Nereye gidiyorsunuz?
hemen geetmek eecheen mee, neray-eh geedeeyorsoonooz

▶ To the town centre.
Kent merkezine.
kent merkezeeneh

▶ I'd like to book a taxi to the airport for tomorrow.
Yarın için havalimanına bir taksi ayarlamak istiyorum.
yaruhn eecheen havaleemanuhna beer taksee ī-arlamak eesteeyoroom

▶▶ Sure, at what time? How many people?
Elbette, saat kaç için? Kaç kişisiniz?
elbetteh sa-at kach eecheen, kach keesheeseeneez

▶ How much is it to Taksim?
Taksim ne kadar tutar?
takseem neh kadar tootar

▶ Right here is fine, thanks.
Müsait bir yerde, teşekkürler.
mewsa-eet beer yerdeh teshekkewrler

▶ Can you wait here and take us back?
Bekleyip bizi geri götürebilir misiniz?
beklay-eep beezee geree gurtewrebeeleer meeseeneez

▶▶ How long are you going to be?
Ne kadar süre kalacaksınız?
neh kadar sewreh kalajaksuhnuhz

24. Trains

to change trains	aktarma yapmak	aktarma yapmak
platform	peron	peron
return	gidiş-dönüş	geedeesh-durnewsh
single	gidiş	geedeesh
station	istasyon	eestasyon
stop	durak	doorak
ticket	bilet	beelet

▶ How much is...?
... ne kadar?
... neh kadar

▶ A single, second class to...
... 'a bir adet ikinci sınıf gidiş.
... a beer adet eekeenjee suhnuhf geedeesh

▶ Two returns, second class to...
... 'a iki adet ikinci sınıf gidiş-dönüş.
... a eekee adet eekeenjee suhnuhf geedeesh-durnewsh

▶ For today.
Bugün için.
boogewn eecheen

▶ For tomorrow.
Yarın için.
yaruhn eecheen

▶ For next Tuesday.
Gelecek salı için.
gelejek saluh eecheen

▶▶ There's a supplement for the Boğaziçi Ekpresi.
Boğaziçi Ekpresi için fark ödenmesi gerekiyor.
bo-azeechee ekpresee eecheen fark urdenmesee gerekeeyor

▶▶ Do you want to make a seat reservation?
Yer ayırtmak istiyor musunuz?
yer ī-uhrtmak eesteeyor moosoonooz

▶▶ You have to change at Bursa.
Bursa'da aktarma yapmanız lazım.
boorsada aktarma yapmanuhz lazuhm

▶ Is this seat free?
Bu yer boş mu?
boo yer bosh moo

▶ Excuse me, which station are we at?
Affedersiniz, hangi istasyondayız?
affederseeneez hangee eestasyondi-uhz

▶ Is this where I change for İzmir?
İzmir için burada mı aktarma yapmam lazım?
eezmeer eecheen boorada muh aktarma yapmam lazuhm

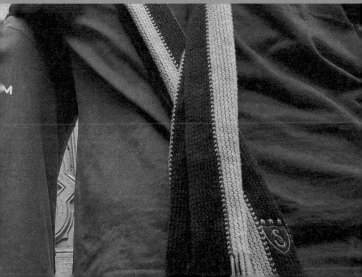

ENGLISH
→ **TURKISH**

A

a, an bir

about: about 20 yirmi civarında
jeevaruhnda

  at about 5 o'clock saat beş
  civarında sa-at

  a film about Turkey Türkiye
  hakkında bir film tewrkee-yeh
  hakkuhnda

above: above the...
  ...-in üstünde ewstewndeh

abroad yurt dışında duh-shuhnda

absolutely! (I agree) kesinlikle!
keseenleekleh

absorbent cotton hidrofil
pamuk

accelerator gaz pedalı
pedaluh

accept kabul etmek

accident kaza

  there's been an accident
  bir kaza oldu

accommodation kalacak yer
kalajak

accurate doğru doh-roo

ache ağrı a-ruh

  my back aches sırtım ağrıyor
  suhrtuhm a-ruh-yor

across: across the... (road etc)
  ...-un karşı tarafında karshuh
  tarafuhnda

adapter adaptör adaptur

address adres

  what's your address?
  adresiniz nedir?

address book adres defteri

admission charge giriş ücreti
geereesh ewjretee

adult yetişkin yeteesh-keen

advance: in advance önceden
urnjeden

Aegean Ege egeh

aeroplane uçak oochak

after: after the... ...-den sonra

  after you siz buyrun boo-iroon

  after lunch öğle yemeğinden
  sonra

afternoon öğleden sonra ur-leden

  in the afternoon öğleden
  sonra

  this afternoon bugün öğleden
  sonra boogewn

aftershave tıraş losyonu tuhrash

aftersun cream güneş sonrası
kremi gewnesh sonrasuh

afterwards sonra

again yine yeeneh

against: against the...
  ...-e karşı -eh karshuh

age yaş yash

ago: a week ago bir hafta önce
urnjeh

  an hour ago bir saat önce

agree: I agree olur

Aids Aids

air hava

  by air uçakla oochakla

air-conditioning klima,
havalandırma –duhrma

airmail: by airmail uçak
postasıyla oochak postasuhla

airmail envelope uçak zarfı
zarfuh

airport havaalanı hava-alan**uh**

  to the airport, please
  havaalanına, lütfen
  –alan**uh**na le**w**tfen

airport bus havaalanı otobüsü
  otob**ew**sew

aisle seat korid**o**r yanı yan**uh**

alarm clock çalar saat chal**a**r
  sa-**at**

alcohol alk**o**l

alcoholic alkollü alkoll**ew**

all: all the boys bütün **o**ğlanlar
  be**wtewn**

  all the girls bütün kızlar

  all of it heps**i**

  all of them onların hepsi
  onlar**uh**n

  that's all, thanks hepsi
  bu kad**a**r, teşekkür eder**i**m
  teshekke**wr**

allergic: I'm allergic to... ...-a
  alerjim var aler**J**eem

allowed: is it allowed? serb**e**st
  mi?

all right pek**i**

  I'm all right ben iyiy**i**m

  are you all right? iy**i** mis**i**n?

almond bad**e**m

almost neredeyse n**e**redayseh

alone yalnız y**a**lnuhz

alphabet alfabe **a**lfabeh

a a	b beh	c jeh
ç cheh	d deh	e eh
f feh	g geh	ğ
		yoomoosha**k** geh
h ha	ı uh	i ee

j Jeh	k ka	l leh
m meh	n neh	o o
ö ur	p peh	r reh
s seh	ş sheh	u oo
ü ew	t teh	v veh
y yeh	z zeh	

already bile beel**eh**

  the film has already started
  film başladı bile bashl**a**duh

also de deh, da

although halde h**a**ldeh

altogether tümüyle tewm**ew**leh

always hep

am: I am ... (ben) ...-im

a.m. (from midnight to 4 a.m.)
  gece gej**eh**
  (from 4 a.m. to noon) sabah sabaH

amazing (surprising) şaşılacak
  shash**uh**lajak
  (very good) şahane shah**a**neh

ambulance cankurtaran
  jankoortar**a**n

  call an ambulance! bir
  cankurtaran çağırın! cha-
  uhruhn

America Am**e**rika

American (adj) Amerik**a**n

  I'm American Amerikal**ı**yım
  –luh-y**uh**m

among: among the...
  ...-in arasında arasuhnd**a**

amount mikt**a**r
  (money) tut**a**r

amp: a 13-amp fuse on üç
  amperl**i**k sig**o**rta

Anatolia Anad**o**lu

and ve veh

angry kızgın kuhz**guh**n

animal hayvan h**ī**van

ankle ayak bileği **ī**-ak beeleh-**ee**

anniversary (wedding) evlenme yıldönümü evlen**meh yuhl**-durnewm**ew**

annoy: this man's annoying me bu adam beni rahatsız ediy**or** rahats**uh**z

annoying can sıkıcı jan suhkuhj**uh**

another başka bir bash**ka**

can we have another room? bize başka bir oda verebil**ir** misin**iz**? beez**eh**

another beer, please bir bira dah**a**, lütfen l**ew**tfen

antibiotics antibiyotik

antifreeze antifriz

antihistamine antihistamin

antique: is it an antique? bu antika mı? muh

antique shop antikacı anteekaj**uh**

antiseptic antiseptik

any: do you have any...? sizde ... var mı? seezd**eh** – muh

sorry, I don't have any üzgünüm, hiç yok **ew**zgewnewm heech

anybody kimse k**ee**mseh

does anybody speak English? İngilizce bil**en** var mı? **ee**ngeeleezjeh – muh

there wasn't anybody there orada kimse y**o**ktu k**ee**mseh

anything bir şey shay

anything else? başka bir şey? bash**ka**

nothing else, thanks hepsi bu kadar, teşekkür eder**im** teshekk**ewr**

would you like anything to drink? bir şey içmek ist**er** misin**iz**? eechmek

I don't want anything, thanks hiç bir şey ist**e**miyorum, teşekkür eder**im** heech

apart from... ...-den başka bash**ka**

apartment apartman dairesi da-**ee**resee, daire da-**ee**reh

apartment block apart**ma**n

aperitif aperetif

apology özür urz**ew**r

appendicitis apandisit

appetizer ordövr ord**ur**vr, meze mez**eh**

apple elma

appointment randev**u**

good morning, how can I help you? günaydın, buyrun? gewnid**uh**n boo-iroon

I'd like to make an appointment randev**u** alm**a**k istiyorum

what time would you like? saat kaç için istersin**iz**? sa-**at** kach eech**een**

three o'clock üç için

I'm afraid that's not possible, is four o'clock all right? korkarım o mümkün değil, saat dörtte olur mu? korkar**uhm** o mewm**kewn** deh-**eel** sa-at durt**teh**

yes, that will be fine evet, o çok iyi chok

the name was? isim neydi? nay**dee**

apricot kayısı kī-uhs**uh**

April nisan

are: we are... biz...-iz

you are... siz...-siniz

they are... onlar...-dırlar duhrlar

area (place) semt

(space) alan

area code şehir kodu sheh-heer

arm kol

Armenia Ermenistan

Armenian (*adj*: person) Ermeni

arrange: will you arrange it for us? bunu bizim için ayarlar mısınız? icheen i-arlar muhsuhn**uhz**

arrival varış var**uhsh**

arrive varmak

when do we arrive? ne §zaman varacağız? neh – varaja-uhz

has my fax arrived yet? faksım geldi mi?

we arrived today bugün geldik

art sanat

art gallery sanat galerisi

artist sanatçı sanatch**uh**

as: as big/small as... ... kadar büy**ük**/küç**ük**

as soon as possible en kısa zamanda kuh**sa**

ashtray kül tablası kewl tablasuh

Asia Asya

ask (question etc) sormak

I didn't ask for this ben bunu istemedim

could you ask him/her to...? ondan...-mesini isteyebilir misiniz?

asleep: he/she's asleep uyuyor oo-y**oo**-yor

aspirin aspirin

asthma astım ast**uhm**

astonishing şaşırtıcı shashuhr-tuhj**uh**

at: at the hotel otelde oteld**eh**

at the station istasyonda

at six o'clock saat altıda sa-at altuhda

at Ali's Ali'de alee-d**eh**

Athens Atina

athletics atletizm

ATM bankamatik

at sign, @ 'at' işareti et eesharet**ee**

attractive çekici chekeej**ee**

aubergine patlıcan patluh**jan**

August ağustos a-oost**os**

aunt (maternal) teyze tayz**eh**

(paternal) hala

Australia Avustralya

Australian (*adj*) Avustralya

I'm Australian Avustralyalıyım –yal**uh**-yuhm

automatic otomatik

autumn sonbahar

  in the autumn sonbaharda

avenue cadde jadd**eh**

average (ordinary) sıradan
suhrad**a**n

  (not good) orta

  on average ortalama olarak

awake: is he/she awake?
uyanık mı? oo-yan**uh**k muh

away: go away! çekil git!
chek**ee**l geet

  is it far away? uzakta mı?
muh

awful berbat

axle aks

B

baby bebek

baby food mama

baby's bottle biber**o**n

baby-sitter çocuk bakıcısı
cho**j**ook bakuhjuhs**uh**

> Travel tip Don't be surprised
> if your child receives an
> affectionate pinch on the
> cheek from a passer-by, often
> accompanied by the word
> *maşallah*, which serves to
> both praise your offspring
> and ward off the evil eye, or
> if a waiter unselfconsciously
> picks a child up and waltzes
> them off into the kitchen to
> show their workmates how
> sweet they are.

back (of body) sırt suhrt

  (back part) arka

  at the back arkada

  **can I have my money
back?** paramı geri alabilir
miyim? param**uh**

  to come back geri gelmek

  to go back dönmek durnmek

backache sırt ağrısı suhrt
a-ruhs**uh**

bacon beykın bayk**u**hn

bad kötü kurt**ew**

  not bad fena değil deh-**eel**

badly kötü kurt**ew**

bag çanta chanta

  (handbag) el çantası
chantas**uh**

  (suitcase) bav**u**l

baggage bagaj baga**ɹ**

baggage check emanet

baggage claim bagaj alım baga**ɹ**
al**uh**m

bakery fırın fuhr**uh**n

balcony balk**o**n

  a room with a balcony
balkonl**u** bir oda

bald kel

ball top

ballet bale bal**eh**

ballpoint pen tükenmez kalem
tewkenm**e**z

banana muz

band (musical) orkestra

bandage sargı sarg**uh**

Bandaids flaster, yara bandı
band**uh**

bank (money) banka

bank account banka hesabı hesab**uh**

bar bar

a bar of chocolate bir paket çikolata cheekola**ta**

barber's berber

bargain (*verb*) pazarlık etmek pazarl**uh**k

how much do you want for this? bunun için ne kadar istiyorsunuz? eechee**n** neh

80 lira seksen lira

that's too much – I'll give you 50 lira o çok fazla – size elli lira veririm chok – seeze**h**

I'll let you have it for 65 lira size altmış beş liraya bırakırım besh – buhrak**uh**ruhm

can't you make it cheaper?/OK it's a deal daha ucuza olmaz mı?/ tamam, anlaştık oojo**o**za – muh/anlast**uh**k

basket sepet

bath banyo

can I have a bath? banyo yapabilir miyim?

bathroom banyo

with a private bathroom banyolu oda

bath towel havlu

bathtub küvet kewvet

battery pil

bay koy

(large) körfez kurfe**z**

bazaar çarşı charsh**uh**, pazar

be olmak

beach plaj plaJ

on the beach plajda

beach mat plaj yaygısı plaJ yiguhs**uh**

beach umbrella plaj şemsiyesi shemsee-yes**ee**

> **Travel tip** All beaches are free in theory, but luxury compounds straddling routes to the sand will control access in various ways. Never pay a fee for a beach-lounger or umbrella unless the seller provides you with a ticket.

beans fasulye fahs**ool**-yeh

  French beans ayşekadın
fasulyes**i** **i**shekaduhn

  broad beans bakl**a**

bear ayı **ī-uh**

beard sak**a**l

beautiful güzel gewz**e**l

because çünkü ch**e**wnkew

  because of… … nedeniyle
neden**ee**leh

bed yat**a**k

  I'm going to bed now ben
artık yatıyorum art**uh**k yatuh-
y**o**room

bed and breakfast pansiy**o**n

bedroom yatak odası odas**uh**

beef sığır eti suh-**uh**r

beer bir**a**

  two beers, please ik**i** bira,
lütfen l**e**wtfen

before önce **u**rnjeh

begin başlamak bashlam**a**k

  when does it begin? ne
zaman başlıyor? neh – bashluh-y**o**r

beginner acemi ajem**ee**

beginning: at the beginning
başlangıçta bashlanguh**ch**ta

behind: behind the…
…-in arkasında arkasuhnd**a**

  behind me arkamd**a**

beige bej be**J**

Belgian (*adj*) Belçika b**e**lcheeka

Belgium Belçika

believe inanmak

below: below the…
…-in altında altuhnd**a**

belt kem**e**r

bend (in road) viraj veera**J**

berth (on ship) ranza, yat**a**k

beside: beside the…
…-in yanında yanuhnd**a**

best en iy**i**

better dah**a** iyi

  are you feeling better?
kendiniz**i** daha iyi hissediy**o**r
musun**u**z?

between: between the…
… lerin arasında arasuhnd**a**

beyond: beyond the…
…-in ötesinde urtees**ee**nd**eh**

bicycle bisikl**e**t

big büyük bew-y**e**wk

  too big fazla büyük

  it's not big enough yeterince
büyük değil yeter**ee**nj**eh** – deh-**ee**l

bike bisikl**e**t

  (motorbike) motosiklet

bikini bik**i**ni

bill hes**a**p

  (US) kâğıt par**a** ka-**uh**t

  **could I have the bill,
please?** hesap, lütfen l**e**wtfen

bin çöp kutus**u** churp

bin liners çöp torbası torbas**uh**

bird kuş koosh

birthday doğum günü doh-**oo**m
gewn**e**w

  happy birthday! doğum
gününüz kutl**u** ols**u**n!
gewnewn**e**wz

biscuit bisküvi beesk**e**w-vee

bit: a little bit birazcık beerazj**uh**k

  a big bit büyük bir parça bew-
y**e**wk beer parch**a**

a bit of... bir parça...

a bit expensive/small biraz pahalı/küçük

bite (by insect) sokma

(by dog) ısırma uhs**uh**rma

bitter (taste etc) acı aj**uh**

black siyah see-ya**H**, kar**a**

Black Sea Karadeniz

blanket battaniye batt**a**nee-yeh

bleach (for toilet) tuval**e**t temizleyicisi temeezlay-eejee-see

bless you! çok yaşa! chok yash**a**

blind kör kur

blinds jaluzi Ja**l**oozee

blister su toplaması toplamas**uh**

I have a blister on my heel topuğum su topladı topoo-**oo**m soo toplad**uh**

blocked (road) kapalı kapal**uh**

(sink, pipe) tıkalı tuhkal**uh**

blond (adj) sarışın saruh-sh**uh**n

blood kan

high blood pressure yüksek tansiy**o**n yewks**e**k

blouse bluz

blow-dry (noun) fön furn

I'd like a cut and blow-dry lütfen kesip fönleyin l**e**wtfen – furnlayeen

blue mavi

blusher allık all**uh**k

boarding house pansiy**o**n

boarding pass biniş kartı ben**ee**sh kart**uh**

boat gemi

(small) kayık kī-**uh**k

---

body vücut vewj**oo**t

boiled egg haşlanmış yumurt**a** hashlanm**uh**sh

boiler kaz**a**n

bone kem**i**k

bonnet (of car) motor kapağı kapa-**uh**, kap**u**t

book (noun) kit**a**p

(verb: seat etc) ayırtmak ī-uhrtmak

can I book a seat? bir yer ayırtabilir miyim? ī-uhrtabeel**ee**r

bookshop, bookstore kitapçı keet**a**p-chuh

boot (footwear) çizme cheezm**eh**

(of car) bagaj baga**J**

border (of country) sınır suhn**uh**r

bored: I'm bored canım sıkılıyor jahn**uh**m suhkuhluh-yor

boring sıkıcı suhkuh-j**uh**

born: I was born in Manchester Manchester'de doğdum –d**eh** doh-d**oo**m

I was born in 1960 bin dokuz yüz altmış'da doğdum

borrow ödünç almak urdewnch

may I borrow...?...-i ödünç
alabilir miyim?

Bosphorus İstanbul Boğazı
eestanbool bo-azuh

both ikisi de eekeesee deh

bother: sorry to bother you
rahatsız ettiğim için özür
dilerim rahatsuhz ettee-eem
eecheen urzewr

bottle şişe sheesheh

bottle-opener şişe açacağı
achaja-uh

bottom (of person) popo

at the bottom of the hill
tepenin eteğinde eteh-eendeh

at the bottom of the street
yolun alt kısmında kuhsmuhnda

box kutu

(large) sandık sanduhk

box office bilet gişesi geeshesee

boy oğlan oh-lan

boyfriend erkek arkadaş arkadash

bra sütyen sewt-yen

bracelet bilezik

brake fren

brandy konyak

brass pirinç peereench

bread ekmek

white bread beyaz ekmek
bayaz

brown bread kara ekmek

wholemeal bread kepekli
ekmek

break (verb) kırmak kuhrmak

I've broken the... ...'i kırdım
kuhrduhm

I think I've broken my wrist
sanırım bileğimi kırdım sanuhruhm

break down arıza yapmak
aruhza

I've broken down arabam
arıza yaptı yaptuh

breakdown (mechanical) arıza

breakdown service araç
kurtarma arach

breakfast kahvaltı kaнvaltuh

break-in: I've had a break-in
evime hırsız girdi eveemeh
huhrsuhz

breast göğüs gur-ews

breathe nefes almak

breeze esinti

bridge köprü kurprew

brief kısa kuhsa

briefcase evrak çantası
chantasuh

bright (light etc) aydınlık īduhnluhk

(colour) canlı janluh

bright red ateş kırmızısı atesh
kuhrmuhzuhsuh

brilliant (person) çok zeki chok

(idea) parlak

bring getirmek

I'll bring it back later sonra
geri getiririm

Britain Büyük Britanya bew-yewk

British İngiliz eengeeleez

brochure broşür broshewr

broken bozuk

(leg etc) kırık kuhruhk

bronchitis bronşit bronsheet

brooch broş brosh

broom süpürge sewrpewrg**eh**

brother erk**e**k kardeş kard**e**sh

brother-in-law (husband's/wife's brother) kayınbirader kī-uhn-beerad**er**

  (sister's husband) enişte eneesht**eh**

brown kahverengi ka**H**v**e**rengee

bruise çürük chewr**ew**k

brush (for cleaning) fırça fu**H**rcha

  (for hair) saç fırçası sach fu**H**rchas**uh**

  (artist's) resim fırçası

bucket kov**a**

buffet car yemekl**i** vag**o**n

buggy (for child) pus**e**t

building bin**a**

bulb (light bulb) amp**u**l

Bulgaria Bulgarist**a**n

Bulgarian (*adj*: person) Bulg**a**r

bumper tamp**o**n

bunk ranz**a**

bureau de change kambiy**o**

burglary hırsızlık huhrsuhzl**uh**k

burn (*noun*) yanık yan**uh**k

  (*verb*) yanm**a**k

burnt: this is burnt bu yanmış yah**n**m**uh**sh

burst: a burst pipe patlamış bor**u** patla**muh**sh

bus otobüs otob**ew**s

  what number bus is it to...?
  ...-'a kaç numaralı otobüs gidiy**o**r? kach noomaral**uh**

  when is the next bus to...?...-'a bund**a**n sonr**a**ki otobüs ne zam**a**n? neh

what time is the last bus?
son otobüs saat kaçta? sa-**a**t ka**ch**ta

business iş eesh

bus station otobüs garajı otob**ew**s gara**J**uh, otog**a**r

bus stop otobüs durağı doora-**uh**

bust göğüs gur-**ew**s

bus terminal otog**a**r

busy (restaurant etc) kalabalık kalabal**uh**k

  I'm busy tomorrow yar**ı**n meşgulüm meshg**oo**lewm

but am**a**

butcher's kas**a**p

butter tereyağı ter**a**ya-uh

button düğme dewm**eh**

buy satın almak sat**uh**n

  where can I buy...?
  nerede... bulabilirim? nered**eh**

by: by bus/car otob**ü**s/otomob**i**l ile eel**eh**

  written by... ... tarafından yazılan tarafu**h**nd**a**n yazu**h**lan

  by the window pencere yanında yan**uh**nda

by the sea deniz kenarında kenar**uh**nda

by Thursday perşembey**e** kad**a**r

bye (general use) hoşça kalın hosh-cha kal**uh**n

(said by person leaving) hoşça kal h**o**sh-cha

(said to person leaving) güle güle gewl**eh**

Byzantine B**i**zans

C

cabbage lahana la**H**ana

cabin (on ship) kamar**a**

cable car teleferik

café (for men) kahve ka**H**veh, kahvehane ka**H**veh-**H**aneh, çayhane chi**H**aneh

(for families) pastane pastaneh, cafe kaf**eh**

cagoule naylon yağmurluk n**i**lon ya-moorl**oo**k

cake past**a**

cake shop pastane pastaneh

call (verb) çağırmak cha-uhrmak

(verb: to phone) telef**o**n etm**e**k

what's it called? ona ne denir? neh

he/she is called... adı... ad**uh**

please call the doctor lütfen doktor**u** çağırın l**e**wtfen – cha-uhr**uh**n

please give me a call at 7.30 a.m. tomorrow lütfen

yarın sabah yedi buçukta bana bir telefon edin

please ask him/her to call me lütfen beni aramasını söyleyin arama-suhn**uh** suh-ilay-**ee**n

call back: I'll call back later s**o**nra tekr**a**r uğrarım oo-rar**uhm**

(phone back) s**o**nra tekr**a**r ararım arar**uhm**

call round: I'll call round tomorrow yarın uğrarım oo-rar**uhm**

camcorder video kamer**a**

camel deve dev**eh**

camera fotoğraf makinesi foto-raf

camera shop fotoğrafçı foto-rafch**uh**

camp (verb) kamp yapm**a**k

can we camp here? bur**a**da kamp yapabilir miy**i**z?

camping gas tüpgaz tewpg**a**z

campsite kamping, kamp yeri

can teneke kutu tenek**eh**

a can of beer bir kutu bira

can: can you...? ...-ebil**i**r misiniz?

can I have...? bana... verebil**i**r misin**i**z?

I can't... ...-em**e**m

Canada Kan**a**da

Canadian (adj) Kan**a**da

I'm Canadian Kan**a**dalıyım kanadaluh-yuhm

canal kan**a**l

cancel iptal etm**e**k

candies şeker shek**e**r

candle mum moo**m**

canoe kan**o**

canoeing kano kullanma**k**

can-opener konserve açacağı kons**e**rveh achaja-uh

cap (hat) kask**e**t

(of bottle) kap**a**k

car otomob**i**l, araba

by car otomobil il**e** eel**eh**

carafe sürahi sewr**a**hee

a carafe of house white, please bir sürahi beyaz şarabınızdan, lütfen bay**a**z sharabuhnuhzd**a**n l**ew**tfen

caravan karav**a**n

caravan site kamp**i**ng

carburettor karbürat**ö**r karbewrat**u**r

card (birthday etc) kart

here's my (business) card buyrun, kartviz**i**tim b**oo**-iroon

cardigan hırka huh**r**ka

cardphone kartlı telef**o**n kartl**uh**

careful dikkatl**i**

be careful! dikkatli ol**u**n!

caretaker kapıcı kapuhj**uh**

car ferry ferib**o**t

car hire kiralık otomob**i**l keeral**uh**k

carnival karnav**a**l

car park otopar**k**

car rental kiralık otomob**i**l keeral**uh**k

carpet halı hal**uh**

carriage (of train) vag**o**n

carrier bag naylon torba nil**o**n

carrot havuç hav**oo**ch

carry taşımak tashuhma**k**

carry-cot portbebe portbeb**eh**

carton kut**u**

carwash (place) otomobil yıkama yer**i** yuhkam**a**

case (suitcase) valiz, bav**u**l

cash (*noun*) nakit par**a**

(*verb*) paraya çevirmek par**ī**-a cheveerm**e**k

will you cash this cheque for me? ben**i**m için bu çeki boz**a**r mısınız? eech**ee**n – muhsuhn**uh**z

cash desk k**a**sa

cash dispenser bank**a**matik

> **Travel tip** The simplest way to get hold of money in Turkey is to use the widespread ATM network – screen prompts are given in English on request. It's safest to use ATMs attached to banks during normal working hours so help can be summoned if your card is eaten (not uncommon).

cashier kasiy**e**r

cassette kas**e**t

cassette recorder kasetli teyp tayp

castle kale kal**eh**

casualty department acil servis aj**ee**l

cat kedi ked**ee**

catacomb yeraltı mezarları yeralt**uh** mezarlar**uh**

catch (*verb*: ball etc) yakalama**k**

where do we catch the bus to İzmir? İzmir otobüsüne nereden binebiliriz? **eezmeer**

cathedral katedral

Catholic Katolik

cauliflower karnabahar

cave mağara ma-ara

ceiling tavan

celery sap kerevizi

cemetery mezarlık mezarluhk

centigrade santigrat

centimetre santimetre santeemetreh

central merkezi

central heating kalorifer

centre merkez

how do we get to the city centre? şehir merkezine nasıl gidilir? sheh-heer merkezeeneh nasuhl

certainly kesinlikle keseenleekleh

certainly not kesinlikle hayır hi-**uhr**

chair iskemle eeskemleh

champagne şampanya shampanya

change (*noun*: money) bozuk para

(*verb*: money) bozmak

can I change this for...? bunu… ile değiştirebilir miyim? eeleh deh-eeshteereh-beeleer

I don't have any change hiç bozuk param yok heech

can you give me change for a 100 lira note? bana bir yüz lira bozabilir misiniz?

do we have to change (trains)? aktarma yapmamız lazım mı? yapmam**uh**z laz**uh**m muh

yes, change at Bursa/no, it's a direct train evet, Bursa'da değiştirin b**oo**rsa-da deh-eeshteer**ee**n/hayır, bu tren dir**e**kt gid**e**r hī-**uh**r

changed: to get changed üstünü değiştirmek ewstewn**ew** deh-eeshteerm**e**k

chapel kilise keelees**eh**

charge (noun) alınan para aluhn**a**n
(verb) para alm**a**k

charge card kredi kartı kart**uh**

cheap ucuz ooj**oo**z

do you have anything cheaper? daha ucuz bir şey var mı? shay var muh

check (verb) kontrol etmek
(US: noun) çek chek
see **cheque**
(US: bill) hes**a**p
see **bill**

could you check the..., please?...-i kontrol eder misiniz, lütfen? l**e**wtfen

checkbook çek defteri chek

check card çek kartı kart**uh**

check-in bagaj kayıt baga**J** kī-**uh**t, check-in

check in (at hotel) yerleşmek yerleshm**e**k
(at airport) check-in yaptırmak yaptuhrm**a**k

where do we have to check in? nerede check-in yaptırmamız lazım? n**e**rede – yaptuhrmam**uh**z laz**uh**m

cheek yan**a**k

cheerio! eyvallah! ayvalla**H**

cheers! (toast) şerefe! sheref**eh**

cheese peynir payn**ee**r

chemist's eczane ejzan**e**h

cheque çek chek

do you take cheques? çek kabul ediyor musun**u**z?

cheque book çek defteri chek

cheque card çek kartı kart**uh**

cherry kir**a**z

chess satranç satr**a**nch

chest göğüs gur-**e**ws

chewing gum çiklet cheekl**e**t

chicken tav**u**k

chickenpox suçiçeği soochech**e**h-ee

child çocuk choj**oo**k

children çocuklar choj**oo**klar

child minder çocuk bakıcısı choj**oo**k bakuhjuhs**uh**

children's pool çocuk havuz**u**

children's portion çocuk porsiy**o**nu

chin çene chen**eh**

china porsel**e**n

Chinese (adj) Çin cheen

chips patates kızartması kuhzartmas**uh**
(US) çips cheeps

chocolate çikolata cheekol**a**ta

milk chocolate sütlü çikolata sewtl**ew**

plain chocolate sade çikolata sa-d**eh**

a hot chocolate kak**a**o

choose seçmek sech**mek**

Christian Hıristiyan huhreestee-yan

Christian name ad

Christmas No**e**l

Christmas Eve No**e**l Gecesi gejes**ee**

merry Christmas! İyi Noell**e**r! ee-y**ee**

church kilise keelees**eh**

cider elma şırası shuhras**uh**

cigar p**u**ro

cigarette sigar**a**

cigarette lighter çakmak chakm**ak**

cinema sin**e**ma

circle daire da-eer**eh**

(in theatre) balk**o**n

citadel iç kale eech kal**eh**

city şehir sheh-h**eer**

city centre şehir merkez**i**

clean (adj) tem**i**z

can you clean these for me? lütfen b**a**na bunları temizl**e**r misiniz? l**ew**tfen – bunlar**uh**

cleaning solution (for contact lenses) temizleme sıvısı temeezlem**eh** suhvuhs**uh**

cleansing lotion temizleme losyon**u**

clear dur**u**

(obvious) açık ach**uh**k

clever akıllı akuhll**uh**

cliff yar

climbing dağcılık da-juhl**uh**k

cling film jelatin ɉelat**ee**n

clinic klin**i**k

cloakroom vestiy**e**r

clock saat sa-**at**

close (verb) kapatm**ak**

DIALOGUE

what time do you close? saat kaçta kapatıyorsunuz? sa-**at** k**a**chta kapatuh-**yor**–

we close at 8 p.m. on weekdays and 6 p.m. on Saturdays haft**a** içinde akşam sekizde, cumartesileri akşam altıda kapatıyoruz eecheend**eh** aksham sek**ee**zdeh joomarteseeler**ee** – alt**uh**da kapatuh-yor**oo**z

do you close for lunch? öğlenleri kapatıyor musun**uz**? ur-lenler**ee** kapatuh-y**or**

yes, between 1 and 3.30 p.m. ev**e**t, saat birle üçbuçuk arasında sa-**at** beerl**eh** ewchboochook aras**uh**nda

---

closed kapalı kapal**uh**

cloth (fabric) kumaş koom**a**sh

(for cleaning etc) bez

clothes giysiler gee-is**ee**ler

clothes line çamaşır ipi chamash**uhr**

clothes peg çamaşır mandalı mandal**uh**

cloud bul**u**t

cloudy bulutlu

clutch (in car) debriyaj debree-ya**J**

coach (bus) yolcu otobüsü yol**joo**
otobews**ew**

(on train) vag**o**n

see **bus**

coach station otobüs garajı
gara**Juh**

coach terminal otogar

coach trip otobüsle gezi
otob**ew**sleh

coast sahil sa**Hee**l

on the coast sahilde
sa**Hee**ld**eh**

coat (long coat) p**a**lto

(jacket) ceket jek**et**

coathanger askı ask**uh**

cockroach ham**a**m böceği
bur**j**eh-ee

cocoa kak**a**o

coconut hindistancevizi
–jevee**zee**

code (for phoning) kod numarası
noomaras**uh**

**what's the (dialling) code
for İzmir?** İzmir'in kodu
nedir?

coffee kahve ka**Hveh**

two coffees, please ik**i**
kahve, lütfen l**ew**tfen

coin madeni par**a**

Coke K**o**ka K**o**la

cold soğuk so-**ook**

I'm cold üşüyorum ewsh**ew**-
yoroom

I have a cold soğuk aldım
ald**uh**m

collapse: he's collapsed
yığılıverdi yuh-uhl**uh**verdee

collar yak**a**

collect toplam**a**k, biriktirm**ek**

I've come to collect...
...-ı almaya geldim -uh almi-a

collect call ödemeli konuşma
urdemel**ee** konooshm**a**

college kolej kole**J**

colour renk

**do you have this in other
colours?** bun**u**n başka
renkleri de bulun**u**r mu sizde?
bashk**a** – deh – seezd**eh**

comb tar**a**k

come (arrive) gelm**ek**

where do you come from?
siz nerelisiniz?

I come from Edinburgh
ben Edinburgluy**um**

come back dönmek durnm**ek**

I'll come back tomorrow
yar**ı**n tekr**a**r gelirim

come in girm**ek**

comfortable rah**a**t

compact disc Compact Disc,
CD see dee

company (business) şirket
sheerk**et**

compartment (on train)
kompartıman kompartuhm**a**n

compass pusul**a**

complain şikayet etmek sheekī-et

complaint şikayet

I have a complaint
bir şikay**e**tim var

completely tamamen

computer bilgisayar beelgeesi-ar

concert konser

concussion beyin sarsıntısı bayeen sarsuhn-tuhsuh

conditioner (for hair) saç kremi sach

condom prezervatif

conference konferans

confirm doğrulamak dohroolamak

congratulations! tebrikler!

connecting flight aktarmalı sefer aktarmaluh

connection bağlantı ba-lantuh

conscious şuuru yerinde shoo-ooroo yereendeh

constipation kabızlık kabuhzluhk

consulate konsolosluk

contact (verb) ilişki kurmak eeleeshkee

contact lenses kontak lensleri

contraceptive prezervatif, koruyucu koroo-yoojoo

convenient uygun oo-igoon

that's not convenient o pek uygun değil deh-eel

cook (verb) pişirmek peesheermek

not cooked pişmemiş peeshmemeesh

cooker ocak ojak

cookie bisküvi beeskewvee

cooking utensils mutfak aletleri

cool serin

copper bakır bakuhr

cork mantar

corkscrew tirbuşon teerbooshon

corner: on the corner köşe başında kursheh bashuhnda

in the corner köşede kurshedeh

cornflakes mısır gevreği muhsuhr gevreh-ee

correct (right) doğru doh-roo

corridor koridor

cosmetics makyaj malzemesi

cost (verb) mal olmak

how much does it cost? fiyatı nedir? fee-yatuh

cot çocuk yatağı chojook yata-uh

cotton pamuk

cotton wool hidrofil pamuk

couch (sofa) kanape kanapeh

couchette yatak, kuşet

cough (noun) öksürük urksew-rewk

cough medicine öksürük şurubu shoorooboo

could: could you give...? ...verebilir misiniz?

could I have...? ...alabilir miyim?

I couldn't... ...-amadım -amaduhm

country (nation) ülke ewlkeh

(countryside) kırsal alanlar kuhrsal

countryside kırlar kuhrlar, şehir dışı sheh-heer duhshuh

couple (two people) çift cheeft

a couple of... (two) bir çift...

(a few) bir iki tane... taneh

courgette kabak

courier kurye koor-yeh

course (main course etc) yemek çeşidi chesheedee

of course elbette elbetteh

of course not tabii değil tabee-ee deh-eel

courtyard avlu

cousin (male) kuzen

(female) kuzin

cow inek

crab yengeç yengech

cracker (biscuit) kraker

craft shop el sanatları dükkanı sanatlaruh dewk-kanuh

crash (noun) çarpışma charpuhshma

I've had a crash kaza yaptım yaptuhm

crazy deli

cream (in cake etc) krema

(lotion) krem

(colour) krem rengi

creche kreş kresh

credit card kredi kartı kartuh

do you take credit cards? kredi kartı kabul ediyor musunuz?

can I pay by credit card? kredi kartıyla ödeyebilir miyim? kartuh-ila urdayebeeleer

which card do you want to use? hangi kartla ödemek istersiniz? urdemek

Access/Visa Access'le/ Visa'yla

yes, sir peki efendim

what's the number? numarası nedir? noomarasuh

and the expiry date? ve ne zamana kadar geçerli? veh neh – gecherlee

credit crunch kredi krizi krehdee kreezee

Crete Girit geereet

crisps çips cheeps

crockery tabak takımları takuhmlaruh

crossing (by sea) geçiş gecheesh

crossroads kavşak kavshak

crowd kalabalık kalabaluhk

crowded kalabalık

crown (on tooth) kuron

cruise vapur gezisi

crutches koltuk değnekleri deh-neklleree

cry (verb) ağlamak a-lamak

cucumber salatalık salataluhk

cup fincan feenjan

a cup of…, please lütfen bir fincan… lewtfen

cupboard dolap

cure (verb) tedavi etmek

curly kıvırcık kuhvuhrjuhk

current (electrical) akım akuhm

(in water) akıntı akuhntuh

curtains perdeler

cushion yastık yastuhk

custom gelenek

Customs Gümrük gewmrewk

cut (noun) kesik

(verb) kesmek

I've cut my finger parmağımı kestim parma-uh**muh**

cutlery çatal bıçak chatal buh**ch**ak

cycling bisiklete binmek beeseeklet**eh**

cyclist bisikletli

Cypriot (*adj*) Kıbrıs **kuh**bruhs

(person) Kıbrıslı **kuh**bruhsluh

Cyprus Kıbrıs

D

dad bab**a**

daily her gün g**ewn**

(*adj*) günlük gewnl**ewk**

damage (*verb*) zar**a**r vermek

damaged has**a**r görmüş gurm**ew**sh

I'm sorry, I've damaged this özür dilerim, bun**u** bozd**um** urz**ewr**

damn! Allah kahrets**i**n!

damp (*adj*) neml**i**

dance (*noun*) dans

(*verb*) dans etmek

would you like to dance? dans etmek ist**e**r misin**i**z?

dangerous tehlikel**i**

Danish (*adj*) Danim**a**rka

(language) Danim**a**rkaca – m**a**rkaja

Dardanelles Çanakkale Boğazı chan**a**kkaleh bo-az**uh**

dark (*adj*: colour) koy**u**

(skin, hair) esm**e**r

it's getting dark hav**a** kararıyor kararuh-y**or**

date: what's the date today? bugün ayın kaçı? boog**ewn** ī-**uh**n kach**uh**

let's make a date for next Monday gelecek pazartesi için randevulaşalım gelej**ek** – eech**ee**n randevoolashal**uh**m

dates (fruit) hurm**a**

daughter kız evl**a**t kuhz

daughter-in-law gel**i**n

dawn (*noun*) şafak shaf**a**k

at dawn gün ağarırken g**ewn** a-ar**uh**rken

day gün g**ewn**

the day after ertesi gün

the day after tomorrow öbür gün urb**ewr**

the day before bir gün önce urnj**eh**

the day before yesterday evvelki gün

every day her gün

all day bütün gün bewt**ewn**

in two days' time iki gün içinde g**ewn** eecheend**eh**

have a nice day! iyi günl**e**r!

day trip günlük gezi gewnl**ewk**

dead ölü url**ew**

deaf sağır sa-**uh**r

deal (business) iş eesh

it's a deal anlaştık anlasht**uh**k

death ölüm url**ew**m

decaffeinated coffee kafeinsiz kahve kafeh-eens**eez** ka**H**v**eh**

December aralık aral**uh**k

decide kar**a**r vermek

we haven't decided yet
henüz karar vermedik hen**ewz**

decision karar

deck (on ship) güverte ge**ww**verteh

deckchair şezlong shez**long**

deep der**in**

definitely kesinlikle
kese**enleek**leh

definitely not kesinlikle değil
deh-**eel**

degree (qualification) diploma

delay (noun) gecikme geje**ek**meh

deliberately kasten

delicatessen şarküteri
shark**ew**ter**ee**

delicious nefis

deliver teslim etmek

delivery (of mail) dağıtım
da-uht**uh**m

Denmark Danimarka

dental floss diş ipi d**eesh**

dentist dişçi d**eesh-chee**

it's this one here işte
buradaki ee**sh**teh

this one? bu mu?

no, that one hayır, şu hī-**uhr**
shoo

here? buradaki mi?

yes evet

dentures takma diş d**eesh**

deodorant deodoran

department bölüm burl**ewm**

department store büyük
mağaza bew-y**ewk** ma-**a**za

departure kalkış kalk**uh**sh

departure lounge giden
yolcular salon**u**

depend: it depends duruma
göre gur-r**eh**

it depends on... ...-a bağlı
ba-l**uh**

deposit (noun) depozito

dervish derviş derv**eesh**

description tanım tan**uh**m

dessert tatlı tatl**uh**

destination gidilecek yer
geedeelej**ek**

diabetic (noun) şeker hastası
sheker hastas**uh**

diabetic foods şeker hastaları
için diyet yemeği –lar**uh**
eeche**en** – yemeh-**ee**

dial (verb) çevirmek chev**eer**mek

dialling code telefon kodu

dialling tone çevir sesi chev**eer**

diamond elmas

diaper çocuk bezi choj**ook**

diarrhoea ishal

**do you have something
for diarrhoea?** sizde ishale
karşı bir ilaç var mı? seezd**eh**
eeshal**eh** karsh**uh** beer eel**a**ch var
muh

diary (business etc) ajanda aJ**a**nda
(for personal experiences) günce
gewnj**eh**

dictionary sözlük surzl**ewk**

didn't see **not**

Didyma Didim

die ölmek urlmek

diesel mazot

diet perhiz perh**eez**

I'm on a diet perhiz
yapıyorum yap**uh**-yoroom

**I have to follow a special
diet** özel bir rejim izlem**e**m
gerekiy**o**r urz**e**l beer re**J**eem

difference fark

what's the difference? ne
fark var? neh

different başka ba**sh**ka

this one is different bu farklı
farkl**uh**

a different table başka bir
masa

difficult zor

difficulty zorl**u**k

dinghy sandal

dining room yem**e**k salon**u**

dinner (evening meal) akşam
yemeği aksham yemeh-ee
(midday meal) öğle yemeği urleh

to have dinner akşam yemeği
yemek

direct (adj) dir**e**kt

is there a direct train? direkt
gid**e**n bir tren var mı? muh

direction yön yurn

which direction is it? h**a**ngi
yönde? yurnd**eh**

is it in this direction? bu
yönde mi?

directory enquiries bilinmeyen
numaral**a**r beel**ee**nmayen

dirt pisl**i**k, kir

dirty kirl**i**

disabled özürlü urzewrl**ew**

**is there access for the
disabled?** özürlüler için giriş
var mı? urzewrlewler eech**ee**n
geer**ee**sh var muh

disappear kaybolmak k**i**bolmak

it's disappeared ortad**a**n
kayboldu k**i**boldoo

disappointed hayal kırıklığına
uğramış h**ī**-al kuhruhkluh-uhna
oo-ram**uh**sh

disappointing düş kırıcı dewsh
kuhruhj**uh**

disaster felak**e**t

disco disk**o**

discount ind**i**rim

is there a discount? indirim
var mı? muh

disease hastalık hastal**uh**k

disgusting iğrenç eer**e**nch

dish (meal) yemek
(bowl) tabak

dishcloth bulaşık bezi boolash**uh**k

disinfectant (noun) dezenfekt**a**n

disk (for computer) disk**et**

disposable diapers/nappies
kâğıt çocuk bez**i** ka-**uh**t chojo**ok**

distance uzaklık oozak**luh**k

  in the distance uzak**ta**

distilled water arı su ar**uh** soo

district semt

disturb rahatsız etmek rahats**uh**z

diversion (detour) geçici güzergah
gecheej**ee** gewzerga**H**

diving board trampl**en**

divorced boşanmış boshanm**uh**sh

dizzy: I feel dizzy başım
dönüyor bash**uh**m durnew-y**o**r

do (*verb*) yapmak

  what shall we do? ne
  yapalım? neh yapal**uh**m

  how do you do it? onu nasıl
  yapıyorsunuz? nas**uh**l yap**uh**–

  will you do it for me? ben**i**m
  için bun**u** yapar mısınız?
  eech**ee**n – muhsuhn**uh**h

  how do you do? nasılsınız?
  nas**uh**l-suhnuhz

  nice to meet you
  tanıştığımıza memn**u**n
  old**u**m tanuhshtuh-uhm**uh**za

  what do you do? (work) ne
  iş yapıyorsunuz? neh eesh

  I'm a teacher, and you?
  öğretmenim, ya siz?
  ur-retmen**ee**m

  I'm a student öğrenciyim
  ur-renjee-y**ee**m

  **what are you doing this
  evening?** bu akşam ne
  yapıyorsunuz?

**we're going out for a
drink, do you want
to join us?** bir şey
içmeye gidiyor**u**z, bize
katılmak ister misin**i**z?
shay eechmay**eh** – beez**eh**
katuhlmak

do you want cream?
kr**e**ma ist**e**r misin**i**z?

I do, but she doesn't ben
ister**i**m **a**ma o istemiy**o**r

doctor dokt**o**r

  we need a doctor bize bir
  doktor lazım beez**eh** – laz**uh**m

  please call a doctor lütfen
  bir doktor çağırın l**ew**tfen – cha-
  uhr**uh**n

  where does it hurt? neres**i**
  acıyor? aju**h**-y**o**r

  right here tam burası
  booras**uh**

  does that hurt now? şimdi
  acıyor mu? sheemd**ee**

  yes ev**e**t

  take this to the chemist
  alın bun**u**, eczaneye
  götürün al**uh**n – ejzanay**eh**
  gurtewr**ew**n

document belge belg**eh**

dog köpek kurp**e**k

doll beb**e**k

dome kubbe koobb**eh**

domestic flight iç hat seferi eech

donkey eşek esh**e**k

don't! yapma!

don't do that! onu yapma!
see **not**

> **Travel tip** If you venture
> much off the tourist track,
> accept that being stared
> at is part of the experience
> and not considered rude. In
> some parts of the southeast,
> you may also be mobbed
> by small children wishing to
> guide you around the local
> ruins or begging for pens,
> sweets or money.

door kapı kapuh

doorman kapıcı kapuhjuh

double çift cheeft

double bed iki kişilik yatak
keesheeleek

double room iki kişilik oda

down (direction) aşağı asha-**uh**

  down here burda aşağıda

  put it down over there
onu şuraya bırakın shoorī-a
buhrak**uh**n

  it's down there on the right
şurada, aşağıda sağda shoorada
– sa-da

  it's further down the road
yolun daha aşağısında asha-
uhsuhnda

download (*verb*) indirmek
eendeermek

downmarket (restaurant etc)
gösterişsiz gurstereesh-seez

downstairs alt kat

dozen düzine dewzeeneh

  half a dozen yarım düzine
yar**uh**m

drain (in sink) pis su borusu

  (in street) kanalizasyon

draught beer fıçı birası fuhchuh
beerasuh

draughty: it's draughty cereyan
yapıyor jerayan yapuh-yor

drawer çekmece chekmejeh

drawing çizim cheezeem

dreadful berbat

dream (*noun*) rüya rew-**ya**

dress (*noun*) elbise elbiseh

dressed: to get dressed
giyinmek

dressing (for cut) pansuman

  salad dressing sos

dressing gown (for women)
sabahlık sabaHluhk

  (for men) robdöşambr
robdurshambr

drink (alcoholic) içki eechkee

  (non-alcoholic) içecek eechejek,
meşrubat meshroobat

  (*verb*) içmek eechmek

  a cold drink soğuk meşrubat
so-**ook**

  can I get you a drink?
içecek bir şey ister misiniz?
shay

  **what would you like (to
drink)?** ne içki alırsınız? neh
eechkee aluhrsuhnuhz

  no thanks, I don't drink
hayır teşekkür, ederim alkol
almıyorum hī-uhr teshekkewr –
almuh-yoroom

  **I'll just have a drink
of water** sadece biraz su
istiyorum sa-dejeh

drinking water içme suyu eechm**eh**

   is this drinking water? bu içme suyu mu?

drive (*verb*) sürmek sewrm**ek**

   we drove here buraya arabayla geldik b**oo**ri-a arab**ī**la

   I'll drive you home ben sizi arabayla evinize götürürüm eveeneez**eh** gurtewr-ewr**ewm**

driver (of car) sürücü sewrewj**ew**

   (of bus) şoför shof**ur**

driving licence şoför ehliyeti

drop: just a drop, please (of drink) yalnız bir damla, lütfen yaln**uh**z – l**ew**tfen

drugs (narcotics) uyuşturucu oo-yooshtooroj**oo**

drunk (*adj*) sarhoş sarh**osh**

drunken driving içkili araba kullanmak eechkeel**ee**

dry (*adj*) kur**u**

   (wine) sek

dry-cleaner kuru temizleyici temeezl**a**yeejee

duck ördek urd**ek**

due: he/she was due to arrive yesterday dün gelmesi gerekiyord**u** dewn

   when is the train due? tren kaçta gelecek? k**a**chta gelej**ek**

dull (pain) don**u**k

   (weather) sıkıntılı suhkuhntuhl**uh**

dummy (baby's) emz**i**k

during sırasında suhra-s**uh**nda

dust toz

dustbin çöp tenekesi churp

dusty t**o**zlu

Dutch (*adj*) Hollanda

   (language) Hollandaca holl**a**ndaja

duty-free (goods) gümrüksüz eşya gewmr**ewk**sewz esh-y**a**

duty-free shop duty-free

duvet yorg**a**n

DVD DVD

E

each (every) her

   how much are they each? tanesi kaça? k**a**cha

ear kul**a**k

earache: I have earache kulağım ağrıyor koola-**uhm** a-ruh-y**or**

early erk**en**

   early in the morning sabah erkend**e**n sab**a**H

   I called by earlier daha önce uğramıştım **u**rnjeh oo-ramuhsht**uhm**

earring(s) küpe kewp**eh**

east doğu doh-**oo**

   in the east doğud**a**

Easter Paskalya

easy kolay ko-l**ī**

eat yem**ek**

   we've already eaten, thanks biz yedik, teşekkür ederiz teshekk**ewr**

eau de toilette kolonya

EC AT a teh

economy class ekonomi sınıfı suhnuhf**uh**

Edinburgh Edinburg

egg yumurta

eggplant patlıcan patluhjan

either: either... or... ya... ya...

either of them ikisinden biri

elastic (*noun*) lastik

elastic band lastik bant

elbow dirsek

electric elektrikli

electrical appliances elektrikli aletler

electric fire elektrik sobası sobasuh

electrician elektrikçi elektreekchee

electricity elektrik

elevator asansör asansur

else: something else başka bir şey bashka beer shay

somewhere else başka bir yer

DIALOGUE

would you like anything else? başka bir şey ister misiniz?

no, nothing else, thanks hayır, hepsi bu kadar, teşekkür ederim hı-**uh**r – teshekk**ewr**

email e-posta eh-posta

(*verb*) e-postayla yollamak eh-postila

embassy elçilik elcheeleek

emergency acil durum ajeel

this is an emergency! bu acildir! ajeeldeer

emergency exit tehlike çıkışı tehleekeh chukuhshuh

---

empty boş bosh

end (*noun*) son

(*verb*) bitmek

at the end of the... (street etc) ...-un sonunda

when does it end? ne zaman bitiyor?

engaged (toilet, telephone) meşgul meshgool

(to be married) nişanlı neeshanluh

engine (car) motor

England İngiltere eengeeltereh

English (*adj*) İngiliz eengeeleez

(language) İngilizce eengeeleezjeh

I'm English ben İngilizim

do you speak English? İngilizce biliyor musunuz?

enjoy: to enjoy oneself eğlenmek eh-lenmek

DIALOGUE

how did you like the film? filmi nasıl buldunuz? nasuhl

I enjoyed it very much, did you enjoy it? benim çok hoşuma gitti, ya sizin? chok hoshooma

enjoyable zevkli

enlargement (of photo) büyültme bew-yewltmeh

enormous dev

enough yeter

there's not enough yetmez

it's not big enough yeterince büyük değil yetereenjeh bew-yewk deh-eel

that's enough bu kadar yeter

entrance giriş geer**ee**sh
envelope zarf
Ephesus Ef**es**
epileptic (*adj*) saralı saral**uh**
equipment donatım donat**uh**m
error hat**a**
especially özellikle urzelleekl**eh**
essential şart shart
  it is essential that...
  ...-sı şarttır -shuh shart**tuhr**
EU AB a beh
Eurocheque Eu**r**ocheque
Eurocheque card Eurocheque
  kardı kard**uh**
Europe A**v**rupa
European (*adj*) Avrupa
  (person) Avrupalı avroopal**uh**
even... ... bile beel**eh**
  even if... ...-se bile -seh
evening akşam aksh**am**

this evening bu akşam
in the evening akşamleyin
  aksh**am**layeen
evening meal akşam yemeği
  yemeh-**ee**
eventually son**u**nda
ever hiç heech

> **DIALOGUE**
>
> **have you ever been to
> Antalya?** hiç Antalya'ya
> gittiniz mi?
> **yes, I was there two
> years ago** evet, iki yıl
> önce ordaydım yuhl **u**rnjeh
> ordid**uh**m

every her
  every day her gün gewn
everyone h**e**rkes
everything her şey shay
everywhere her yer

exactly! çok doğru! chok d**oh**-roo

exam sınav suhn**av**

example örnek urn**ek**

  for example örneğin urn**eh**-een

excellent mükemmel
  mewk**emmel**
  (food) nefis
  (hotel) çok güzel chok gewz**el**
  excellent! mükemmel!

except... ... hariç h**areech**

excess baggage fazla bagaj
  bag**aJ**

exchange rate döviz kur**u**
  durv**eez**

exciting heyecan verici hay**ejan**
  vereej**ee**

excuse me (to get past) p**ardon**
  (to get attention) affed**ersiniz**
  (to say sorry) özür dilerim urz**ewr**

exhaust (pipe) egz**o**s borus**u**

exhausted (tired) bitk**in**

exhibition sergi

exit çıkış chuhk**uh**sh

  where's the nearest exit?
  en yakın çıkış nerede? yak**uh**n –
  nered**eh**

expect beklem**ek**

expensive pahalı paн**aluh**

experienced tecrübeli
  tejrewbel**ee**

explain açıklamak achuhklam**ak**

  can you explain that? on**u**
  açıklar mısınız? achuhkl**ar**
  muhsuhn**uh**z

express (mail, train) ekspr**es**

extension (telephone) dahili
  numara daнeel**ee**

what is your extension?
dahili numaranız nedir?
noomar**anuh**z

  extension 221, please iki
  yüz yirmi bir numara, lütfen
  yewz – l**ew**tfen

extension lead uzatm**a** kablos**u**

**extra: can we have an extra
one?** lütfen bir tane daha
l**ew**tfen – tan**eh**

  **do you charge extra for
  that?** bun**u**n için ayrıca para
  alıyor musun**u**z? eech**een** iruhj**a**
  para aluh-y**or**

extraordinary çok garip chok
  gar**eep**

extremely son derece derej**eh**

eye göz gurz

  **will you keep an eye on
  my suitcase for me?** ben**im**
  için bav**u**luma göz kul**a**k ol**u**r
  musun**u**z? eech**een**

eyebrow pencil kaş kalemi kash

eye drops göz damlası gurz
  damlas**uh**

eyeglasses (US) gözlük gurzl**ewk**

eyeliner eyeliner

eye make-up remover
  göz makyajı çıkarıcısı gurz
  makyaJ**uh** chuhkaruh-juhs**uh**

eye shadow far

F

face yüz yewz

factory fabrika

Fahrenheit Fahrenhayt –h**ī**t

faint (*verb*) bayılmak bī-uhlm**ak**

she's fainted bayıldı
bī-uhld**uh**

I feel faint kendimi çok halsiz
hissediy**o**rum chok

fair (funfair) panayır panī-**uh**r

(trade) fuar fwar

(*adj*: just) **a**dil, haklı hakl**uh**

fairly oldukça old**oo**kcha

fake takl**i**t

fall (*verb*) düşmek dewshm**e**k

she's had a fall düştü
dewsht**ew**

(US: autumn) s**o**nbahar

in the fall s**o**nbaharda

false sahte sa**H**t**e**h

Famagusta Mag**o**sa

family aile a-**ee**leh

famous ünlü ewnl**ew**

fan (electrical) vantilatör
vant**ee**lat**u**r

(handheld) yelpaze yelpaz**eh**

(sports) tarafta**r**

(of pop star etc) hayran h**i**ran

fanbelt vantilatör kayışı
vant**ee**latur kī-uhsh**uh**

fantastic fantast**i**k, hay**a**li

far uz**a**k

DIALOGUE

is it far from here? burad**a**n
uzak mı? muh

no, not very far hayır, pek
uzak değil hī-**uh**r – deh-**ee**l

well, how far? pek**i** ne kad**a**r
uzak? neh

it's about 20 kilometres
yaklaşık yirm**i** kilometre
yaklash**uh**k – keelometr**eh**

fare yol parası paras**uh**

farm çiftlik cheeftl**ee**k

fashionable m**o**da

fast hızlı huhzl**uh**

fat (person) şişman sheeshm**a**n

(on meat) yağ ya

father bab**a**

father-in-law kayınpeder
kī-**uh**npeder

faucet musl**u**k

fault hat**a**

sorry, it was my fault özür
diler**i**m, hata bendeydi urz**ew**r –
bend**a**ydee

it's not my fault hata bende
değil bend**eh** deh-**ee**l

faulty arızalı aruhzal**uh**

favourite gözde gurzd**eh**

fax faks

fax (*verb*: person) -a faks çekmek
chekm**e**k

(document) fakslam**a**k

February şubat shoob**a**t

feel hissetm**e**k

I feel hot sıcak bastı suhj**a**k
bast**uh**

I feel unwell kendimi kötü
hissediy**o**rum kurt**ew**

I feel like going for a walk
canım yürüyüşe çıkmak
istiyor jan**uh**m yewrew-yewsh**e**h
ch**uh**km**a**k

how are you feeling?
kendin**i**zi nasıl
hissediy**o**rsunuz? nas**uh**l

I'm feeling better kendimi
dah**a** iy**i** hissediy**o**rum

felt-tip (pen) keçe uçlu kalem kecheh oochloo

fence parmaklık parmakluhk

fender tampon

ferry feribot

festival festival

> **Travel tip** During the Şeker and Kurban festivals travel becomes almost impossible – without advance planning you won't get a seat on any long-distance coach, train or plane. Many shops and all banks, museums and government offices close during these national holidays, although corner grocery shops and most resort shops stay open.

fetch gidip getirmek

I'll fetch him/her gidip onu çağırayım cha-uhrï-uhm

will you come and fetch me later? sonra gelip beni alır mısınız? aluhr muhsuhnuhz

feverish ateşli ateshlee

few: a few birkaç beerkach

a few days birkaç gün gewn

fiancé(e) nişanlı neeshanluh

field tarla

fight (noun) kavga

figs incir eenjeer

file dosya dos-ya

fill in doldurmak

do I have to fill this in? bunu doldurmam gerekli mi?

fill up doldurmak

fill it up, please lütfen depoyu doldurun lewtfen depo-yoo

filling (in cake, sandwich) iç eech (in tooth) dolgu

film film

filter coffee süzme kahve sewzmeh kaнveh

filter papers filtre kağıdı feeltreh ka-uhduh

filthy pis pees

find (verb) bulmak

I can't find it bulamıyorum boolamuh-yoroom

I've found it buldum

find out sorup öğrenmek ur-renmek

could you find out for me? benim için öğrenir misiniz? eecheen ur-reneer

fine (weather) güzel gewzel (punishment) ceza jeza

finger parmak

finish (verb) bitirmek

I haven't finished yet henüz bitirmedim henewz

when does it finish? ne zaman bitiyor? neh

fire (in hearth, campfire etc) ateş at**esh**

  (blaze) yangın yang**uhn**

  fire! yangın var!

  can we light a fire here?
b**u**rada ateş yakabil**i**r miy**i**z?

  it's on fire yanıyor yan**uh**-yor

fire alarm yangın alarmı yang**uh**n
alarm**uh**

fire brigade itfaiye eetfa-ee-y**eh**

fire escape yangın merdiveni
yang**uh**n

fire extinguisher yangın
söndürücü surndewrew-j**ew**

first ilk, birinci beer**ee**njee

  I was first ilk bend**i**m

  at first ilk önce **u**rnjeh

  the first time ilk kez

  first on the left sold**a**n birinci

first aid ilk yardım yard**uh**m

first aid kit ilk yardım çantası
chantas**uh**

first class (travel etc) birinci sınıf
beer**ee**njee suhn**uh**f

first floor birinci kat

  (US) zem**i**n kat

first name ad

fish (noun) balık bal**uh**k

fish restaurant balık lokantası
bal**uh**k lokantas**uh**

fishing village balıkçı köyü
bal**uh**kchuh kur-y**ew**

fishmonger's balıkçı

fit (attack) nöbet nurbet

fit: it doesn't fit me bana
uymuyor oo-imoo-y**o**r

fitting room soyunma odası
odas**uh**

fix (arrange) halletmek

  can you fix this? (repair) bun**u**
tam**i**r edebil**i**r misiniz?

fizzy gazlı gazl**uh**

flag bayrak b**i**rak

flannel el havlus**u**

flash (for camera) flaş flash

flat (noun: apartment) apartm**a**n
dairesi da-**ee**resee, daire da-**ee**reh

  (adj) düz dewz

  I've got a flat tyre lastiğim
patladı lastee-**ee**m patlad**uh**

flavour tat

flea pire peer**eh**

flight uçak seferi oochak

flight number sefer sayısı
s**i**-uhs**uh**h

flippers paletl**e**r

flood sel

floor (of room) yer

  (storey) kat

  on the floor yerde yerd**eh**

florist çiçekçi cheech**e**kchee

flour un

flower çiçek cheech**e**k

flu grip greep

**fluent: he speaks fluent
Turkish** akıcı bir Türkçesi var
akuhj**uh** beer tewrkchesee

fly (noun) sinek

  (verb) uçmak oochmak

fly in inm**e**k

fly out uçmak oochmak

fog sis

foggy: it's foggy sisli

folk dancing halk oyunları
oyunlar**uh**

folk music halk müziği mewzee-ee

follow takip etmek

   follow me beni takip edin

food yiyecek yee-yejek

food poisoning gıda zehirlenmesi guhda

food shop/store bakkal

foot (of person, measurement) ayak ī-ak

   on foot yayan yī-an

football (game) futbol

   (ball) top

football match futbol maçı machuh

for için eecheen

   do you have something for...? (headache/diarrhoea etc)... için bir şeyiniz var mı? shayeeneez var muh

   who's the imam bayıldı for? imam bayıldı kim için? bi-uhlduh

   that's for me o benim için

   and this one? ya bu?

   that's for her o, bayanın bi-anuhn

   where do I get the bus for İzmir? İzmir otobüsüne nereden binebilirim? eezmeer otobewsewneh

   the bus for İzmir leaves from İstiklal Caddesi İzmir otobüsü İstiklal Caddesi'nden kalkıyor kalkuh-yor

   how long have you been here for? ne zamandan beri buradasınız? neh – booradasuhnuhz

   I've been here for two days, how about you? ben iki gündür buradayım, ya siz? gewndewr booradi-uhm

   I've been here for a week bir haftadır buradayım haftaduhr booradi-uhm

forehead alın aluhn

foreign yabancı yabanjuh

foreigner yabancı

forest orman

forget unutmak

   I forget, I've forgotten unuttum

fork çatal chatal

   (in road) iki yol ağzı a-zuh

form (document) form, formüler formewler

formal (dress) resmi

fortnight on beş gün besh gewn

fortress kale kaleh

fortunately bereket versin

forward: could you forward my mail? mektuplarımı yeni adresime gönderir misiniz? –laruhmuh – adreseemeh gurndereer

forwarding address gönderilecek adres gurndereelejek

foundation cream fondöten fondurten

fountain çeşme cheshm**eh**

foyer giriş holü gee**ree**sh hol**ew**, fuaye fw**ī**-eh

fracture (*noun*) kırık kuhr**uh**k

France Fr**a**nsa

free serb**e**st

  (no charge) bedav**a**

  is it free (of charge)? ücretsiz mi? ewjrets**ee**z

freeway otoy**o**l

freezer buzl**u**k

French (*adj*) Fransız fr**a**nsuhz

  (language) Fransızca fransuhzj**a**

French fries patates kızartması kuhzartmas**uh**

frequent sık suhk

  how frequent is the bus to Edirne? Edirne'ye kaç saatte bir otobüs var? edeern**eh**-yeh kach sa-att**eh**

fresh (breeze) ser**i**n

  (fruit etc) taze taz**eh**

fresh orange juice taze portak**a**l suy**u**

Friday cuma joom**a**

fridge buzdolabı b**oo**zdolabuh

fried kızarmış kuhzarm**uh**sh

fried egg yağda yumurta ya-d**a**

friend arkadaş arkad**a**sh

friendly (person, animal) sokulg**a**n

  (behaviour) dostça d**o**stcha

from -den

  when does the next train from Eskişehir arrive? Eskişehir'den bir sonr**a**ki tren ne zam**a**n geliy**o**r? eskisheheer-den – neh

from Monday to Friday pazartesid**e**n cumay**a**

from next Thursday bir dah**a**ki perşembed**e**n itibar**e**n

front ön urn

  in front önde urnd**eh**

  in front of the hotel otel**i**n önünde urnewnd**eh**

  at the front ön taraft**a**

frost don

frozen donmuş donm**oo**sh

frozen food dondurulmuş yiyecekler dondooroolm**oo**sh yee-yejekl**e**r

fruit meyva mayv**a**

fruit juice meyva suy**u**

fry kızartmak kuhzartm**a**k

frying pan tav**a**

full dol**u**

  it's full of... ... ile dolu eel**eh**

  I'm full doyd**u**m

full board tam pansiy**o**n

fun: it was fun eğlendik eh-lend**ee**k

funeral cenaze jenaz**eh**

funny (strange) gar**i**p

  (amusing) kom**i**k

furniture mob**i**lya

further ileride ileree**d**eh

  it's further down the road yol**u**n ilerisinde eeleree-s**ee**ndeh

how much further is it to Troy? Truva'ya daha ne kadar var? neh

about 5 kilometres yaklaşık beş kilometre yaklashuhk – keelometreh

fuse sigorta

the lights have fused sigorta attı attuh

fuse box sigorta kutusu

fuse wire sigorta teli

future gelecek gelejek

in future gelecekte gelejekteh

G

Gallipoli Gelibolu

gallon galon

game (cards etc) oyun

(match) maç mach

(meat) av eti

garage (for fuel) benzin istasyonu

(for repairs) tamirhane tameerhaneh

(for parking) garaj garaJ

garden bahçe baнcheh

garlic sarmısak sarmuhsak

gas gaz

(US: petrol) benzin

gas cylinder (camping gas) gaz tüpü tewpew

gasoline benzin

gas permeable lenses gaz geçirgen lensler gecheergen

gas station benzin istasyonu

gate kapı kapuh

(at airport) çıkış kapısı chuhkuhsh kapuhsuh

gay homoseksüel homoseksewel

gay bar eşcinsellerin barı eshjeensellereen baruh

gearbox vites kutusu

gear lever vites kolu

gears vitesler

general (adj) genel

gents (toilet) erkekler (tuvaleti)

genuine (antique etc) gerçek gerchek

Georgia Gürcistan gewrjeestan

Georgian (adj) Gürcü gewrjew

German (adj) Alman

(language) Almanca almanja

German measles kızamıkçık kuhzamuhk-chuhk

Germany Almanya

get (fetch) getirmek

(obtain, buy) almak, bulmak

will you get me another one, please? bana bir tane daha getirir misiniz, lütfen? tan**eh** – l**ew**tfen

how do I get to...?...-e nasıl gidebilirim? -eh nas**uh**l

do you know where I can get them? onlardan nerede bulabilirim acaba, biliyor musunuz? n**e**redeh – ajaba

can I get you a drink? bir şey içmek ister misiniz? shay eechm**e**k

no, I'll get this one, what would you like? olmaz, bu sefer ben alacağım, ne istersiniz? alaja-**uh**m neh

a glass of red wine bir bardak kırmızı şarap

get back (return) dönmek durnm**e**k

get in (arrive) gelmek

get off inmek

where do I get off? nerede inmem lazım? n**e**redeh – laz**uh**m

get on (to train etc) binmek

get out (of car etc) inmek

get up (in the morning) kalkmak

gift hediye hedee-y**eh**

gift shop hediyelik eşya dükkanı esh-ya dewkkan**uh**

gin cin jeen

a gin and tonic, please bir cintonik, lütfen l**ew**tfen

girl kız kuhz

girlfriend kız arkadaş arkad**a**sh

give vermek

can you give me some bread/milk? bana biraz ekmek/süt verebilir misiniz?

I gave it to him/her ona verdim

will you give this to...? bunu...-e verir misiniz? -**eh**

give back iade etmek ee-ad**eh**

glad memnun

glass (material) cam jam

(tumbler) bardak

(wine glass) kadeh

a glass of wine bir kadeh şarap

a glass of tea bir bardak çay

glasses gözlük gurzl**ew**k

gloves eldiven

glue (noun) zamk

go gitmek

we'd like to go to the Topkapı Palace Topkapı Sarayı'na gitmek istiyoruz topkapuh sar**ī**-uh-na

where are you going? nereye gidiyorsunuz? n**e**rayeh

where does this bus go? bu otobüs nereye gidiyor?

let's go! haydi gidelim! h**ī**dee

he/she's gone (left) gitti

where has he gone? nereye gitti?

I went there last week oraya geçen hafta gittim or**ī**-a gech**e**n

hamburger to go paket hamburger

go away çekilip gitmek chekeeleep

go away! çekil git! chekeel geet

go back (return) dönmek durnmek

go down (the stairs etc) inmek

go in girmek

go out çıkmak chuhkmak

do you want to go out tonight? bu akşam çıkmak ister misiniz? aksham chuhkmak

go through geçmek gechmek

go up (the stairs etc) çıkmak chuhkmak

goat keçi kechee

goat's cheese keçi peyniri payneeree

God Allah

god tanrı tanruh

goddess tanrıça tanruhcha

goggles koruyucu gözlük koroo-yoojoo gurzlewk

gold altın altuhn

golf golf

golf course golf sahası sahasuh

good iyi

good! iyi!

it's no good boşuna, yararsız boshoona yararsuhz

goodbye (general use) hoşça kalın hosh-cha kaluhn

(said by person leaving) Allahaısmarladık alaha-uhsmarladuhk

(said to person leaving) güle güle gewleh

good evening iyi akşamlar akshamlar

good morning günaydın gewniduhn

good night iyi geceler gejeler

goose kaz

got: we've got to leave gitmemiz gerek

have you got any...? hiç...-nız var mı? heech...-nuhz var muh

government hükümet hewkewmet

gradually giderek

grammar gramer

gram(me) gram

granddaughter torun

grandfather büyükbaba bewyewk-baba

grandmother büyükanne bewyewk-anneh

grandson torun

grapefruit greyfrut grayfroot

grapefruit juice greyfrut suyu

grapes üzüm ewzewm

grass ot

grateful minnettar

gravy sos

great (excellent) fevkalade fevkaladeh

that's great! mükemmel! mewkemmel

a great success büyük bir başarı bewyewk beer basharuh

Great Britain Büyük Britanya

Greece Yunanistan

greedy açgözlü achgurzlew

Greek (*adj*) Yunan

  (language) Rumca r**oo**mja

  (person) Yunanlı yoonanl**uh**

  (*adj*: person, living in Turkey) Rum
room

Greek Cypriot (*adj*) Kıbrıs Rum
kuhbr**uhs**

  (person) Kıbrıslı Rum
kuhbruhsl**uh**

Greek Orthodox Rum Ortod**o**ks

green yeşil yesh**ee**l

green card (car insurance) yeşil
kart

greengrocer's man**a**v

grey gri gree

grill (*noun*) ızgara uhzg**a**ra

grilled ızgara uhzg**a**ra

grocer's bakk**a**l

ground yer

  on the ground yerde yerd**eh**

ground floor zem**i**n kat

group grup

guarantee (*noun*) garant**i**

  is it guaranteed? garantis**i**
var mı? muh

guest mis**a**fir

guesthouse pansiy**o**n

guide (person, book) rehber re**H**ber

guidebook rehb**e**r

guided tour rehberl**i** tur

guitar git**a**r

gum (in mouth) dişeti deeshet**ee**

gun (rifle) tüfek tewf**e**k

  (pistol) tabanca tab**a**nja

gym spor salon**u**

gypsy çingene cheegen**eh**

hair saç sach

hairbrush saç fırçası fuhrchas**uh**

haircut (man's) saç tıraşı tuhr**a**shuh

  (woman's) saç kesme kesm**eh**

hairdresser's (men's) berb**e**r

  (women's) kuaför kwaf**u**r

hairdryer saç kur**u**tma makines**i**
sach

hair gel jel Jel

hairgrips saç tokaları sach
tokalar**uh**

hair spray saç spreyi spray**ee**

half yarım yar**uh**m

  half an hour yarım saat sa-**a**t

  half a litre yarım litre l**ee**treh

  about half that onun yarısı
kad**a**r yaruhs**uh**

half board yarım pansiy**o**n

half-bottle yarım şişe sheesh**eh**

half fare yarım tarife tareef**eh**

half price yarı fiy**a**t yar**uh**

ham jambon J**a**mbon

hamburger hamburger
hamb**oo**rger

hammer (*noun*) çekiç chek**ee**ch

hand el

handbag el çantası chantas**uh**

handbrake el fren**i**

handkerchief mend**i**l

handle (on door) kol

  (on suitcase etc) sap

hand luggage el bagajı bagaJ**uh**

hang-gliding hang-gliding

hangover içkiden gelen baş
ağrısı eechkeeden – bash
a-ruhsuh

  I've got a hangover çok
içtiğim için başım ağrıyor chok
eechtee-eem eecheen bashuhm

happen olmak

  what's happening? ne
oluyor? neh

  what has happened? ne
oldu?

happy mutlu

  I'm not happy about this
bu hiç hoşuma gitmiyor heech
hoshooma

harbour liman

hard sert

  (difficult) zor

hard-boiled egg lop yumurta

hard lenses sert lensler

hardly ancak anjak

  hardly ever hemen hemen hiç
heech

hardware shop nalbur

hat şapka shapka

hate (verb) nefret etmek

have sahip olmak

  can I have a...? bir... rica
edebilir miyim? reeja

  can we have some...?
biraz... rica edebilir miyiz?

  do you have...? sizde...
bulunur mu? seezdeh – muh

  what'll you have? ne
alırsınız? neh aluhrsuhnuhz

  I have to leave now şimdi
gitmek zorundayım sheemdee
– zoroondı-uhm

do I have to...? ...-m lazım
mı? lazuhm muh

hayfever saman nezlesi

hazelnuts fındık fuhnduhk

he o

head baş bash

headache baş ağrısı a-ruhsuh

headlights farlar

headphones kulaklıklar
koolakluhklar

healthy sağlıklı sa-luhkluh

hear duymak doo-imak

hearing aid işitme cihazı
eesheetmeh jeehazuh

heart kalp

heart attack kalp krizi

heat sıcaklık suhjakluhk

heater (in room) ısıtıcı uhsuhtuhjuh
  (in car) radyatör radyatur

heating ısıtma uhsuhtma

heavy ağır a-uhr

heel (of foot, shoe) topuk

  could you heel these?
bunların topuklarını
yapar mısınız? boonlaruhn
topooklaruhnuh – muhsuhnuhz

heelbar kundura tamircisi
tameerjeesee

height (of person) boy

(of mountain) yükseklik yewksekleek

helicopter helikopter

hello merhaba

(answer on phone) alo

helmet (for motorcycle) kask

help (*noun*) yardım yarduhm

(*verb*) yardım etmek

help! imdat!

can you help me? bana yardım edebilir misiniz?

thank you very much for your help yardımınız için çok teşekkür ederim yarduhmuhnuhz eecheen chok teshekkewr

helpful yardımcı yarduhmjuh

hepatitis hepatit

her: her... ...-i,...-si

(emphatic) onun...

it's her towel onun havlusu

I haven't seen her onu görmedim gurmedeem

to her ona

with her onunla

for her onun için eecheen

that's her işte o eeshteh

herbal tea bitkisel çay chī

herbs çeşni veren otlar cheshnee

here burada

here is/are... işte... eeshteh

here you are (offering) buyrun boo-iroon

hers onunki

that's hers şu onunki shoo

hey! hey!

hi! (hello) merhaba!

hide (*verb*) saklamak

high yüksek yewksek

highchair bebek iskemlesi

highway otoyol

hill tepe tepeh

him: I haven't seen him onu görmedim gurmedeem

to him ona

with him onunla

for him onun için eecheen

that's him over there şuradaki o işte shooradakee o eeshteh

hip kalça kalcha

Hippodrome At Meydanı maydanuh

hire kiralamak

for hire kiralık keeraluhk

where can I hire a bike? nereden bir bisiklet kiralayabilirim? keeralī-abeeleereem

his: his... ...-i,...-si

(emphatic) onun...

it's his car onun otomobili

that's his şu onunki shoo

hit (*verb*) vurmak

hitch-hike otostop yapmak

hobby merak

hold (*verb*) tutmak

hole delik

holiday tatil

on holiday tatilde tateeldeh

Holland Hollanda

home ev

at home (in my house etc) evde evdeh

(in my country) bizde beezdeh

we go home tomorrow
yarın evimize gidiyor**uz** yar**uh**n
eveemeez**eh**

honest dürüst dew**rew**st

honey bal

honeymoon balayı ba**l**i-uh

hood (US) motor kapağı kapa-**uh**,
kap**ut**

hookah nargile nargeel**eh**

hope um**ut**

  I hope so umarım öyledir
oomar**uh**m uh-iled**eer**

  I hope not umarım öyle
değildir uh-il**eh** deh-ee**ldeer**

hopefully inşallah eenshallah

horn (of car) klaks**o**n, k**o**rna

horrible korkunç kork**oo**nch

horse at

horse riding binicilik
beeneejeel**eek**

hospital hastane hastan**eh**

hospitality kon**u**ksever**lik**

  **thank you for your
hospitality** konukseverliğiniz
için teşekkürler
kon**oo**kseverlee-een**eez** ich**ee**n
teshekkew**ler**

hot sıcak suhj**ak**

  (spicy) acı aj**uh**

  I'm hot sıcak bastı bast**uh**

  it's hot today bugün hava
sıcak boog**ewn** – suhj**ak**

hotel ot**el**

hotel room ot**el** odası odas**uh**

hour saat sa-**at**

house ev

hovercraft hoverkr**aft**

---

how nasıl nas**uhl**

  how many? kaç tane? kach
tan**eh**

  how do you do? memn**un**
old**um**!

  how are you? nasılsınız?
nas**uhl**-suhn**uh**z

  fine, thanks, and you?
iyiyim, teşekkür ederim, ya
siz? teshekkew**r**

  how much is it? kaça?
kach**a**

  22 lira yirmi iki lira

  I'll take it alıyorum al**uh**-
yoroom

---

humid neml**i**

hungry: I'm hungry acıktım
ajuhkt**uhm**

  are you hungry? acıktınız
mı? ajuhktuhn**uh**z muh

hurry (verb) acele etm**ek** aj**e**leh

  I'm in a hurry acelem var
aj**e**lem

  there's no hurry aceleye
ger**ek** yok aj**e**lay**eh**

  hurry up! çabuk ol! chab**ook**

hurt (verb) incitmek eenjeetm**ek**,
acımak ach**uh**mak

  it really hurts gerçekten
çok acıyor gerchekten chok
aj**uh**-y**or**

husband koca koj**a**

hydrofoil kızaklı tekne kuhzakl**uh**
tekn**eh**, hidrofoil h**ee**drofoyl

I

I ben

ice buz booz

  with ice buzlu

  no ice, thanks buz istemez,
teşekkür ederim teshekkewr

ice cream dondurma

ice-cream cone dondurma
külahı kewl-ahuh

iced coffee buzlu kahve kaнveh

ice lolly eskimo

idea fikir

idiot aptal

if eğer eh-er

ignition kontak

ill hasta

  I feel ill kendimi hasta
hissediyorum

illness hastalık hastaluhk

imitation (leather etc) taklit

immediately hemen

important önemli urnemlee

  it's very important çok
önemlidir chok

  it's not important önemli
değil deh-eel

impossible imkansız eemkansuhz

impressive etkileyici etkeelay-
eejee

improve iyileştirmek eeyeelesh–,
geliştirmek geleeshteermek

  **I want to improve my
Turkish** Türkçemi geliştirmek
istiyorum tewrkchemee
geleeshteermek

in: it's in the centre merkezde
merkezdeh

  in my car arabamda

  in İstanbul İstanbul'da

  in two days from now iki
güne kadar gewneh

  in five minutes beş dakika
içinde eecheendeh

  in May mayısta

  in English İngilizce
eengeeleezjeh

  in Turkish Türkçe tewrkcheh

  is he in? orda mı? muh

inch inç eench

include dahil etmek daнeel

  does that include meals?
buna yemekler dahil mi?

  is that included? bu dahil
mi?

inconvenient elverişsiz
elvereesh-seez

incredible inanılmaz
eenanuhlmaz

Indian (adj) Hint

indicator sinyal

indigestion hazımsızlık hazuhm-
suhzluhk

indoor pool kapalı havuz kapaluh

indoors içerde eecherdeh

inexpensive ucuz oojooz

infection enfeksiyon

infectious bulaşıcı boolashuhjuh

inflammation iltihap

informal fazla resmi olmayan
olmi-an

information bilgi

  do you have any

information about…?
sizde… hakkında bilgi var mı?
hakkuhnda – muh

information desk danışma
masası danuhshma masasuh

injection enjeksiyon enJeksee-yon

injured yaralı yaraluh

  she's been injured yaralandı
  yaralanduh

inner tube (for tyre) iç lastik eech

innocent masum

insect böcek burjek

insect bite böcek sokması
  sokmasuh

  **do you have anything for
  insect bites?** sizde böcek
  sokmasına karşı bir şey
  bulunur mu? seezdeh – karshuh
  beer shay

insect repellent böcek ilacı
  eelachuh

inside: inside the hotel otelin
  içinde eecheendeh

  let's sit inside içerde oturalım
  eecherdeh otooraluhm

insist: I insist ısrar ediyorum

insomnia uykusuzluk
  oo-ikoosoozlook

instant coffee neskafe neskafeh

instead yerine yereeneh

  give me that one instead
  yerine şunu verin shoonoo

  instead of… …-in yerine

insulin insülin eensewleen

insurance sigorta

intelligent zeki

interested: I'm interested in…
  …-e ilgi duyuyorum -eh

interesting ilginç eelgeench

  that's very interesting
  çok ilginç chok

international uluslararası
  oolooslararasuh

Internet internet

Travel tip Many hotels,
pensions and even hostels
in tourist areas have
internet access, as do an
ever-increasing number of
cafés. The Turkish-character
keyboard may cause some
confusion: the dotless Turkish
'ı' is located where you'd
expect the conventional
Western 'i' to be – which can
be found second key from the
right, middle row.

interpret tercüme etmek
  terjewmeh

interpreter tercüman terjewman

intersection kavşak kavshak

interval (at theatre) ara

into: into the… …-in içine
  eecheeneh

  I'm not into… … ilgimi
  çekmiyor chekmee-yor

introduce tanıştırmak
  tanuhshtuhrmak

  may I introduce…? size…-i
  tanıştırabilir miyim? seezeh…-
  ee tanuhsh-tuhrabeeleer

invitation davet

invite davet etmek

Iran İran eeran

Iraq Irak uhrak

Ireland İrlanda eerlanda

Irish İrlanda

  I'm Irish İrlandalıyım
  eerlandal**uh**-yuhm

iron (for ironing) ütü ewt**ew**

  can you iron these for me?
  bunları benim için ütüler
  misiniz? boonlar**uh** – eech**een**
  ewtewler

is -dir

Islam İslam ees**lam**

Islamic İslami

island ada

İstanbul İstanbul eestanbool

it o

  it is... o...-dir

  is it...? ... mu?

  where is it? nerede? neredeh

  it's him/her odur

  it was... ... idi

Italian (adj: person) İtalyan
eetaly**an**

  (language) İtalyanca eetaly**an**ja

Italy İtalya

itch: it itches kaşınıyor
kash**uh**nuh-y**or**

J

jack (for car) kriko

jacket ceket jek**et**

jam reçel rech**el**

jammed: it's jammed takıldı
tak**uh**ld**uh**

January ocak oj**ak**

jar (noun) kavanoz

jaw çene chen**eh**

jazz caz jaz

jealous kıskanç kuhskanch

jeans blucin blooj**een**

jellyfish denizanası –s**uh**

jersey kaza**k**

jetty iskele eeskeleh

jeweller's kuyumcu koo-
yoomjoo

jewellery mücevherat mew-
jevherat

Jewish Yahudi

job iş eesh

jogging koşu koshoo

  to go jogging koşu yapmak

joke şaka shaka

journey yolculuk yoljool**ook**

  have a good journey! iyi
  yolculuklar!

jug sürahi sewrahee

  a jug of water bir sürahi su

juice: ... juice ... suyu

July temm**uz**

jump (verb) atlamak

jumper kaza**k**

jump leads buji telleri booJee

junction kavşak kavshak

June hazir**an**

just (only) sadece sa-dej**eh**

  just two sadece iki tane tan**eh**

  just for me yalnız benim için
  yaln**uh**z – eech**een**

  just here tam burada

  not just now şimdi değil
  sheemdee deh-**eel**

  we've just arrived henüz
  geldik hen**ewz**

K

kebab kebap
  (mild) Bursa kebabı kebab**uh**
  (very spicy) Urfa kebabı
keep tutmak
  keep the change üstü kalsın
  ewst**ew** kals**uh**n
  can I keep it? bende kalabilir
  mi? bend**eh**
  please keep it sizde kalsın
  seezd**eh**
ketchup keçap kech**a**p
kettle çaydanlık chïdanl**uh**k
key anahtar anaHt**a**r
  the key for room 201,
  please iki yüz bir numaralı
  odanın anahtarı, lütfen yewz
  beer noomaral**uh** odan**uh**n
  anaHtar**uh** l**ew**tfen

keyring anahtarlık anaHtarl**uh**k
kidneys (in body) böbrekler
  burbrekl**e**r
  (food) böbr**e**k
kill (*verb*) öldürmek urldewrm**e**k
kilo kil**o**
kilometre kilometre
  keelometr**eh**
  how many kilometres
  is it to...?... buradan kaç
  kilometre? kach
kind (generous) nazik, iyi
  that's very kind çok
  naziksiniz chok

which kind do you want? hangisinden istiyorsunuz?	DIALOGUE
I want this/that kind bu/ şu türden istiyorum shoo tewrd**e**n	

king kral

kiosk büfe bewfeh

kiss (*noun*) öpücük urpewjewk
(*verb*) öpmek urpmek

kitchen mutfak

Kleenex kâğıt mendil ka-uht

knee diz

knickers külot kewlot

knife bıçak buhchak

knitwear örgü urgew

knock (*verb*) vurmak

knock down çarpmak charpmak
  he's been knocked down
  araba çarpmış charpmuhsh

knock over (object) devirmek
(pedestrian) çarpmak charpmak,
çiğnemek chee-nemek

know (somebody) tanımak
tanuhmak
(something) bilmek
  I don't know bilmiyorum
  I didn't know that onu
  bilmiyordum
  **do you know where I
  can find…?** …-i nerede
  bulabilirim, biliyor musunuz?
  neredeh

L

label etiket

ladies' (toilets) bayanlar bī-anlar

ladies' wear kadın giyim eşyası
kaduhn – esh-yasuh

lady bayan bī-an

lager bira

lake göl gurl

lamb (meat) kuzu

lamp lamba

lane (motorway) şerit shereet
(small road) dar yol

language dil

language course dil kursu

laptop dizüstü bilgisayar
deezewstew beelgeesi-ar

large büyük bewyewk

last (final) son
  last week geçen hafta gechen
  last Friday geçen cuma
  last night dün gece dewn gejeh
  **what time is the last train
  to Ankara?** Ankara'ya son
  tren kaçta? kachta

late geç gech
  sorry I'm late geciktiğim için
  özür dilerim gejeektee-eem
  eecheen urzewr
  the train was late tren gecikti
  gejeektee
  we must go – we'll be late
  gitmemiz gerek – geç kalacağız
  kalaja-uhz
  it's getting late geç oluyor
  gech

later daha sonra
  I'll come back later sonra
  tekrar gelirim
  see you later görüşmek üzere
  gurewshmek ewzereh
  later on daha sonra

latest en son
  by Wednesday at the latest
  en geç çarşambaya kadar gech

laugh (*verb*) gülmek gewlmek

launderette, laundromat
otomatlı çamaşırhane otomatl**uh**
chamash**uh**r-haneh

laundry (clothes) çamaşır
chamash**uh**r

(place) çamaşırhane
chamash**uh**r-haneh

lavatory tuval**e**t

law k**a**nun

lawn çimen cheem**e**n

lawyer avuk**a**t

laxative müshil m**e**ws-heel,
laks**a**tif

lazy temb**e**l

lead (electrical) kabl**o**

where does this lead to?
bu nereye çıkıyor? n**e**rayeh
chuhkuh-y**o**r

leaf yapr**a**k

leaflet broşür brosh**e**wr

leak (*noun*) sızıntı suhzuhnt**uh**
(*verb*) sızmak suhzm**a**k

the roof leaks dam akıyor
akuh-y**o**r

learn öğrenmek ur-renm**e**k

least: not in the least hiç de
değil heech deh deh–**ee**l

at least en azından en
azuhnd**a**n

leather der**i**

leave (*verb*) bırakmak buhrakm**a**k
(go away) ayrılmak **ī**ruhlm**a**k

I am leaving tomorrow yarın
hareket ediyorum yar**uh**n

he left yesterday dün gitti
d**e**wn

may I leave this here? bun**u**
bur**a**da bırakabilir miyim?
buhraka-bee**ee**r

I left my coat in the bar
palto**mu** barda bıraktım
buhrakt**uh**m

**when does the bus for
Bursa leave?** Bursa otobüsü
ne zam**a**n kalkıyor? neh –
kalkuh-y**o**r

Lebanon Lübnan lewbn**a**n

leeks pırasa puhr**a**sa

left sol

on the left solda

to the left sola

turn left sola dönün durn**e**wn

there's none left hiç kalmadı
heech kalmad**uh**

left-handed sol**a**k

left luggage (office) eman**e**t

leg bacak baj**a**k

lemon lim**o**n

lemonade limon**a**ta

lemon tea limonlu çay leemonl**oo**
ch**ī**

lend ödünç vermek urd**e**wnch

will you lend me your... ?
...-inizi ödünç verir misiniz?
urd**e**wnch

lens (of camera) objektif
obj**e**kteef

lesbian sevici seve**e**jee

less dah**a** az

less than... ...-den daha az

less expensive daha az pahal**ı**

lesson ders

let (allow) -a izin vermek

will you let me know? bana
haber verir misiniz?

I'll let you know ben size
haber veririm seez**eh**

**let's go for something
to eat** hadi gidip bir şeyler
yiyelim shay**ler**

let off bırakmak buhrakmak

will you let me off at…?
beni…-da bırakır mısınız?
buhrak**uhr** muhsuhn**uhz**

letter mektup

**do you have any letters
for me?** bana mektup var
mı? **muh**

letterbox mektup kutusu

lettuce yeşil salata yesh**eel**

lever (*noun*) manivela

library kütüphane kewtewp-haneh

licence izin belgesi

(driving) ehliyet

lid kapak

lie (*verb*: tell untruth) yalan
söylemek suh-ilemek

lie down uzanmak

life hayat hī-at

lifebelt can kemeri jan

lifeguard cankurtaran
jankoortaran

life jacket can yeleği jan yeleh-**ee**

lift (in building) asansör asans**ur**

could you give me a lift?
beni de arabanıza alır mısınız?
deh arabanuh**za** al**uhr**

would you like a lift?
sizi de götürebilir miyim?
gurtewrebeel**eer**

light (*noun*) ışık uhshu**hk**

(not heavy) hafif

do you have a light? (for
cigarette) ateşiniz var mı?
atesheen**eez** var muh

light green açık yeşil achu**hk**
yesh**eel**

light bulb amp**ul**

I need a new light bulb bana
yeni bir ampul lazım laz**uhm**

lighter çakmak chakmak

lightning şimşek sheemshek

like (*verb*) hoşlanmak hoshlanmak,
sevmek

I like it beğendim beh-end**eem**

I like going for walks
yürüyüşe çıkmayı severim
yewrew-yewsh**eh** chuhkmī-**uh**

I like you sizden
hoşlanıyorum hoshlan**uh**-yoroom

I don't like it hoşuma
gitmiyor hoshooma

do you like…?… sever
misiniz?

I'd like a beer bir bira
istiyorum

I'd like to go swimming
yüzmeye gitmek istiyorum
yewzmay**eh**

would you like a drink? bir
şey içmek ister misiniz? shay
eechmek

**would you like to go for
a walk?** yürüyüşe çıkmak
ister misiniz? yewrew-yewsh**eh**
chuhkmak

what's it like? nasıl bir şey?
nas**uhl**

I want one like this bunun
gibi bir şey istiyorum

lime misket limonu

lime cordial konsantre limon
suyu konsantreh

line (on paper) çizgi cheezgee

(phone) hat

**could you give me an
outside line?** bana bir dış hat
verir misiniz? duhsh

lips dudaklar

lip salve dudak merhemi

lipstick ruj rooJ

liqueur likör leekur

listen dinlemek

listen! dinle! deenleh

litre litre leetreh

a litre of white wine bir litre
beyaz şarap bayaz sharap

little küçük kewchewk

just a little, thanks yalnız
çok az bir şey, teşekkür
ederim yalnuhz chok – shay
teshekkewr

a little milk biraz süt sewt

a little bit more biraz daha

live (verb) yaşamak yashamak

we live together birlikte
yaşıyoruz beerleekteh yashuh-
yorooz

DIALOGUE

where do you live? nerede
oturuyorsunuz? neredeh

I live in London Londra'da
oturuyorum

lively (person) canlı janluh

(town) hareketli

liver (in body) karaciğer
karajee-er

(food) ciğer

loaf somun

lobby (in hotel) lobi

lobster istakoz

local yerel

**can you recommend a
local restaurant?** yöröde
bir lokanta tavsiye edebilir
misiniz? yuredeh – tavsee-yeh

lock (noun) kilit

(verb) kilitlemek

it's locked kilitli

lock in içeri kilitlemek
eecheree

lock out dışarıda bırakmak
duhsharuhda buhrakmak

I've locked myself out
dışarıda kaldım duhsharuhda
kalduhm

locker (for luggage etc) emanet
kasası kasasuh

lollipop lolipop

London Londra

long uzun

**how long will it take to
fix it?** tamir etmesi ne kadar
sürer? neh – sewrer

how long does it take? ne
kadar sürer?

a long time uzun süre
sewreh

one day/two days longer bir
gün/iki gün daha

long-distance call şehirlerarası
konuşma sheheerler-arasuh
konooshma

look: I'm just looking, thanks
şöyle bir bakıyorum, teşekkür
ederim shuh-ileh beer bakuhyoroom teshekkewr

you don't look well
iyi görünmüyorsunuz
gurewnmew–

look out! dikkat!

can I have a look? bir
bakabilir miyim?

look after -a bakmak

look at -a bakmak

look for aramak

I'm looking for... ...-i
arıyorum aruh-yoroom

look forward to iple çekmek
eepleh chekmek

I'm looking forward to it
onu iple çekiyorum eepleh
chekee-yoroom

loose (handle etc) gevşek
gevshek

lorry kamyon

lose kaybetmek kī-betmek

I'm lost, I want to get to...
yolumu kaybettim,...-'e gitmek
istiyordum kībetteem...-eh

I've lost my bag çantamı
kaybettim chantamuh

lost property (office) kayıp eşya
kī-uhp esh-ya

lot: a lot, lots çok chok

not a lot çok değil deh-eel

a lot of people bir çok insan

a lot bigger çok daha büyük

I like it a lot çok beğendim
beh-endeem

lotion losyon

loud (noise) gürültülü gewrewl-
tewlew

(voice) yüksek sesle yewksek
sesleh

lounge (in house, hotel) salon
(airport) yolcu salonu yoljoo

love (*noun*) sevgi
(*verb*) sevmek

I love Turkey Türkiye'ye
aşığım tewrkee-yeh-yeh ashuh-
uhm

lovely çok güzel chok gewzel

low alçak alchak

luck şans shans

good luck! bol şanslar!

luggage bagaj bagaJ

luggage trolley eşya arabası
esh-ya arabasuh

lump (on body) yumru

lunch öğle yemeği urleh
yemeh-ee

lungs akciğerler akjee-erler

luxurious (hotel, furnishings) lüks
lewks

luxury lüks

M

macaroon acıbadem kurabiyesi
ajuhbadem

machine makina

mad (insane) deli
(angry) kızgın kuhzguhn

magazine dergi

maid (in hotel) kat görevlisi
gurevleesee

maiden name kızlık adı
kuhzluhk aduh

mail (*noun*) posta

(*verb*) postalamak

is there any mail for me?
bana mektup var mı? muh

mailbox mektup kutusu

main esas

main course ana yemek

main post office merkez
postanesi

main road (in town) ana cadde
jaddeh

(in country) anayol

mains switch şalter shalter

make (brand name) marka

(*verb*) yapmak

I make it 37 lira benim
hesabıma göre otuz yedi lira
ediyor hesabuhma gureh

what is it made of? neden
yapılmış? yapuhlmuhsh

make-up makyaj makyaJ

man adam

manager yönetici yurneteejee

can I see the manager?
yöneticiyi görebilir miyim?
yurneteejee-yee gurebeeleer

manageress yönetici bayan

manual düz dewz

(car) düz vitesli

many çok chok

not many az

map (city plan) şehir planı sheh-
heer planuh

(road map, geographical) harita

March mart

margarine margarin

market pazar, çarşı charshuh

marmalade portakal reçeli
rehchelee

married: I'm married evliyim

are you married?
evli misiniz?

mascara rimel

match (football etc) maç mach

matches kibrit

material (fabric) kumaş
koomash

matter: it doesn't matter
önemli değil urnemlee deh-eel

what's the matter?
ne oluyor? neh

mattress şilte sheelteh

May mayıs mī-uhs

**may: may I have another
one?** bir tane daha alabilir
miyim? taneh

may I come in? girebilir
miyim?

may I see it? onu görebilir
miyim? gurebeeleer

may I sit here? buraya
oturabilir miyim? boorī-a

maybe belki

mayonnaise mayonez
mī-onez

me beni, bana

that's for me o benim için
eecheen

send it to me onu bana
gönderin

me too ben de deh

meal yemek

did you enjoy your meal?
yemek hoşunuza gitti mi?
hoshoonooza

**it was excellent, thank
you** mükemmeldi, teşekkür
ederim mewkemmeldee
teshekkewr

mean: what do you mean?
ne demek istiyorsunuz? neh

**what does this word
mean?** bu kelimenin
anlamı ne? anlamuh neh

it means... in English
İngilizcede... demektir
eengeeleezjedeh

measles kızamık kuhzamuhk

meat et

meat restaurant kebapçı
kebapchuh

mechanic tamirci tameerjee

medicine ilaç eelach

Mediterranean Akdeniz

medium (*adj*: size) orta

medium-dry dömi sek durmee

medium-rare orta pişmiş
peeshmeesh

medium-sized orta büyüklükte
bewyew-klewkteh

meet buluşmak boolooshmak
(at airport) karşılamak
karshuhlamak

nice to meet you memnun
oldum

where shall I meet you?
nerede buluşalım? neredeh
boolooshaluhm

meeting toplantı toplantuh

meeting place buluşma yeri
boolooshma

melon kavun

memory stick hafıza çubuğu
hafuhza chooboo-**oo**

men adamlar

mend onarmak

**could you mend this
for me?** bunu benim için
onarabilir misiniz? eecheen

menswear erkek giyim eşyası
esh-yasuh

mention (*verb*) bahsetmek
baнsetmek

don't mention it bir şey değil
shay deh-**eel**

menu yemek listesi

**may I see the menu,
please?** yemek listesini
görebilir miyim, lütfen?
gurebeeleer – lewtfen

see Menu Reader

message mesaj mesaJ

**are there any messages
for me?** bana mesaj var mı?
muh

**I want to leave a message
for...** ... için bir mesaj
bırakmak istiyorum eecheen –
buhrakmak

metal metal

metre metre metreh

microwave (oven) mikro dalga

midday öğle üzeri ur-**leh**
ewzeree

at midday öğleyin ur-layeen

middle: in the middle ortada

in the middle of the night
gece yarısı gej**eh** yaruhs**uh**

the middle one ortadak**i**

midnight gece yarısı

at midnight gece yarısı

might: I might come belki
gelir**im**

I might not go gitmeyebilir**im**

**I might want to stay
another day** bir gün daha
kalm**ak** isteyebilir**im**

migraine migr**en**

mild (taste) haf**if**

(weather) ılıman uhluhm**an**

mile mil

milk süt sewt

milkshake milkşeyk meelkshayk

millimetre milimetre
meeleem**e**treh

minaret minare meenar**eh**

minced meat kıyma kuh-ima

mind: never mind zar**a**r yok

I've changed my mind
fikrim**i** değiştirdim deh-
eeshteerd**eem**

**do you mind if I open
the window?** pencereyi
açmamın bir mahzur**u** var
mı? penjeray**ee** achmamuh**n**
beer ma**H**zoor**oo**

no, I don't mind hayır,
benim için farketm**ez** h**ī-uhr**
eech**een**

mine: it's mine o benim,
benimk**i**

mineral water maden suy**u**

mints nane şekeri nan**eh** sheker**ee**

minute dak**i**ka

in a minute birazd**an**

just a minute bir dak**i**ka

mirror ayna in**a**

Miss Bayan b**ī-an**

miss: I missed the bus otobüs**ü**
kaçırdım kachuhrd**uhm**

missing eksik eks**ee**k

one of my ... is missing
...lerimden bir**i** eksik

there's a suitcase missing
bir bav**ul** eksik

mist sis

mistake (*noun*) hata

I think there's a mistake
sanırım bir yanlışlık var
sanuhr**uhm** – yanluhshluh**k**

sorry, I've made a mistake
özür dilerim, hata yaptım
urz**ewr** – yaptuh**m**

misunderstanding yanlış
anlam**a** –luh**sh**

**mix-up: sorry, there's been
a mix-up** özür dilerim, bir
karışıklık olmuş urz**ewr** –
karuhshuhkluh**k** olm**oo**sh

mobile (phone) cep telefonu jep
telefon**oo**

modern modern modair**n**

modern art gallery çağdaş
sanat galerisi cha-dash

moisturizer nemlendirici krem
–reej**ee**

**moment: I'll be back in a
moment** hem**en** geliyorum

monastery manastır manast**uhr**

Monday paz**a**rtesi

money para

month ayı

monument anıt anuht

moon ayı

moped moped

more daha

can I have some more water, please? biraz daha su alabilir miyim, lütfen? lewtfen

more expensive/interesting daha pahalı/ilginç

more than 50 elliden fazla

more than that ondan daha fazla

a lot more çok daha fazla chok

would you like some more? biraz daha ister misiniz?

no, no more for me, thanks hayır, teşekkür ederim, bu kadar yeter bana hı-**uhr** – teshekkewr

how about you? ya siz?

I don't want any more, thanks ben daha fazla istemiyorum, teşekkür ederim

morning sabah sabaH

this morning bu sabah boo

in the morning sabahleyin sabaHlayeen

mosaic mozaik moza-**eek**

mosque cami jamee

mosquito sivrisinek

mosquito repellent sivrisinek ilacı eelaj**uh**

most: I like this one most of all en çok bundan hoşlanıyorum chok – hoshlan**uh**-yoroom

most of the time çoğu zaman choh-**oo**

most tourists çoğu turist

mostly çoğunlukla choh-oonl**oo**kla

mother anne anneh

mother-in-law kayınvalide kı-uhnvaleed**eh**

motorbike motosiklet

motorboat deniz motoru

motorway otoyol

mountain dağ da

in the mountains dağlarda da-larda

mountaineering dağcılık da-juhl**uh**k

mouse fare far**eh**

moustache bıyık buhy**uh**k

mouth ağız a-**uh**z

mouth ulcer aft, pamukçuk pamookch**oo**k

move (*verb:* oneself) hareket etmek

(something) oynatmak

(house) taşınmak tashuhnmak

he's moved to another room başka bir odaya taşındı bashka beer odǐ-a tashuhnd**uh**

could you move your car? arabanızı çeker misiniz? arabanuhz**uh** cheker

could you move up a little? biraz yukarı gider misiniz? yookar**uh**

where has it moved to?

nereye taşındı? nerayeh
tashuhnduh

**where has it been moved
to?** (painting etc) nereye
kaldırıldı? kalduhruhlduh

movie film

movie theater sinema

MP3 format MP üç formatı
em-peh ewch formatuh

Mr Bay bī

Mrs Bayan bī-an

Ms Bayan

much çok chok

much better/worse çok daha
iyi/daha kötü

much hotter çok daha sıcak

not much pek değil deh-eel

not very much çok fazla değil

I don't want very much çok
fazla istemiyorum

mud çamur chamoor

mug (for drinking) kupa

I've been mugged saldırıya
uğradım salduhruh-ya
oo-raduhm

mum anne anneh

mumps kabakulak

museum müze mewzeh

Travel tip Museums are
generally open from 8.30 or
9 a.m. until 5.30 or 6 p.m.,
except Mondays, while
İstanbul's palaces are usually shut on Mondays and
Thursdays. Major archaeo-
logical sites are open from
8.30 a.m. to 6.30 p.m. in
summer, but winter opening
hours tend to be shorter. All
tourist sites are closed on the
mornings of public holidays.

---

mushrooms mantar

music müzik mewzeek

musician müzisyen

Muslim (adj: person) Müslüman
mewslewman

mussels midye meed-yeh

must: I must... ...-meliyim

I mustn't drink alcohol
alkol almamam lazım lazuhm

mustard hardal

my -im, -ım -uhm, -um, -üm
-ewm, -m

myself: I'll do it myself kendim
yaparım yaparuhm

by myself yalnız başıma
yalnuhz bashuhma

N

nail (finger) tırnak tuhrnak
   (metal) çivi cheevee
nailbrush tırnak fırçası tuhrnak
   fuhrchasuh
nail varnish tırnak cilası jeelasuh
name ad
   my name's John adım John
      aduhm
   what's your name? adınız
      nedir? aduhnuhz
   what is the name of this
      street? bu caddenin adı ne?
      jaddeneen aduh neh
napkin peçete pecheteh
nappy çocuk bezi chojook
narrow (street) dar
nasty (person, weather, taste)
   iğrenç eegrench
   (cut, accident) kötü kurtew
national ulusal
nationality vatandaşlık
   vatandashluhk
natural doğal doh-al
nausea mide bulantısı meedeh
   boolantuhsuh
navy (blue) lacivert lajeevert
near: near the... ...-in
   yakınında yakuhnuhnda
   is it near the city centre?
      şehir merkezine yakın mı? muh
   do you go near Aya
      Sophia? Ayasofya'nın
      yakınından geçecek misiniz?
      i-asofya-nuhn yakuhnuhndan
      gechejek

where is the nearest...?
   en yakın... nerede? neredeh
nearby yakında yakuhnda
nearly neredeyse neredayseh
necessary gerekli
neck boyun
necklace kolye kol-yeh
necktie kravat
need: I need... ...-e ihtiyacım
   var -eh eeнtee-yajuhm
   do I need to pay? para
      ödemem gerekiyor mu?
      urdemem
needle iğne ee-neh
neither: neither (one) of them
   hiç biri heech
   neither... nor... ne... ne... neh
nephew yeğen yeh-en
net (in sport) ağ a
Netherlands Hollanda
network map şebeke planı
   shebekeh planuh
never hiçbir zaman heechbeer

new yeni
news (radio, TV etc) haber
newsagent's gazete bayii
   gazeteh bī-ee-ee
newspaper gazete
newspaper kiosk gazete satış
   büfesi satuhsh bewfesee

New Year Yeni Yıl yuhl

  Happy New Year! Yeni Yılınız Kutlu Olsun! yuhluhnuhz

New Year's Eve Yılbaşı Gecesi yuhlbashuh gejesee

New Zealand Yeni Zelanda

New Zealander: I'm a New Zealander Yeni Zelandalıyım zelandaluhyuhm

next bir sonraki

  the next turning/street on the left solda, bir sonraki sapak/cadde

  at the next stop bir sonraki durakta

  next week gelecek hafta gelejek

  next to... ...-in bitişiğinde beeteeshee-eendeh

nice (food, day) güzel gewzel

  (person, looks, view) hoş hosh

Nicosia Lefkoşe lefkosha

niece yeğen yeh-en

night gece gejeh

  at night geceleyin gejelay-een

  good night iyi geceler gejeler

  do you have a single room for one night? bir gece için tek kişilik bir odanız var mı? gejeh eecheen tek keesheeleek beer odanuhz var muh

  yes, madam evet, efendim

  how much is it per night? gecesi ne kadar? gejesee neh

  it's 120 lira for one night bir gece için yüz yirmi lira yewz

  thank you, I'll take it tutuyorum, teşekkür ederim teshekkewr

nightclub gece kulübü koolewbew

nightdress gecelik gejeleek

night porter gece bekçisi bekcheesee

no hayır hī-uhr

  I've no change hiç bozuğum yok heech bozoo-oom

  there's no... left hiç... kalmadı kalmaduh

  no way! katiyen olmaz!

  oh no! (upset) hay aksi! hī

nobody hiç kimse heech keemseh

  there's nobody there hiç kimse yok orda

noise gürültü gewrewltew

noisy: it's too noisy fazla gürültülü

non-alcoholic alkolsüz –sewz

none hiç heech

nonsmoking compartment sigara içmeyenlere mahsus kompartıman eechmayenlereh maHsoos kompartuhman

noon öğle ur-leh

no-one hiç kimse heech keemseh

nor: nor do I ne de ben neh deh

normal normal nor-mal

north kuzey koozay

in the north kuzeyde koozaydeh

to the north kuzeye koozayeh

north of Ankara Ankara'nın kuzeyi ankara-nuhn

northeast kuzeydoğu koozaydoh-**oo**

northern kuzey

Northern Ireland Kuzey İrlanda eerlanda

northwest kuzey batı batuh

Norway Norveç norvech

Norwegian (*adj*) Norveç
(language) Norveççe norvech-cheh

nose burun

nosebleed burun kanaması kanamasuh

not değil deh-eel

  no, I'm not hungry hayır, aç değilim hī-uhr ach deh-eeleem

  I don't want any, thank you hiç istemiyorum, teşekkür ederim heech – teshekkewr

  it's not necessary gerekli değil deh-eel

  I didn't know that onu bilmiyordum

  not that one – this one o değil – bu

note (banknote) kâğıt para ka-**uh**t

notebook not defteri

notepaper (for letters) mektup kağıdı ka-uhd**uh**

nothing hiç bir şey heech beer shay

  nothing for me, thanks ben bir şey istemem, teşekkür ederim teshekkewr

  nothing else hepsi o kadar

novel roman

November kasım kasuhm

now şimdi sheemdee

number (amount) sayı si-**uh**
(telephone) numara

  I've got the wrong number yanlış numara yanluhsh

  what is your phone number? telefon numaranız nedir? noomaranuhz

number plate plaka

nurse hasta bakıcı bakuhjuh

nursery slope acemi pisti ajemee

nut (for bolt) somun

nuts fıstık fuhstuhk

O

occupied (toilet) meşgul meshgool

o'clock:... o'clock saat... sa-at

October ekim

odd (strange) tuhaf

of -in

off (lights) kapalı kapaluh

  it's just off İstiklal Caddesi/ Taksim Meydanı hemen daha İstiklal Caddesi'ne/ Taksim Meydanı'na çıkmadan eesteeklal jaddesee-neh/taks**ee**m maydanuh-na chuhkmadan

  we're off tomorrow yarın ayrılıyoruz yaruhn iruhluh-yorooz

offensive çirkin cheerkeen

office büro bewro

officer (said to policeman) memur bey bay

often sık sık suhk

not often ara sıra suhra

how often are the buses?
otobüsler ne kadar sık? neh

oil (for car, for salad) yağ ya

ointment merhem

OK tamam

are you OK? iyi misin?

is that OK with you? siz ne
dersiniz? neh

is it OK to...? ...-nin bir
mahzuru var mı? muh

that's OK, thanks tamam,
teşekkür ederim teshekkewr

I'm OK (nothing for me) ben
böyle iyiyim buh-ileh

(I feel OK) ben iyiyim

is this train OK for...? ... için
bu tren doğru mu? eecheen –
doh-roo

I said I'm sorry, OK özür
diledim ya urzewr

old (person) yaşlı yashluh

(thing) eski

DIALOGUE

how old are you? kaç
yaşındasınız? kach
yashuhnda-suhnuhz

I'm 25 yirmi beş yaşındayım
yashuhndī-uhm

and you? ya siz?

old-fashioned eski moda

old town (old part of town)
eski şehir sheh-heer

olive oil zeytinyağı zayteenya-uh

olives zeytin

black/green olives siyah/
yeşil zeytin yesheel

omelette omlet

on: on the... ...-in üstünde
ewstewndeh

(light) açık achuhk

on the street/beach
caddede/plajda jaddedeh/plaJda

is it on this road? bu yol
üzerinde mi? ewzereendeh

on the plane uçakta oochakta

on Saturday cumartesi günü
gewnew

on television televizyonda

I haven't got it on me
yanımda değil yanuhmda deh-
eel

this one's on me (drink) bu
benden

the light wasn't on ışık
yanmıyordu uhshuhk yanmuh-
yordoo

what's on tonight? bu akşam
ne var? neh

once (one time) bir kere kereh

at once (immediately) hemen

one bir

the white one beyaz olan

one-way ticket gidiş bileti
geedeesh

onion soğan soh-an

online (book, check) online

only yalnız yalnuhz

only one yalnız bir tane taneh

it's only 6 o'clock saat henüz
altı sa-at henewz

I've only just got here ancak
şimdi geldim anjak sheemdee

on/off switch açıp/kapama
düğmesi achuhp – dew-mesee

open (adj) açık ach**uh**k

  (verb) açmak ach**mak**

  when do you open? saat
kaçta açıyorsunuz? sa-**at** k**a**chta
ach**uh**–

  I can't get it open
açamıyorum ach**a**muh–

  in the open air açık havad**a**

opening times açılış ve
kapanış saatleri ach**uh**l**uh**sh veh
kapan**uh**sh sa-**a**tleree

open ticket açık bilet ach**uh**k

operation (medical) ameli**ya**t

operator (telephone) santr**al**
memur**u**

**opposite: the opposite
direction** aksi yön yurn

  the bar opposite karşıdaki
bar karshuhdak**ee**

  opposite my hotel otelim**in**
karşısında karshuhs**uh**nda

optician gözlükçü gurzlewkch**ew**

or veya vay-**a**

orange (fruit) portak**al**

  (colour) turuncu tooroonj**oo**

orange juice portak**al** suy**u**

orchestra orkestr**a**

order: can we order now?
(in restaurant) yemekler**i** şimdi
söyleyebilir miy**i**z? sh**ee**emdee
suh-il**a**yebeel**ee**r

  **I've already ordered,
thanks** ben ısmarladım,
teşekkür ederim uhsmarlad**uh**m
teshekk**ew**r

  I didn't order this ben bun**u**
ısmarl**a**madım

  out of order boz**u**k

ordinary olağan ola-**a**n

other diğer dee-**e**r

  the other one öbürü
urbewr**ew**

  the other day geçen gün
gech**e**n gewn

  I'm waiting for the others
diğerlerin**i** bekl**i**yorum

  do you have any others?
başka var mı? bashk**a** var muh

otherwise yoks**a**

our -miz, -mız -mu**h**z, -muz,
-müz -me**w**z

ours bizimk**i**

out: he's out yok, dışarda
duhshard**a**

  **three kilometres out of
town** şehrin üç kilometre
dışında shehr**ee**n ewch
keelometr**eh** duhsh**uh**nda

outdoors açık havad**a** ach**uh**k

outside: outside the…
…-in dışında duhsh**uh**nda

  can we sit outside? dışarda
oturabilir miy**i**z? duhshard**a**

oven fırın fuhr**uh**n

over: over here burada

  over there orada

  over 500 beş y**ü**zden fazl**a** besh

  it's over bitt**i**

**overcharge: you've
overcharged me** bend**e**n
fazl**a** par**a** aldınız alduhn**uh**z

overcoat palto

**overlooking: I'd like a room
overlooking the courtyard**
avluy**a** bak**a**n bir oda isti**yo**rum

overnight (travel) gece gej**e**h

overtake geçmek gechm**ek**

owe: how much do I owe you? size borcum ne kad**a**r? seez**eh** borj**oo**m neh

own: my own... benim kend**i**...-m

   are you on your own? tek ba**ş**ına mısınız? bashuhn**a** muhsuhn**uh**z

   I'm on my own tek ba**ş**ımayım bashuhm**ī**-**uhm**

owner sahib**i**

P

pack (*verb*) paketlem**ek**

   a pack of... bir pak**et**...

package (parcel) paket, kol**i**

package holiday pak**et** tur

packed lunch pikn**i**k paket**i**

packet: a packet of cigarettes bir pak**et** sigar**a**

padlock asm**a** kil**i**t

page (of book) sayf**a** s**ī**f**a**

   could you page Mr...? Sayın...-i ça**ğ**ırtabilir misiniz? s**ī**-**uhn**...-ee cha-uhrtabeel**eer**

pain a**ğ**rı a-r**uh**

   I have a pain here şuramda bir a**ğ**rı var shooramd**a** beer a-r**uh** var

painful ızdıraplı uhzduhrapl**uh**

painkillers a**ğ**rı kesiciler a-r**uh** keseejeel**er**

paint (*noun*) boy**a**

painting res**i**m

pair: a pair of... bir çift... cheeft

Pakistani (*adj*: person) Pakistanl**ı** –l**uh**

palace saray sar**ī**

pale solg**u**n

   pale blue uçuk mavi ooch**oo**k

pan tencere tenjer**eh**

panties külot kewl**o**t

pants (underwear: men's) don (women's) külot kewl**o**t (US) pantol**o**n

pantyhose külotlu çorap kewlotl**oo** chorap

paper kâğıt ka-**uh**t (newspaper) gazete gazet**eh**

   a piece of paper bir parça kağıt parch**a**

paper handkerchiefs kağıt mend**i**l

parcel kol**i**

pardon (me)? (didn't understand/hear) ef**e**ndim?

parents anne baba ann**eh**

park (*noun*) park (*verb*) park etm**ek**

   can I park here? buraya park edebil**i**r miyim? boor**i**-a

parking lot otopark

> **Travel tip** Heed the signposted no-parking zones, especially in resorts, as towing is common and although the fines aren't too heavy the hassle of finding the pound and negotiating language barriers is considerable. Generally, it's wisest to patronize the covered or open *otoparks*.

part (*noun*) parça parcha

partner (boyfriend, girlfriend etc) arkadaş arkadash

party (group) grup

(celebration) parti

pass (in mountains) geçit gecheet

passenger yolcu yoljoo

passport pasaport

password şifre sheefreh

past: in the past geçmişte gechmeeshteh

   just past the information office danışma bürosunu geçer geçmez danuhshma bewrosoonoo gecher gechmez

path patika, yol

pattern desen

pavement kaldırım kalduhruhm

   on the pavement kaldırımda

pay (*verb*) ödemek urdemek

   can I pay, please? ödeyebilir miyim, lütfen? urdayebeeleer

   it's already paid for ödendi bile urdendee beeleh

   who's paying? kim ödüyor? urdew-yor

   I'll pay ben ödeyeceğim urdayejeh-eem

   no, you paid last time, I'll pay olmaz, siz geçen sefer ödediniz, ben ödeyeceğim gechen – urdedeeneez ben urdayejeh-eem

pay phone umumi telefon

peaceful sakin

peach şeftali sheftalee

peanuts yerfıstığı yerfuhstuh-**uh**

pear armut

peas bezelye bezelyeh

peculiar (strange) tuhaf

pedestrian crossing yaya geçidi yï-a gecheedee

pedestrian precinct yayalara mahsus bölge maнsoos burlgeh

peg (for washing) mandal

(for tent) kazık kazuhk

pen mürekkepli kalem mewrek-keplee

pencil kurşun kalem koorshoon

penfriend mektup arkadaşı arkadashuh

penicillin penisilin

penknife çakı chakuh

pensioner emekli

people insanlar

   the other people in the hotel oteldeki diğer kişiler dee-er keesheeler

   too many people fazla sayıda insan sï-uhda

pepper biber

   green pepper yeşil biber yesheel

   red pepper kırmızı biber kuhrmuhrzuh

peppermint (sweet) nane şekeri naneh shekeree

per: per night bir gecesi gejesee

   how much per day? gündeliği kaça? gewndelee-ee kacha

per cent yüzde yewzdeh

perfect mükemmel mewkemmel

perfume parfüm parfewm

perhaps belki

perhaps not belki de değil deh deh-**eel**

period (of time) süre sewr**eh**

(menstruation) adet dönemi

perm perma

permit (*noun*) izin

person kişi keeshee

petrol benzin

petrol can benzin bidonu

petrol station
benzin istasyonu

pharmacy eczane ejzaneh

phone (*noun*) telefon

(*verb*) telefon etmek

phone book telefon rehberi reHberee

phone box telefon kulübesi koolewbesee

phonecard telefon kartı kart**uh**

phone charger şarj aleti sharJ aletee

phone number telefon numarası noomaras**uh**

photo fotoğraf foto-raf

excuse me, could you take a photo of us? affedersiniz, bir fotoğrafımızı çekebilir misiniz? foto-rafuhmuhz**uh** chekebeel**eer**

phrasebook konuşma kılavuzu konooshma kuhlavooz**oo**

piano piyano

pickpocket yankesici yankeseej**ee**

pick up: will you be there to pick me up? beni almaya gelecek misiniz? almi-**a** gelej**ek**

picnic piknik

picture resim

pie (meat) etli börek bur-r**ek**

(fruit) turta

piece parça parcha

a piece of... bir parça...

pill doğum kontrol hapı doh-**oom** – hahp**uh**

I'm on the pill doğum kontrol hapı alıyorum hap**uh** aluh-y**o**room

pillow yastık yast**uh**k

pillow case yastık kılıfı kuhluhf**uh**

pin (*noun*) toplu iğne ee-neh

pineapple ananas

pineapple juice ananas suyu

pink pembe pemb**eh**

pipe (for smoking) pipo

(for water) bor**u**

pistachio antep fıstığı fuhst**uh**-uh

pity: it's a pity yazık yaz**uh**k

pizza pizza

place (*noun*) yer

is this place taken? bu yerin sahibi var mı? muh

at your place sende send**eh**, sizin evde evd**eh**

at his place onda, onun evinde eveend**eh**

plain (not patterned) düz dewz

plane uçak ooch**ak**

by plane uçakla uch**a**kla

plant bitki

plaster cast alçı alch**uh**

plasters flast**er**, yar**a** bandı band**uh**

plastic plast**i**k

   (credit cards) kred**i** kartları kartlar**uh**

plastic bag naylon torb**a** n**ī**lon

plate tab**a**k

platform per**o**n

   which platform is it for Bursa? Burs**a** tren**i** hang**i** perond**a**n kalkıyor? kalkuh-y**o**r

play (*verb*) oynam**a**k

   (*noun*: in theatre) oy**u**n

playground çocuk bahçes**i** choj**oo**k ba**H**chesee

pleasant hoş hosh

please lütfen le**w**tfen

   yes please lütfen

   could you please…? lütfen…-ebil**i**r miydiniz? mee-ideen**ee**z

   please don't do that lütfen yapmayın

   pleased to meet you! tanıştığımıza memn**u**n old**u**m! tanuhsht**u**h-uhm**u**hz**a**

pleasure: my pleasure rica eder**i**m r**ee**ja

plenty: plenty of… bol bol…

   there's plenty of time bol bol vak**i**t var

   that's plenty, thanks teşekkür eder**i**m, yet**er** teshekk**e**wr

pliers kerpet**e**n

plug (electrical) fiş feesh

   (in sink) tıkaç tuhk**a**ch

   (for car) buji b**oo**Jee

plumber tesisatçı teseesatch**uh**

p.m.: …p.m. (afternoon) öğleden s**o**nra… ur-led**e**n

   (evening) akşam… aksham

poached egg kaynar suy**a** kırılmış yumurt**a** kīnar – kuhruhlm**uh**sh

pocket cep jep

point: two point five ik**i** nokta beş

   there's no point anlamı yok anlam**uh**

points (in car) kesic**i** platinl**er** keseej**ee**

poisonous zehirl**i**

police pol**i**s

   call the police! pol**i**s çağırın! cha-**uh**ruhn

policeman pol**i**s

police station pol**i**s karakol**u**

policewoman kadın pol**i**s kad**uh**n

polish (*noun*) cila jeel**a**

polite naz**i**k

polluted kirl**i**

pony midill**i**

pool (for swimming) hav**u**z

poor (not rich) fak**i**r

   (quality) kalites**i**z

pop music pop müz**i**k mewz**ee**k

pop singer pop şarkıcısı sharkuhjuhs**uh**

popular sevil**e**n

population nüfus newf**oo**s

pork dom**u**z et**i**

port (for boats) liman

   (drink) porto şarabı sharab**uh**

porter (in hotel) kapıcı kapuhj**uh**

portrait portre portreh

posh kibar

possible mümkün mewmk**ew**n

   is it possible to...? ...-mak
   mümkün mü? mew

   as... as possible
   olduğunca... oldoo-oonja

post (*noun*: mail) posta

   (*verb*) postalamak

   **could you post this for
   me?** bunları benim için
   postalayabilir miydiniz?
   boonlar**uh** – eeche**en** postalï-
   abee**leer** mee-ideen**eez**

postbox posta kutus**u**

postcard kartpostal

postcode posta kod**u**

poster (for room) poster

   (in street) afiş af**eesh**

poste restante postrest**a**nt

post office postane post**a**neh

potato patates

pots and pans mutfak eşyası
esh-yas**uh**

pottery (objects) seramik, toprak
eşya esh-y**a**

pound (money) sterlin

   (weight) libre le**e**breh

power cut elektrik kesilmesi

power point priz

**practise: I want to practise
my Turkish** Türkçe pratik
yapmak istiyorum tewrkcheh

prawns karides

prayer dua

prayer mat seccade sejjadeh

prefer: I prefer... ... tercih
ederim terjee**H**

pregnant gebe gebe**h**

premium süper sewp**e**r

prescription (for medicine) reçete
reche**teh**

present (gift) hediye hedee-y**eh**

president (of country)
cumhurbaşkanı joomH**oo**r-
bashkan**uh**

pretty güzel gewz**e**l

   it's pretty expensive oldukça
   pahalı old**oo**kcha

price fiy**a**t

priest rahip

prime minister başbakan
bashbakan

printed matter matbua

priority (in driving) öncelik
urnjeleek

prison hapishane
hapeeshaneh

private özel urz**e**l

private bathroom özel banyo

probably belki

problem problem

   no problem! hiç sorun değil!
   heech – deh-**ee**l

program(me) (*noun*) program

promise: I promise söz
veriyorum surz

**pronounce: how is this
pronounced?** bu nasıl telaffuz
edilir? nas**u**hl

properly (repaired, locked etc)

hakkıyla hakk**uh**-yuhla, iyice **ee**-yeejeh

protection factor korum**a** faktörü fakt**u**rew

Protestant Protest**a**n

public convenience umum**i** hel**a**

public holiday resm**i** tat**i**l

pudding (dessert) sütlü tatlı sewtl**ew** tatl**uh**, pud**i**ng

pull çekmek chekm**e**k

pullover kaz**a**k

puncture (*noun*) lastik patlaması patlamas**uh**

purple eflat**u**n

purse (for money) par**a** çantası chantas**uh**

    (US) el çantası chantas**uh**

push itm**e**k

pushchair pus**e**t

put koym**a**k

    where can I put...? ...-**i** nereye koyabilir**i**m? n**e**rayeh

    could you put us up for the night? bu gece biz**i** kon**u**k edebilir misin**i**z? gej**e**h

pyjamas pijama pee**J**ama

Q

quality kalite kaleet**e**h

quarantine karantin**a**

quarter çeyrek chayr**e**k

quayside: on the quayside rıhtımda ru**H**tuhmd**a**

question sor**u**

queue (*noun*) kuyruk koo-ir**oo**k

quick çabuk chab**oo**k

    that was quick ne kadar çabuk oldu neh

    what's the quickest way there? oraya en çabuk nasıl gidilir? nas**uh**l

    fancy a quick drink? çabucak bir şey içelim ist**e**r misin? chaboo**j**ak beer shay eechel**ee**m

quickly hızla huhzl**a**

quiet (place, hotel) sakin sak**ee**n

quiet! gürültü yapmayın! gewrewlt**ew** yapmı-uhn

quite (fairly) oldukça old**oo**kcha

    (very) tamam**e**n, pek, çok chok

    that's quite right çok doğru chok doh-r**oo**

    quite a lot oldukça çok old**oo**kcha

R

rabbit tavşan tavsh**a**n

race (for runners, cars) yarış yar**uh**sh

racket (tennis, squash) rak**e**t

radiator radyatör rad-yat**u**r

radio r**a**dyo

    on the radio rady**o**da

rail: by rail trenle tr**e**nleh

railway demiryol**u**

rain (*noun*) yağmur ya-m**oo**r

    in the rain yağmurd**a**

    it's raining yağmur yağıyor ya-uh-y**o**r

raincoat yağmurl**u**k

Ramadan Ramazan

rape (*noun*) ırza geçme uhrza gechmeh

rare (uncommon) nadide nadeedeh

(steak) az pişmiş peeshmeesh

rash (on skin) isilik

raspberry ahududu aнoodoodoo

rat sıçan suhchan

rate (for changing money) kur

rather: it's rather good oldukça iyi oldookcha

I'd rather... ...-yi tercih ederim terjeeн

razor ustura

(electric) elektrikli tıraş makinesi tuhrash

razor blades jilet Jeelet

read okumak

ready hazır hazuhr

are you ready? hazır mısınız? muhsuhnuhz

I'm not ready yet henüz hazır değilim henewz – deh-eeleem

when will it be ready? ne zaman hazır olur? neh

it should be ready in a couple of days bir kaç güne kadar hazır olur kach gewneh

real gerçek gerchek

really gerçekten gerchekten

I'm really sorry gerçekten üzgünüm ewzgewnewm

that's really great gerçekten çok iyi chok

really? (doubt) yok canım? januhm

(polite interest) sahi mi?

rear lights arka lambalar

rearview mirror dikiz aynası inasuh

reasonable (prices etc) akla yakın yakuhn

receipt makbuz

recently geçenlerde gechenlerdeh

reception (in hotel) resepsiyon

(for guests) davet

at reception resepsiyonda

reception desk resepsiyon masası masasuh

receptionist resepsiyon memuru

recognize tanımak tanuhmak

recommend: could you recommend...? ... tavsiye edebilir misiniz? tavsee-yeh

record (*noun*: music) plak

red kırmızı kuhrmuhzuh

red wine kırmızı şarap sharap

refund (*noun*) iade ee-adeh

can I have a refund? paramı geri alabilir miyim? paramuh

region bölge burlgeh

registered: by registered mail taahhütlü ta-a-hewtlew

registration number kayıt numarası ki-uht noomarasuh

regular gas normal nor-mal

relative (*noun*) akraba

religion din deen

remember: I don't remember hatırlamıyorum hatuhrlamuh-yoroom

I remember hatırlıyorum
hatuhrluh-**yo**room

do you remember? hatırlıyor
musun**uz**?

rent (*noun:* for apartment etc) kir**a**
(*verb:* car etc) kiralam**a**k

for rent kiralık keeral**uhk**

rented car kiralık otomob**i**l
keeral**uhk**

repair (*verb*) onarm**a**k

can you repair it? on**u**
onarabil**i**r misin**i**z?

repeat tekrarlam**a**k

could you repeat that?
onu tekrarlar mısınız?
muhsuhn**uhz**

reservation rezervasy**o**n

**I'd like to make a
reservation** bir rezervasyon
yapm**a**k ist**i**yorum

I have a reservation
rezervasyon**um** var

**yes sir, what name
please?** ev**e**t ef**e**ndim, is**i**m
n**e**ydi lütfen? nay**dee**

reserve (*verb*) ayırtm**a**k ī-uhrtm**a**k

**can I reserve a table
for tonight?** bu akş**a**m
için bir mas**a** ayırtabil**i**r
miy**i**m? aksh**a**m eech**ee**n –
ī-uhrtabeel**ee**r

**yes madam, for how many
people?** ev**e**t ef**e**ndim, k**a**ç
kiş**i** için? kach keesh**ee**

for two ik**i** kiş**i** için

and for what time? ve sa**a**t
k**a**ç için? veh sa-**a**t

for eight o'clock sek**i**z için

**and could I have your
name, please?** adın**ı**zı
alab**i**l**i**r miy**i**m, lütfen?
aduhnuhzuh-abeel**ee**r –
l**e**wtfen

see **alphabet** *for spelling*

rest: I need a rest dinlenm**e**ye
iht**i**yacım var –may**eh** ee**H**tee-
yaj**uh**m

the rest of the group grub**u**n
ger**i** kal**a**n kısm**ı** kuhsm**uh**

restaurant lok**a**nta, restor**a**n

restaurant car yem**e**kli vag**o**n

restroom tuval**e**t tooval**e**t
see **toilet**

retired: I'm retired emekl**i**yim

return: a return to... ....-**e**
bir gid**i**ş dön**ü**ş bil**e**t -eh beer
geed**ee**sh durn**ew**sh

return ticket gid**i**ş dön**ü**ş bil**e**ti
see **ticket**

reverse charge call ödem**e**li
konuşm**a** urdemel**ee** konooshm**a**

reverse gear ger**i** vit**e**s

revolting iğr**e**nç ee-r**e**nch

Rhodes Rod**o**s

rib kab**u**rga

rice (uncooked) pir**i**nç peer**ee**nch
(cooked) pil**a**v

rich (person) zeng**i**n
(food) ağ**ı**r a-**uh**r

ridiculous gül**ü**nç gewl**ew**nch

right (correct) doğr**u** doh-r**oo**

(not left) sağ sa

you were right haklıymışsınız
hakluh-imuhsh-suhn**uh**z

that's right doğru

this can't be right bu doğru
olam**a**z

right! tam**a**m!

is this the right road for...?
bu yol...-e gider mi? -eh

on the right sağda sa-d**a**

turn right sağ**a** dönün durn**ew**n

right-hand drive sağdan
direksiyonl**u** sa-d**a**n

ring (on finger) yüzük yewz**ew**k

I'll ring you siz**i** telefo**n**la
arar**ı**m ar**a**ruhm

ring back ger**i** aram**a**k
(telefonl**a**)

ripe (fruit) olg**u**n

rip-off: it's a rip-off tam bir
kazık kaz**uh**k

rip-off prices kazık fiyatl**a**r

risky rizikol**u**

river nehir neh-H**eer**

road yol

is this the road for...?
bu... yol**u** mud**u**r?

down the road yol**u**n
ilerisinde eelereeseend**eh**

road accident trafik kazası
kazas**uh**

road map karayol**u** haritası
hareetas**uh**

roadsign trafik işareti eesharet**ee**

rob: I've been robbed
soyuld**u**m

rock kaya kī-**a**
(music) rock müziği mewzee-**ee**

on the rocks (with ice) buzl**u**

roll (bread) sandviç ekmeği
sandv**ee**ch ekmeh-**ee**

roof dam

roof rack üst bagaj yeri ewst
bagaɹ

room oda

  in my room odamda

room service oda servisi

rope halat

rosé (wine) pembe şarap pembeh
sharap

roughly (approximately) kabaca
kabaja

round: it's my round bu sefer
sıra bende suhra bendeh

roundabout (for traffic) göbek
gurbek

round trip ticket gidiş dönüş
bileti

route yol

  what's the best route? en iyi
hangi yoldan gidilir?

rubber (material) lastik

  (eraser) silgi

rubber band lastik bant

rubbish (waste) çöp churp

  (poor quality goods) uyduruk
şeyler oo-idooruhk shayler

  rubbish! (nonsense) saçma!
sachma

rucksack sırt çantası suhrt
chantasuh

rude kaba

rug (for floor) kilim

  (blanket) battaniye battanee-yeh

ruins harabeler

rum rom

  rum and coke rom ve koka
kola veh

run (verb: person) koşmak koshmak

**how often do the buses
run?** otobüslerin arası ne
kadar? arasuh neh

I've run out of money param
bitti

rush hour kalabalık saatler
kalabaluhk sa-atler

S

sad üzgün ewzgewn

saddle (for horse) eyer ay-er

  (for bike) sele seleh

safe (not in danger) güvenli
gewvenlee

  (not dangerous) güvenilir

safety pin çengelli iğne
chengellee ee-neh

sail (noun) yelken

sailboard (noun) yelkenli sörf surf

sailboarding sörf yapmak

salad salata

salad dressing salata sosu

sale: for sale satılık satuhluhk

salmon som balığı baluh-**uh**

salt tuz

same: the same aynı **ı**nuh

  the same as this bunun
aynısı **ı**nuhsuh

  the same again, please
aynısından bir tane daha,
lütfen **ı**nuhsuhndan beer taneh –
lewtfen

  it's all the same to me
benim için hepsi bir eecheen

sand kum koom

sandals sandal

sandwich sandviç sandveech

sanitary napkin kadın bağı kaduhn ba-uh

sanitary towel kadın bağı

sardines sardalya

Saturday cumartesi joomartesee

sauce sos

saucepan tencere tenjereh

saucer fincan tabağı feenjan taba-uh

sauna sauna sa-oona

sausage sosis

say (*verb*) demek, söylemek suh-ilemek

   how do you say... in Turkish? Türkçe... nasıl denir? tewrkcheh... nasuhl

   what did he/she say? ne dedi? neh

   he/she said... ... dedi

   could you say that again? tekrarlar mısınız? muhsuhnuhz

scarf (for neck) atkı atkuh (for head) eşarp esharp

scenery manzara

schedule (US) tarife tareefeh

scheduled flight tarifeli sefer

school okul

scissors: a pair of scissors makas

scooter küçük motosiklet kewchewk

scotch viski

Scotch tape seloteyp selotayp

Scotland İskoçya eeskoch-ya

Scottish İskoç

I'm Scottish İskoçyalıyım eeskoch-yaluh-yuhm

scrambled eggs karılmış sahanda yumurta karuhlmuhsh

scratch (*noun*) çizik cheezeek

screw (*noun*) vida

screwdriver tornavida

sea deniz

   by the sea deniz kıyısında kuh-yuhsuhnda

seafood deniz ürünleri ewrewnleree

seafood restaurant balık lokantası baluhk lokantasuh

seafront sahil saheel

   on the seafront sahilde saнeeldeh

seagull martı martuh

Sea of Marmara Marmara Denizi

search (*verb*) aramak

seashell deniz kabuğu deneez kaboo-oo

seasick: I feel seasick beni deniz tuttu

   I get seasick beni deniz tutar

seaside: by the seaside deniz kenarında kenaruhnda

seat oturacak yer otoorajak

   is this anyone's seat? bu yerin sahibi var mı? muh

seat belt emniyet kemeri

sea urchin deniz kestanesi

seaweed yosun

secluded kuytu koo-itoo

second (*adj*) ikinci eekeenjee (of time) saniye sanee-yeh

just a second! bir saniye! beer

second class (travel) ikinci sınıf eekee**njee** suhn**uhf**

second floor ikinci kat eek**ee**njee
(US) birinci kat beer**ee**njee

second-hand eld**e**n düşme dewshm**eh**

see görmek gurmek

can I see? görebilir miyim? gurebeel**eer**

have you seen...? ...-i gördünüz mü? -ee gurdewn**ewz** mew

I saw him/her this morning on**u** b**u** sab**a**h gördüm gurd**ew**m

see you! görüşürüz! g**u**rewshewrewz

I see (I understand) anlıyorum anl**uh**-yoroom

self-catering apartment pansiy**on** (yem**e**k pişirme olan**a**klı) peesheerm**eh** olanakl**uh**

self-service self servis

sell satm**a**k

do you sell...? ... satıyor musun**u**z? satuh-y**o**r

Sellotape seloteyp sel**o**tayp

send göndermek gurndermek

I want to send this to England bun**u** İngiltere'ye göndermek ist**i**yorum **ee**ngeeltereh-yeh

senior citizen yaşlı vatandaş yashl**uh** vatand**a**sh

separate ayrı **i**r**uh**

separated: I'm separated eşimden ayrı yaşıyorum esheemd**e**n – yashuh-yor**oo**m

separately (pay, travel) ayrı ayrı **i**r**uh**

September eylül aylewl

septic mikropl**u**

serious ciddi jeedd**ee**

service charge (in restaurant) servis ücreti ewjret**ee**

service station servis istasyon**u**

serviette peçete pecheteh

set menu tabldot tabld**o**t

several birkaç beerka**ch**

sew dikmek

could you sew this back on? bun**u** yerine dikebilir misin**i**z? yereen**eh**

sex seks
(gender) cinsiyet jeensee-y**et**

sexy cazibeli jazeebel**ee**

shade: in the shade gölgede gurlged**eh**

shake: let's shake hands tokalaşalım tokalashal**uh**m

shallow (water) sığ suh

shame: what a shame! ne yazık! neh yaz**uh**k

shampoo (noun) şampuan shampoo-**an**

shampoo and set yıkama ve mizanpli y**uh**kama veh

share (verb: room, table etc) paylaşmak p**i**lashm**a**k

sharp (taste, knife) keskin
(pain) şiddetli sheeddetl**ee**

shattered (very tired) yorgunluktan bitmiş beetm**ee**sh

shaver tıraş makinesi tuhr**a**sh

shaving foam tıraş köpüğü kurpew-**ew**

shaving point tıraş makinesi prizi

she o

  is she here? o burada mı? muh

sheep's cheese beyaz peynir bay**az** payneer

sheet (for bed) çarşaf charshaf

shelf raf

shellfish kabuklu deniz ürünleri ewrewnler**ee**

sherry şeri sheree

ship gemi

  by ship gemiyle gemee-il**eh**

shirt gömlek gurmlek

shit! şimdi hapı yuttuk! sheemdee hap**uh**

shock (*noun*) şok shok

  I got an electric shock from the... ...-den elektrik çarptı charpt**uh**

shock-absorber amortisör amorteesur

shocking korkunç kork**oo**nch

shoe ayakkabı ï-akkab**uh**

  a pair of shoes bir çift ayakkabı cheeft

shoelaces ayakkabı bağı ba-uh

shoe polish ayakkabı cilası jeelas**uh**

shoe repairer kundura tamircisi –jees**ee**

shop dükkân dewkkan

shopping: I'm going shopping ben alış-verişe çıkıyorum

al**uh**sh-ver**ee**sheh ch**uh**kuh-y**o**room

shopping centre alış-veriş merkezi

shop window vitrin

shore sahil sa**h**eel

short kısa kuhs**a**

shortcut kestirme kesteerm**eh**

shorts şort short

should: what should I do? ne yapmam lazım? neh – laz**uh**m

  you should... ...-malıydınız -maluh-iduhn**uh**z

  you shouldn't... ...-mamalıydınız

  he should be back soon birazdan gelmesi lazım

shoulder omuz om**oo**z

shout (*verb*) bağırmak ba-uhrm**a**k

show (in theatre) gösteri gursteree

  could you show me? bana gösterebilir misiniz? gursterebeel**ee**r

shower (in bathroom) duş doosh

  (rain) sağanak sa-anak

  with shower duşlu dooshl**oo**

shower gel duş jeli doosh

shut (*verb*) kapatmak

  when do you shut? saat kaçta kapatıyorsunuz? sa-**a**t kacht**a** kapat**uh**-yorsoonooz

  when does it shut? ne zaman kapanıyor? neh kapanuh-yor

  they're shut kapalılar kapal**uh**-lar

I've shut myself out anahtarı
içerde unuttum anaHtaruh
eecherdeh

shut up! kapa çeneni!
chenenee

shutter (on camera) örtücü
urtewjew, obtüratör obdewratur

(on window) kepenk

shy çekingen chekeengen

sick (ill) hasta

I'm going to be sick (vomit)
kusacağım galiba koosaja-uhm

side yan

the other side of the street
caddenin öbür tarafı urbewr
tarafuh

side lights park lambaları
lambalaruh

side salad garnitür salata
garneetewr

side street yan sokak

sidewalk kaldırım kalduhruhm

on the sidewalk kaldırımda

sight: the sights of... ...-nin
görmeye değer yerleri gurmayeh
deh-er

**sightseeing: we're going
sightseeing** geziye çıkıyoruz
gezee-yeh chuhkuh-yorooz

sightseeing tour gezi, tur

sign (roadsign etc) işaret eesharet

**signal: he/she didn't give
a signal** (driver, cyclist) işaret
vermedi

signature imza

signpost işaret levhası isharet
levhasuh

silence sessizlik

silk ipek

silly (person) sersem

(thing to do) saçma sachma

silver (noun) gümüş gewmewsh

silver foil aluminyum folyo

similar benzer

simple (easy) kolay kolī

since: since last week geçen
haftadan beri gechen

since I got here buraya
geldiğimden beri boorī-a geldee-
eemden

sing şarkı söylemek sharkuh
suh-ilemek

singer şarkıcı sharkuhjuh

single: a single to... ...-e bir
gidiş bileti -eh beer geedeesh

I'm single bekârım bekaruhm
see **ticket**

single bed tek kişilik yatak
keesheeleek

single room tek kişilik bir oda

sink (in kitchen) evye ev-yeh,
bulaşık lavabosu boolashuhk

sister kız kardeş kuhz kardesh

sister-in-law (wife's sister) baldız
balduhz

(husband's sister) görümce
gurrewmjeh

(brother's wife) yenge yengeh

sit: can I sit here? buraya
oturabilir miyim? boorī-a

is anyone sitting here?
burada oturan var mı? muh

sit down oturmak

sit down oturun

size boy

ski (*noun*) kayak kī-ak
  (*verb*) kayak yapmak
  a pair of skis bir çift kayak
  cheeft
skiing kayakçılık kī-ak-chuhl**uh**k
ski-lift telesiyej telesee-ye↵
skin cilt jeelt
skin-diving balık adamlık bal**uh**k
  adaml**uh**k
skinny sıska suhska
skirt etek
sky gök gurk
sleep (*verb*) uyumak oo-yoomak
  did you sleep well?
  iy**i** uyudunuz mu?
  oo-yoodoon**oo**z
sleeper (on train) yataklı vag**o**n
  yatakl**uh**
sleeping bag uyku tulum**u**
  oo-ik**oo**
sleeping car yataklı vag**o**n
  yatakl**uh**
sleeping pill uyku hapı oo-ik**oo**
  hap**uh**
sleepy: **I'm feeling sleepy**
  uyk**u**m geldi
sleeve kol
slide (photographic) diya
slip (garment) kombinez**o**n
slippers terlik
slippery kaygan kigan
slow yavaş yavash
  slow down! (driving, speaking)
  yavaşla!
slowly yavaşça yavash-cha
  very slowly çok yavaş chok
small küçük kewchewk

smell: **it smells** (smells bad) kötü
  kokuy**o**r kurt**ew**
smile (*verb*) gülümsemek
  gewlewm-semek
smoke (*noun*) duman
  do you mind if I smoke?
  izninizle sigar**a** içebilir miy**i**m?
  –l**eh** – eechebeel**ee**r
  I don't smoke ben sigara
  kullanmıyorum
  koollanmuh–
  do you smoke? sigara içiyor
  musun**u**z? eechee-y**o**r
snack hafif yemek, meze mez**eh**
  just a snack yalnız hafif bir
  şeyler yaln**uh**z – shayler
sneeze (*noun*) hapşırık
  hapshuhr**uh**k
snorkel şnorkel shn**o**rkel
snow (*noun*) kar
  it's snowing kar yağıyor
  ya-uh-y**o**r
so: **it's so good!** öyle iy**i** ki!
  uh-il**eh**
  it's so expensive! öyle pahalı
  ki!
  not so much o kadar çok
  değil chok deh-**ee**l
  not so bad pek kötü değil
  kurt**ew**
  so am I ben de öyle deh
  so do I ben de
so-so şöyle böyle sh**uh**-il**eh**
  b**uh**-il**eh**
soaking solution (for contact
  lenses) koruyucu sıvı koroo-
  yooj**oo** suhv**uh**
soap sabun

soap powder sabun toz**u**

sober ayık ī-**uhk**

sock çorap chor**ap**

socket (electrical) priz

soda (water) mad**e**n sodası sodas**uh**

sofa div**a**n

soft (material etc) yumuşak yoomoosh**a**k

soft-boiled egg rafad**a**n yumurt**a**

soft drink alkolsüz içecek alkols**ewz** eechej**e**k, meşrubat meshroob**a**t

soft lenses yumuşak kont**a**k lensl**e**ri yoomoosh**a**k

sole (of shoe, of foot) tab**a**n

  could you put new soles on these? bunlar**a** pençe yap**a**r mısınız? pench**eh** – muhsuhn**uh**z

some: can I have some water? bir**a**z su alabil**i**r miy**i**m?

  can I have some biscuits? birkaç bisküv**i** alabilir miyim? beerk**a**ch

  can I have some? bir**a**z alabilir miyim?

somebody, someone biris**i**

something bir şey sh**a**y

something to eat yiyecek bir şey yee-yej**e**k

sometimes baz**e**n

somewhere bir yerde beer yerd**eh**

son oğul o-**ool**

song şarkı shark**uh**

son-in-law dam**a**t

soon yakında yak**uh**nd**a**

  I'll be back soon biraz**da**n dön**e**rim

  as soon as possible en kısa zaman**d**a kuhs**a**

sore: it's sore acıyor aj**uh**-yor

sore throat boğaz ağrısı bo-**a**z a-ruhs**uh**

sorry: (I'm) sorry özür dil**e**rim urz**ewr**

  sorry? (didn't hear etc) ef**e**ndim?

sort: what sort of...? ne tür...? neh t**e**wr

soup çorba chorb**a**

sour (taste) ekşi eksh**ee**

south güney gewn**a**y

  in the south güneyde gewnayd**eh**

South Africa Güney Afrik**a**

South African (adj) Güney Afrik**a**

  I'm South African Güney Afrikalıyım –luh-y**uh**m

southeast güney doğu d**oh**-oo

southwest güney batı bat**uh**

souvenir hatıra haнtuhr**a**

Spain İspanya eespany**a**

Spanish (adj: person) İspany**o**l

  (language) İspanyolca eespany**o**lj**a**

spanner som**u**n anahtarı anaнtar**uh**

spare part yedek parça parch**a**

spare tyre yedek last**i**k

spark plug buji b**oo**jee

speak: do you speak English?
İngilizce biliyor musunuz?
eengeeleezjeh

I don't speak...
... bilmiyorum

can I speak to...?
... ile görüşebilir miyim?
eeleh gurew-shebeeleer

can I speak to Sinan?
Sinan'la görüşebilir miyim?
gurewshebeeleer

who's calling? kim arıyor?
aruh-yor

it's Patricia Patricia

I'm sorry, he's not in, can I take a message?
üzgünüm evde değil, mesaj alabilir miyim?
ewzgewnewm evdeh deh-eel mesaJ

no thanks, I'll call back later hayır teşekkür ederim, ben sonra tekrar ararım
hī-uhr teshekkewr – araruhm

please tell him I called
lütfen aradığımı söyleyin
lewtfen araduh-uhmuh suh-ilayeen

spectacles gözlük gurzlewk
speed (*noun*) hız huhz
speed limit azamî hız
speedometer hızölçer huhzurlcher
spell: how do you spell it?
nasıl yazılıyor? nasuhl yazuhluh-yor
see **alphabet**

spend harcamak harjamak
spider örümcek urewmjek
spin-dryer santrifüjlü kurutma makinesi santreefewJlew
splinter kıymık kuh-imuhk
spoke (in wheel) jant Jant
spoon kaşık kashuhk
sport spor
sprain: I've sprained my...
...-m burkuldu
spring (season) ilkbahar
(of car, seat) yay yī
square (in town) meydan maydan
stairs merdiven
stale bayat bī-at
stall: the engine keeps stalling motor sık sık duruyor suhk
stamp (*noun*) pul

a stamp for England, please İngiltere'ye bir pul, lütfen eengeeltereh-yeh – lewtfen
what are you sending?
ne gönderiyorsunuz?
gurnderee-yorsoonooz
this postcard bu kartpostalı
–postaluh

standby yedek, standby
star yıldız yuhlduhz
(in film) film yıldızı
start (*noun*) başlangıç bashlanguhch
(*verb*) başlamak bashlamak

when does it start?
ne zaman başlayacak? neh –
bashlī-ajak

the car won't start araba
çalışmıyor chaluhshmuh-yor

starter (of car) marş marsh

(food) ordövr ordurvr, meze
mezeh

starving: I'm starving çok
acıktım chok ajuhktuhm

state (country) devlet

the States (USA) Birleşik
Amerika beerlesheek

station istasyon

statue heykel haykel

stay: where are you staying?
nerede kalıyorsunuz? neredeh
kaluh-yorsoonooz

I'm staying at... ....-de
kalıyorum -deh kaluh-yoroom

**I'd like to stay another two
nights** iki gece daha kalmak
istiyorum gejeh

steak biftek

steal çalmak chalmak

my bag has been stolen
çantam çalındı chantam
chaluhnduh

steep (hill) dik

steering direksiyon sistemi

step: on the steps merdivende
merdeevendeh

stereo stereo

sterling sterlin

steward (on plane) kabin
memuru

stewardess hostes

sticky tape seloteyp selotayp

sticking plaster flaster, yara
bandı banduh

still: I'm still here hâlâ
buradayım hala booradī-uhm

is he/she still there? hâlâ
orada mı? muh

keep still! kımıldamayın!
kuhmuhl-dami-uhn

sting: I've been stung beni
böcek soktu burjek

stockings çoraplar choraplar

stomach mide meedeh

stomach ache mide ağrısı
a-ruhsuh

stone (rock) taş tash

stop (verb) durmak

please, stop here (to taxi
driver etc) lütfen, burada durun
lewtfen

do you stop near...?
... yakınında duruyor
musunuz? yakuhnuhnda

stop it! kes (artık)! artuhk

stopover ara durak

storm fırtına fuhrtuhna

straight (whisky etc) sek

it's straight ahead dümdüz
ilerde dewmdewz eelerdeh

straightaway hemen şimdi
sheemdee

strange (odd) acayip ajī-eep

stranger yabancı yabanjuh

I'm a stranger here buranın
yabancısıyım booranuhn
–suh-yuhm

strap (on watch, suitcase) kayış
kī-uhsh

(on dress) askı askuh

strawberry çilek cheel**ek**
stream dere der**eh**
street sokak
  on the street sokak**ta**
streetmap şehir planı sheh**eer**
  plan**uh**
string ip
strong (person) güçlü gewchl**ew**
  (drink) sert
stuck: it's stuck sıkıştı
  suhkuhsht**uh**
student öğrenci ur-renj**ee**
stupid aptal
subway (US) m**e**tro
suburb banliyö banlee-y**ur**
suddenly **a**niden
suede süet sew**et**
sugar şeker shek**er**
sugared almonds bad**e**m şeker**i**
suit (man's) takım elbise tak**uh**m
  elbees**eh**
  (woman's) tayyör ti-**ur**
  it doesn't suit me (jacket etc)
  ban**a** yakışmıyor yak**uh**shmuh-
  yor
  it suits you size yakışıyor
  seez**eh** yakuhshuh-y**or**
suitcase bav**ul**
summer yaz
  in the summer yazın yaz**uh**n
sun güneş gewn**esh**
  in the sun güneşte
  gewnesht**eh**
  out of the sun gölgede
  gurlged**eh**
sunbathe güneş b**a**nyosu
  yapm**ak**

sunblock (cream) güneş merhem**i**
  gewn**esh**
sunburn güneş yanığı yanuh-**uh**
sunburnt güneşte yanmış
  gewnesht**eh** yanm**uh**sh
Sunday paz**a**r
sunglasses güneş gözlüğü
  gewn**esh** gurzlew-**ew**
sun lounger şezlong shezl**o**ng
sunny: it's sunny hav**a** güneşli
  gewneshl**ee**
sunroof (in car) güneşlik
  gewneshl**eek**, sunroof
sunset günbatımı gewn-
  batuhm**uh**
sunshade gölgelik gurlgel**eek**,
  güneş şemsiyesi gewn**esh**
  shemsee-yes**ee**
sunshine güneş ışığı uhsh**uh**-uh
sunstroke güneş çarpması
  charpmas**uh**
suntan bronz ten
suntan lotion güneş losyonu
  gewn**esh** los-yon**oo**
suntanned bronzlaşmış
  bronzlashm**uh**sh
suntan oil güneş yağı gewn**esh**
  ya-**uh**
super fevkalade fevkalad**eh**
supermarket süpermarket
  sewpermark**et**
supper akşam yemeği aksh**a**m
  yemeh-**ee**
supplement (extra charge) ek
  ücret ewjr**et**
sure: are you sure? em**i**n
  misin**i**z?
  sure! tabii! tabee-**ee**

surfboard sörf tahtası surf tahta**suh**

surname soy**a**dı

swearword küfür kewf**ewr**

sweater kaz**a**k

sweatshirt svetşört svetsh**urt**

Sweden İsveç eesv**e**ch

Swedish (adj) İsveç

(language) İsveççe eesvech-ch**eh**

sweet (dessert) tatlı tatl**uh**

  it's too sweet fazla tatlı

sweets şeker shek**e**r

swelling şişlik sheeshl**ee**k

swim (verb) yüzmek yewzm**e**k

  I'm going for a swim yüzmeye gidiyorum yewzmay**eh**

  let's go for a swim hadi yüzmeye gidelim

swimming costume mayo mī-**o**

swimming pool yüzme havuzu yewzm**eh**

swimming trunks mayo mī-**o**

switch (noun) elektrik düğmesi dewmes**ee**

switch off kapamak

switch on açmak ach**ma**k

swollen şişmiş sheeshm**ee**sh

Syria Suriye s**oo**ree-yeh

T

table mas**a**

  a table for two iki kişilik bir masa keesheel**ee**k

tablecloth masa örtüsü urtews**ew**

table tennis masatop**u**

table wine sofra şarabı sharab**uh**

tailback (of traffic) taşıt kuyruğu tash**uh**t koo-ir**oo**-oo

tailor terz**i**

take (verb: lead) götürmek gurtewm**e**k

  (accept) alm**a**k

  (room etc) tutm**a**k

  can you take me to the...? beni...-'e götürür müsünüz? -eh gurtew-**rewr** mewsewn**e**wz

  do you take credit cards? kredi kartı kabul ediyor musun**u**z? kart**uh**

  fine, I'll take it tamam, alıyorum aluh-y**o**room

  (room) tamam, tut**u**yorum

  can I take this? (leaflet etc) bun**u** alabilir miy**i**m?

  how long does it take? ne kadar sürer? neh – sew**re**r

  it takes three hours üç saat sürer ewch sa-**at**

  is this seat taken? bu yerin sahibi var mı? muh

  hamburger to take away pak**e**t hamburger

  can you take a little off here? (to hairdresser) buradan biraz alır mısınız? al**uh**r muhsuhn**uh**z

talcum powder talk pudrası tahlk poodras**uh**

talk (verb) konuşmak konoosh**ma**k

tall (person) uz**u**n boylu

  (building) yüksek yewks**e**k

tampons tamp**o**n

tan (noun) bronz ten

to get a tan güneşte yanmak
gewnesh**teh**, bronzlaşmak
bronzlash**mak**

tank (of car) depo

tap musluk

tape (for cassette) teyp tayp

tape measure şerit metre sheret
metre**h**, mezür mez**ewr**

tape recorder teyp tayp

taste (*noun*) tat

can I taste it? tadına
bakabilir miyim? tad**uhna**

taxi taksi

will you get me a taxi? bana
bir taksi bulur musun**uz**?

where can I find a taxi?
nerede bir taksi bulabilir**im**?
nered**eh**

**to the airport/to the
... Hotel, please**
havaalanına/Hotel ....-'e,
lütfen hava-alan**uhna** – ...-**eh**
l**ewt**fen

how much will it be? ne
kadar tutar? neh

16 lira on altı lira alt**uh**

**that's fine right here,
thanks** tamam burası
iy**i**, teşekkürler booras**uh** –
teshekk**ewr**ler

taxi-driver taksi şoförü shofur**ew**

taxi rank taksi durağı doora-**uh**

tea (drink) çay ch**ī**

tea for one/two, please bir/
iki çay, lütfen l**ewt**fen

teabags torba çay

teach: could you teach me?
bana öğretir misiniz? ur-ret**eer**

teacher öğretmen ur-ret**men**

team ekip

(sporting) takım tak**uhm**

teaspoon çay kaşığı ch**ī** kashuh-
uh

tea towel kurulama bezi

teenager (male/female) delikanlı
deleekanl**uh**, genç kız gench kuhz

telephone telefon

see **phone**

television televizyon

**tell: could you tell him/
her...?** ona ....-i söyler misiniz?
suh-iler

temperature (weather) sıcaklık
suhjakl**uhk**

(fever) ateş atesh

temple tapınak tapuhnak

tennis tenis

tennis ball tenis topu

tennis court tenis kortu

tennis racket tenis raketi

tent çadır chad**uhr**

term (at university, school) dönem
durnem

terminus (rail) son istasyon

terrible berbat

terrific müthiş mewt-he**esh**

text (*verb*) mesaj atmak mesa**ɹ**
atmak

text (message) SMS mesajı
mesa**ɹuh**

than -den

smaller than -den küçük
kewch**ewk**

thank: thank you teşekkür
ederim *teshekkewr*

thanks teşekkürler
teshekkewrler

thank you very much çok
teşekkür ederim *chok*

thanks for the lift arabanıza
aldığınız için teşekkür ederim
–nuhza alduh-uhnuhz

no thanks hayır, teşekkür
ederim *hī-uhr*

thanks teşekkürler
don't mention it bir şey
değil *shay deh-eel*

that: that rug (nearby) şu kilim
shoo

(further away) o kilim

that one (nearby) şu

(further away) o

I hope that... umarım ki...
oomaruhm

that's nice o iyi

is that...? şu... mı? *muh*

that's it (that's right) tamam işte
eeshteh

the (there is no word for 'the')

theatre tiyatro

their onların -leri *onlaruhn*

theirs onlarınki

them onları *onlaruh*

for them onlar için *eecheen*

with them onlarla

to them onlara

who? – them kim? – onlar

then (at that time) o zaman

(after that) sonra

there orada

over there şurada *shoorada*,
orada

up there yukarıda *yookaruhda*

is there/are there...?
... var mı? *muh*

there is/there are... ... var

there you are (giving
something) buyrun *boo-iroon*

thermal spring kaplıca *kapluhja*

thermometer termometre
termometreh

thermos flask termos

these: these men/women
bu adamlar/kadınlar

I'd like these bunları
istiyorum *boonlaruh*

they onlar

thick kalın *kaluhn*

(stupid) kalın kafalı *kafaluh*

thief hırsız huhr**suhz**

thigh but boot

thin ince een**jeh**

thing şey shay

my things benim eşyam
esh-**yam**

think düşünmek dewshewn**mek**

I think so bence öyle ben**jeh**
uh-il**eh**

I don't think so bence öyle
değil deh-**eel**

I'll think about it
düşüneceğim dewshewne**jeh**-
eem

third party insurance mecburi
trafik sigortası mejboor**ee** –
seegortas**uh**

thirsty: I'm thirsty susadım
soosad**uhm**

this: this rug bu kilim

this one bu

this is my wife bu eşim
esh**eem**

is this...? bu... mi?

those: those men (nearby)
şu adamlar shoo

(further away) o adamlar

which ones? – those
hangileri? – şunlar shoon**lar**

thread (noun) iplik

throat boğaz bo-**az**

throat pastilles boğaz
pastilleri

through içinden eecheen**den**

does it go through...?
(train, bus) ...-den geçiyor mu?
gechee-**yor**

throw (verb) atmak, fırlatmak
fuhrlat**mak**

throw away (verb) at**mak**

thumb başparmak bash**parmak**

thunderstorm gök gürültülü
fırtına gurk gewrewltewl**ew**
fuhrtuhn**a**

Thursday perşembe pershem**beh**

ticket bil**et**

ticket office (bus, rail) bilet gişesi
geeshes**ee**

tide gel-git olayı olї-**uh**

tie (necktie) krav**at**

tight (clothes etc) dar

it's too tight fazla dar

tights külotlu çorap kewlotl**oo**
chor**ap**

till (cash desk) kas**a**

time zam**an**

what's the time? saat kaç?
sa-**at** kach

this time bu sef**er**

last time geçen sefer gech**en**

next time gelecek sefer gelej**ek**

three times üç kez

timetable tarife taree**feh**

tin (can) konserve kutusu
konserveh

tinfoil alüminyum folyo
alewmeen-yoom

tin-opener konserve açacağı
konserveh achaja-**uh**

tiny minik

tip (to waiter etc) bahşiş baH-sheesh

tired yorgun yorgoon

   I'm tired yorgunum
yorgoonoom

tissues kâğıt mendil ka-uht

to: to Bursa/London Bursa'ya/
Londra'ya londri-a

   to Turkey/England
Türkiye'ye/İngiltere'ye tewrkee-
yeh-yeh/**ee**ngheeltereh-yeh

   to the post office postaneye
postanay**eh**

toast (bread) kızarmış ekmek
kuhzarm**uh**sh

today bugün boog**ewn**

toe ayak parmağı i-ak parma-**uh**

together beraber

   we're together (in shop etc)
beraberiz

toilet tuvalet toovalet

   where is the toilet? tuvalet
nerede? neredeh

   I have to go to the toilet
tuvalete gitmem lazım
toovalet**eh** – lahz**uh**m

toilet paper tuvalet kâğıdı
ka-uhduh

tomato domates

tomato juice domates suyu

tomato ketchup ketçap ketchap

tomorrow yarın yar**uh**n

   tomorrow morning yarın
sabah sabaH

   the day after tomorrow
öbür gün urb**ewr** gewn

toner (cosmetic) toner

tongue dil

tonic (water) tonik

tonight bu gece gej**eh**

tonsillitis bademcik iltihabı
bademj**ee**k eelteehab**uh**

too (excessively) fazla

   (also) de deh

   too hot fazla sıcak

   too much çok fazla chok

   me too ben de deh

tooth diş deesh

toothache diş ağrısı a-ruhs**uh**

toothbrush diş fırçası
fuhrchas**uh**

toothpaste diş macunu
majoonoo

top: on top of... ...-in üstünde
ewstewnd**eh**

   at the top en üstte ewstt**eh**

   at the top of... ...-in en
üstünde

top floor üst kat ewst

topless göğüsleri açık gur-
ewsler**ee** ach**uh**k, üstsüz
ewsts**ewz**

torch el feneri

total (noun) toplam

tour (noun) tur

   is there a tour of...? ... turu
var mı? muh

tour guide rehber

tourist turist

tourist information office turizm danışma bürosu danuhshma bewros**oo**

tour operator tur operatörü operat**urew**

towards -e doğru -eh doh-r**oo**

towel havl**u**

tower kule kool**eh**

town kasab**a**

in town şehirde sheheerd**eh**

just out of town şehrin hem**e**n dışında shehr**ee**n – duhshuhnd**a**

town centre şeh**i**r merkez**i**

town hall belediye binası beledee-y**eh**

toy oyuncak o-yoonjak

track (US: platform) per**o**n

tracksuit eşofman eshofman

traditional geleneks**e**l

traffic traf**i**k

traffic jam trafik tıkanıklığı tuhkanuhkl**uh**-uh

traffic lights trafik ışıkları uhshuhk-lar**uh**

trailer (for carrying tent etc) römork rurm**o**rk, trayler tr**ī**ler (US) karav**a**n

trailer park kamp**ı**ng

train tren

by train trenle tr**e**nleh

is this the train for Ankara? bu Ankara treni mi?

sure tab**i**

---

no, you want that platform there hayır, sizin şu öbür peron**a** gitmeniz lazım hī-u**h**r – shoo ewb**ew**r – laz**uhm**

trainers (shoes) spor ayakkabısı ī-akkabuhs**uh**

train station tren istasyon**u**

Travel tip Trains are generally slow because the mountainous terrain results in circuitous routes, but they are the cheapest and safest form of domestic travel. To get accurate schedule information, go to the station in person, scan the placards and then confirm departures with staff. For long distances, it's advisable to get a sleeper, and for maximum privacy book a two-bedded sleeping car rather than a couchette.

tram tramvay tramv**ī**

translate tercüme etm**e**k terjewm**eh**

could you translate that? bun**u** tercüme edebil**i**r misin**i**z?

translation tercüme

translator tercüman

trash çöp churp

trashcan çöp tenekes**i**

travel seyahat sayahat

we're travelling around geziy**o**ruz

travel agent's seyahat acentası sayahat ajentas**uh**

traveller's cheque seyahat çeki chekee

tray tepsi

tree ağaç a-ach

tremendous muazzam moo-azzam

trendy (restaurant, club) şık shuhk, moda

(clothes) modaya uygun modi-a oo-igoon

(person) şık shuhk

trim: just a trim please (to hairdresser) lütfen yalnız uçlarından biraz alın lewtfen yalnuhz oochlaruhndan – aluhn

trip (excursion) yolculuk yoljoolook

I'd like to go on a trip to... bir... gezisi yapmak istiyorum

trolley el arabası arabasuh

trolleybus troleybüs trolaybews

trouble (noun) dert

I'm having trouble with... ... ile başım dertte eeleh bashuhm dertteh

trousers pantolon

Troy Truva

true gerçek gerchek

that's not true o doğru değil doh-roo deh-eel

trunk (US) bagaj bagaJ

trunks (swimming) mayo mī-o

try (verb) denemek

can I have a try? (at doing something) bir deneyebilir miyim? denayebeeleer

try on prova etmek

can I try it on? üstümde deneyebilir miyim? ewstewmdeh denayebeeleer

T-shirt tişört tee-shurt

Tuesday salı saluh

tuna ton balığı baluh-uh

tunnel tünel tewnel

Turk Türk tewrk

Turkey Türkiye tewrkee-yeh

Turkish (adj) Türk

(language) Türkçe tewrkcheh

Turkish bath hamam

Turkish coffee Türk kahvesi tewrk kaнvesee

Turkish Cypriot (adj) Kıbrıs Türk kuнbruhs

(person) Kıbrıslı Türk kuhbruhsluh

Turkish delight lokum

Turkish wrestling yağlı güreş ya-luh gewresh

turn: turn left/right sola/sağa dönün durnewn

turn off: where do I turn off? nereden sapmalıyım? –luh-yuhm

can you turn the heating off? kaloriferi kapatabilir misiniz?

turn on: can you turn the heating on? kaloriferi yakabilir misiniz?

turning (in road) sapak

TV TV tee vee

tweezers cımbız juhmbuhz

twice iki kez

twice as much iki misli meeslee

twin beds çift yatak cheeft

twin room çift yataklı oda yatak**uh**

twist: I've twisted my ankle ayak bileğimi burkt**u**m i-ak beeleh-ee**mee**

type (*noun*) tip teep

another type of... başka tip bir... bashk**a**

typical tip**i**k

tyre last**i**k

U

ugly çirkin cheerk**ee**n

UK Birleşik Krallık beerlesh**ee**k krall**uh**k

ulcer ülser ewls**e**r

umbrella şemsiye shemsee-**yeh**

uncle amca amj**a**

unconscious baygın bīg**uh**n

under: under the... (position) ...-in altında altuhnd**a**

(less than)...-den az

underdone (meat) az pişmiş peeshm**ee**sh

underground (railway) m**e**tro

underpants külot kewl**o**t

understand: I understand anlıyorum anl**uh**-yoroom

I don't understand anlamıyorum anl**a**muh-yuhoroom

do you understand? anlıyor musunuz? anl**uh**-y**o**r

unemployed işsiz eesh-s**ee**z

United States Birleşik Amerika beerlesh**ee**k

university üniversite ewnee-verseet**eh**

unleaded petrol kurşunsuz benzin koorshoons**oo**z

unlimited mileage kilometre kısıtlamasız keelom**e**treh kuhsuhtlamas**uh**z

unlock kilidi açmak achm**a**k

unpack eşyaları bavuldan çıkarmak esh-yalar**uh** – chuhkarm**a**k

until -e kad**a**r -eh

unusual alışılmamış aluhsh**uh**l-mamuhsh

up yukarı yookar**uh**

up there yukarıda yookaruhd**a**

he's not up yet (not out of bed) daha kalkmadı kalkmad**uh**

what's up? (what's wrong?) ne oldu? neh old**oo**

upmarket sükseli sewksel**ee**

upset stomach mide bozukluğu meed**eh** bozookloo-**oo**

upside down baş aşağı bash asha-**uh**

upstairs üst katta ewst

urgent acil aj**ee**l

us biz**i**

with us bizimle beez**ee**mleh

for us bizim için eech**ee**n

USA ABD a beh deh

use (*verb*) kullanm**a**k

may I use...? ...-i kullanabilir miy**i**m?

useful yararlı yararl**uh**

usual olağan ola-**a**n

the usual (drink etc) her zamank**i**

V

vacancy: do you have any vacancies? (hotel) boş odanız var mı? bosh odan**uh**z var muh

vacation tatil

on vacation tatilde tateeld**eh**

vaccination aşılama ashuhlama

vacuum cleaner elektrik süpürgesi sewpewrges**ee**

valid (ticket etc) geçerli gecherl**ee**

how long is it valid for? ne zamana kadar geçerli? neh

valley vadi

valuable (adj) değerli deh-erl**ee**

can I leave my valuables here? değerli eşyalarımı burada bırakabilir miyim? esh-yalaruhm**uh** – buhraka-beel**ee**r

value (noun) değer deh-er

van kamyonet

vanilla vanilya

a vanilla ice cream vanilyalı dondurma vaneel-yal**uh**

vary: it varies değişir deh-eesheer

vase vazo

veal dana eti

vegetables sebze sebz**eh**

vegetarian (noun) etyemez

vending machine otomat

very çok chok

very big çok büyük

very little for me bana azıcık azuhj**uh**k

I like it very much çok beğeniyorum beh-enee-y**o**room

vest (under shirt) fanila

via üzerinden ewzereend**e**n

video video

view manzara

villa villa

village köy kuh-i

vinegar sirke seerk**eh**

vineyard bağ ba

visa vize ve**e**zeh

visit (verb) ziyaret etmek

I'd like to visit… …i ziyaret etmek isterim

vital: it's vital that… …si şart shart

vodka votka

voice ses

voltage voltaj volta**J**

vomit kusmak

W

waist bel

waistcoat yelek

wait (verb) beklemek

wait for me beni bekleyin beklay**ee**n

don't wait for me beni beklemeyin bekl**e**mayeen

can I wait until my partner gets here? eşim gelinceye kadar bekleyebilir miyim? esh**ee**m geleenjay**eh** – beklayebeel**ee**r

can you do it while I wait? beklerken yapabilir misiniz?

could you wait here for me? beni burada bekler misiniz?

waiter garson

waiter! bakar mısınız! muhsuhn**uh**z

waitress garson kız kuhz

waitress! bakar mısınız! muhsuhn**uh**z

wake: can you wake me up at 5.30? beni beş buçukta uyandırır mısınız? oo-yanduhr**uh**r muhsuhn**uh**z

wake-up call telefonla uyandırma oo-yanduhrma

Wales Galler

walk: is it a long walk? yürüyerek uzak mıdır? yewrew-yer**ek** – m**uh**duhr

it's only a short walk yürüyerek çok yakın chok yak**uh**n

I'll walk yürüyeceğim yewrew-yejeh-**eem**

I'm going for a walk ben yürüyüşe çıkıyorum yewrew-yewsheh chuhkuh-y**o**room

wall duvar

wallet cüzdan jewzd**a**n

wander: I like just wandering around amaçsızca dolaşmayı severim amachsuhzja dolashmi-**uh**

want: I want a... bir... istiyorum

I don't want any... ... ist**e**miyorum

I want to go home eve gitm**ek** istiyorum ev**eh**

I don't want to... ...-mek ist**e**miyorum

he wants to... ...-mek ist**i**yor

what do you want? ne istiyorsun**u**z? neh

ward (in hospital) koğuş ko-**oo**sh

warm sıcak suhjak

I'm so warm sıcak bastı bast**uh**

was: he/she/it was -di

wash (verb) yıkamak yuhkam**a**k

can you wash these? bunları yıkayabilir misiniz? boonlar**uh** yuhki-abeele**er**

washer (for bolt etc) rondela

washhand basin lavabo

washing (clothes) çamaşır chamash**uh**r

washing machine çamaşır makinesi

washing powder çamaşır toz**u**

washing-up liquid deterjan deterJan

wasp eşek arısı eshek aruhs**uh**

watch (wristwatch) saat sa-at

will you watch my things for me? eşyalarıma göz kulak olur musunuz? esh-yalaruhma gurz

watch out! dikk**a**t!

watch strap saat kayışı sa-at kī-uhsh**uh**

water su

may I have some water? bir**a**z su verir misiniz?

water pipe nargile nargeele**h**

waterproof (adj) su geçirmez gecheerm**e**z

waterskiing su kayağı kī-**a**-uh

wave (in sea) dalga

way: it's this way bu tara**f**tan

  it's that way şu taraftan shoo

  is it a long way to...? ... buraya uz**a**k mı? boor**ī**-a – muh

  no way! katiyen olm**a**z! katee-y**e**n

DIALOGUE

could you tell me the way to...? ...-e n**e**reden gidilir söyleyebilir misiniz? -eh – suh-ilayebeel**ee**r

go straight on until you reach the traffic lights trafik ışıklarına kad**a**r dümdüz gid**i**n uhshuhklaruhna – dewmd**ew**z

turn left sola dönün durn**ew**n

take the first on the right sağdan ilk yola sapın sa-d**a**n – sap**uh**n

see **where**

we biz

weak (person) zayıf zi-**uh**f, güçsüz g**ew**chsewz

  (drink) hafif

  (tea) açık ach**uh**k

weather hava

DIALOGUE

what's the weather forecast? hava rapor**u** nasıl? n**a**suhl

it's going to be fine hava güzel olacak gewz**e**l olaj**a**k

it's going to rain yağmur yağacak ya-m**oo**r ya-aj**a**k

it'll brighten up later sonra hava açacak achaj**a**k

website internet sitesi eenternet seetes**ee**

wedding düğün dew-**ew**n

wedding ring aly**a**ns

Wednesday çarşamba charsh**a**mba

week hafta

  a week (from) today haftaya bugün haftī-**a** boog**ew**n

  a week (from) tomorrow yarından itibar**e**n bir hafta sonra yaruhnd**a**n

weekend hafta son**u**

  at the weekend hafta sonund**a**

weight ağırlık a-uhrl**uh**k

weird tuhaf tooh**a**f

weirdo kaçık kach**uh**k

welcome: welcome to... ...-e hoş geldiniz -**eh** hosh

  you're welcome (don't mention it) bir şey değil shay deh-**ee**l

well: I don't feel well kendimi iyi hiss**e**tmiyorum

  he/she's not well iyi değil deh-**ee**l

  you speak English very well çok iyi İngilizce konuşuyorsunuz chok – eengeele**e**zjeh konooshoo-yorsoon**oo**z

  well done! afer**i**n!

this one as well bu da

well well! (surprise) hayret! hīret

how are you? nasılsınız? nasuhlsuhnuhz

very well, thanks, and you? çok iyiyim, teşekkür ederim, ya siz? chok – teshekkewr

well-done (meat) iyi pişmiş peeshmeesh

Welsh (adj) Galler

I'm Welsh Galliyim

were: we were -dik

you were -diniz

they were -diler

west batı batuh

in the west batıda

West Indian (adj) Batı Hint batuh

wet ıslak uhslak

what? ne? neh

what's that? o nedir?

what should I do? ne yapsaydım? yapsïduhm

what a view! ne manzara!

what bus do I take? hangi otobüse binmem lazım? lazuhm

wheel tekerlek

wheelchair tekerlekli iskemle eeskemleh

when? ne zaman?

when we get back biz, dönünce dewnewnjeh

when's the train/ferry? tren/feribot kaçta? kachta

where? nerede? neredeh

I don't know where it is nerede olduğunu bilmiyorum oldoo-oonoo

where is the Topkapı museum? Topkapı müzesi nerede? topkapuh mewzesee

it's over there şurada shoorada

could you show me where it is on the map? haritada yerini gösterir misiniz? gurstereer

it's just here tam burada

see **way**

which: which bus? hangi otobüs?

which one? hangisi?

that one şu shoo

this one? bu mu?

no, that one hayır, şu hī-uhr

while: while I'm here ben buradayken booraduhken

whisky viski

white beyaz bayaz

white wine beyaz şarap sharap

who? kim?

who is it? kim o?

the man who... ...-an adam

whole: the whole week bütün hafta bewtewn

the whole lot hepsi

whose: whose is this? bu kimin?

why? niçin? neecheen

why not? neden olmasın?
olmas**uh**n

wide geniş gen**ee**sh

wife hanım han**uh**m

Wi-Fi wifi wī-fi

will: will you do it for me?
bun**u** benim için yap**a**r
mısınız? eech**ee**n – muhsuhn**uh**z

wind (*noun*) rüzgâr rewzg**a**r

window (of house, car) pencere
p**e**njereh

(of shop) vitr**i**n

near the window pencereni̇n
yakınında yakuhnuhnd**a**

in the window (of shop)
vitrinde veetreend**eh**

window seat pencere yanı
yan**uh**

windscreen arab**a** ön camı urn
jam**uh**

windscreen wiper sileceler
seelejek**le**r

windsurfing yelkenli sörf
yelken**lee** surf

windy rüzgârlı rewzgarl**uh**

wine şarap shar**a**p

**can we have some more
wine?** bize bir**a**z dah**a** şarap
ver**i**r misiniz? beez**eh**

wine list şarap listes**i** shar**a**p

winter kış kuhsh

in the winter kışın kuhsh**uh**n

winter holiday kış tatil**i** kuhsh

wire tel

(electric) k**a**blo

wish: best wishes en iy**i**
dileklerimle deeleklereeml**eh**

with ile eel**eh**

I'm staying with... ....-de
kalıyorum -deh kaluh-y**o**room

without -siz

witness tanık tan**uh**k

  will you be a witness for me? ben**i**m için tanıklık ed**e**r misiniz? eech**ee**n tanuhkl**uh**k

woman kadın kad**uh**n

wonderful harikulade –l**a**deh

won't: it won't start çalışmıyor chal**uh**shmuh-yor

wood (material) tahta ta**H**ta

woods (forest) orm**a**n

wool yün yewn

word kelime keleem**eh**

work (noun) iş eesh

  it's not working çalışmıyor chal**uh**shmuh-yor

  I work in... ...-'da çalışıyorum chaluhsh**uh**-yoroom

world dünya dewny**a**

worry: I'm worried kaygılanıyorum k**ī**guhlanuh-y**o**room

worry beads tesbih tesbee**H**

worse: it's worse dah**a** kötü kurt**ew**

worst en kötü

worth: is it worth a visit? ziyar**e**te değer mi? zeeyaret**eh** deh-**e**r

would: would you give this to...? bun**u** ...-e verir misiniz? -**eh**

wrap: could you wrap it up? pak**e**t yap**a**r mısınız? muhsuhn**uh**z

wrapping paper ambalaj kağıdı ambala**J** ka-uhd**uh**

wrist bil**e**k

write yazm**a**k

  could you write it down? yaz**a**r mısınız? muhsuhn**uh**z

  how do you write it? nasıl yazılır? nas**uh**l yazuhl**uh**r

writing paper yazı kâğıdı yaz**uh** ka-uhd**uh**

wrong: it's the wrong key o yanlış anaht**a**r yanl**uh**sh

  this is the wrong train bu yanlış tren

  the bill's wrong hes**a**p yanlış

  sorry, wrong number aff**e**dersiniz, yanlış num**a**ra

  sorry, wrong room aff**e**dersiniz, yanlış **o**da

  there's something wrong with... ...-de bir sor**u**n var -deh

  what's wrong? sor**u**n n**e**dir?

X

X-ray röntgen r**u**rntgen

Y

yacht yat

yard yard**a**

year yıl yuhl

yellow sarı sar**uh**

yes **e**vet

yesterday dün dewn

  yesterday morning dün sabah saba**H**

  the day before yesterday evvel**si** gün gewn

yet henüz hen**ew**z

is it here yet? daha gelmedi mi?

no, not yet hayır, henüz değil hī-uhr – deh-**eel**

you'll have to wait a little longer yet biraz daha beklemeniz lazım lazuhm

yoghurt yoğurt yo-**oort**

you (*pl* or *pol*) siz, sizler

(*sing*, *fam*) sen

this is for you bu sizin için eech**een**

with you sizinle seez**een**leh

young genç gench

your (*pl* or *pol*) -iniz, -nīz

(*emphatic*) sizin

(*sing*, *fam*) -in, -n

(*emphatic*) sen**in**

your camera fotoğraf makinanız

yours (*pl* or *pol*) sizinki

(*sing*, *fam*) seninki

youth hostel gençlik yurdu genchl**eek**

Z

zero sıfır suhf**uhr**

zip fermuar fermoo-ar

could you put a new zip on? fermuarı değiştirir misiniz? fermoo-ar**uh** deh-eeshteer**eer**

zip code posta kodu

zoo hayvanat bahçesi hīvanat baнchee**ee**

zucchini kabak

TURKISH
→ **ENGLISH**

Colloquialisms

The following are words you might well hear. You shouldn't be tempted to use any of the stronger ones unless you are sure of your audience.

Allah aşkına ashkuhna for God's sake

Allah kahretsin! damn!

Allah razı olsun! razuh bless you!

aslan sütü sewtew slang word for raki

baksana be! beh hey you!

bombok shitty

çek arabanı! chek arabanuh get lost!

dangalak wally

defol! get out!; go away!

eline sağlık! eleeneh sa-luhk well done!

eşşoğlu eşşek esh-sholoo esh-shek ass; lout

eyvah! ayvaH alas!

hay Allah! hī damn!

herif bloke, guy

inşallah eenshallah I hope so; hopefully; God willing

işler nasıl? eeshler nasuhl how are things?

kapa çeneni! chenenee shut up!

katiyen olmaz! no way!

kuş beyinli koosh bayeenlee stupid, bird-brained

maşallah! mashallah wonderful! (used to express admiration and wonder, and to avert the evil eye)

ne haber?, ne var ne yok? how are things?

saçma! sachma rubbish!, nonsense!

serseri tramp, vagabond

sudan ucuz oojooz dirt cheap

vay canına! vī januhna I'll be damned!

yapma be! beh really!

A

a! oh!

-a to

AB a beh EU

abartmak to exaggerate

ABD a beh deh USA

abi older brother

abide abeedeh monument

abla elder sister

abone kartı aboneh kartuh season ticket

abonman book of bus tickets

acaba ajaba I wonder

acayip ajī-eep odd, strange

acele ajeleh hurry; urgent

acele edin! hurry up!

  acele et! hurry up!

acele etmek to hurry

acemi ajemee beginner

acemi pisti nursery slope

acenta ajenta agency

acı ajuh bitter; hot, spicy; pain

acıkmak ajuhkmak to be hungry

  acıktım ajuhktuhm I'm hungry

acılı ajuhluh hot

acımak ajuhmak to feel pain; to ache; to hurt

acıyor ajuh-yor it hurts, it's sore

acil ajeel urgent

acildir: bu acildir! ajeeldeer this is an emergency!

acil durum emergency

acil servis casualty department

acil vaka emergency

aç ach hungry; greedy

açgözlü achgurzlew greedy

açık achuhk open; clear, obvious; (switched) on; light

açık bilet open ticket

açık havada outdoors

açık hava tiyatrosu open air theatre

açıklamak achuhk-lamak to explain

açık yüzme havuzu yewzmeh open-air swimming pool

açılır tavan achuhluhr sun roof

açılış saatleri achuhluhsh sa-atleree opening times; collection times

açılış ve kapanış saatleri veh kapanuhsh opening times

açıp/kapama düğmesi achuhp – dew-mesee on/off switch

açmak achmak to open; to switch on

ad name; first name

ada island

adam man

adamlar men

adaptör adaptur adapter

adası adasuh island

adet number; sum; total

âdet custom; menstruation

adı aduh name

adım… aduhm my name is…, I am called…

adınız nedir? aduhnuhz what's your name?

adil fair

adres address

adres defteri address book

aferin! well done!

affedersiniz sorry; excuse me

afiş afeesh poster

afiyet olsun! enjoy your meal!

aft mouth ulcer

ağ a net

ağa a-a formerly a rank of
nobility, now used as a term
of respect

ağabey a-abay elder
brother

ağaç a-ach tree

ağır a-uhr heavy; rich

ağırlık a-uhrluhk weight

ağız a-uhz mouth; dialect

ağlamak a-lamak to cry

ağrı a-ruh ache, pain

ağrı giderici ilaçlar geedereejee
eelachlar painkillers

ağustos a-oostos August

ahali people

ahçı ahchuh cook

ahize aheezeh receiver, handset

Aids aydz Aids

aile a-eeleh family

aile gazinosu a-eeleh family
nightclub

ailesiz girilmez entry only for
families

aileye mahsus only for family
groups

ait: -e ait -eh īt belonging to;
relating to

ait olmak to belong

ajanda aJanda diary (business etc)

akciğerler akjee-erler lungs

Akdeniz Mediterranean

akıl akuhl intelligence

akıllı akuhlluh clever

akım akuhm current (electrical)

akıntı akuhntuh current (in water)

akraba relative

akrabalar relatives

akrep scorpion

aks axle

aksan accent

akşam aksham evening; in the
evening; p.m.

   akşam on 10 p.m.

   bu akşam this evening

   akşamleyin akshamlayeen
in the evening

akşam yemeği yemeh-ee dinner,
evening meal; supper

   akşam yemeği yemek
yemeh-ee to have dinner

aktarma connection

aktarmalı sefer aktarmaluh
connecting flight

aktarma yapmak to change
(trains etc)

aktör aktur actor

aktris actress

akü akew battery

alan area; field; square

alaturka Turkish-style

al bakalım bakaluhm here you are

alçak alchak low

alçı alchuh plaster cast

alerjik alerJeek allergic

alet device; tool

alıcı aluhjuh addressee

alımlı aluhml**uh** attractive

alın alu**h**n forehead

alınan mal değiştirilmez no refund or exchange

alınan para aluhna**n** charge

alıp götürmek alu**h**p gurtewrmek to take away

alışılmamış aluhsh**uh**l-mamuhsh unusual

alışkanlık aluhshkanl**uh**k habit

alış kuru alu**h**sh buying rate

alışmak: -e alışmak -eh aluhshmak to get used to

alışveriş aluhshver**ee**sh shopping

    alışverişe çıkmak aluhshvereesh**eh** chuhkmak to go shopping

alışveriş merkezi shopping centre

Allah God

Allahaısmarladık allaha-uhsmarladuhk goodbye **(said by person leaving)**

Allah aşkına ashkuhn**a** for God's sake

Allah belanı versin! belan**uh** damn you!

Allah kahretsin! damn!

Allah razı olsun raz**uh** bless you

allık all**uh**k blusher

almak to take, to accept; to receive; to buy; to obtain

Alman German (*adj*: person)

Almanca alman**ja** German (language)

Almanya Germany

alo hello

alt bottom (of road etc)

altı alt**uh** six

altın alt**uh**n gold

altıncı alt**uh**nj**uh** sixth

altında alt**uh**nda below, under; at the bottom of

altmış altm**uh**sh sixty

altta underneath

alüminyum folyo alewmeen-y**oo**m tinfoil

alyans wedding ring

ama but

...-amadım -amaduhm I couldn't

aman! goodness!; heavens!; careful!

ambalaj kağıdı ambala**J** ka-uhd**uh** wrapping paper

amca am**j**a (paternal) uncle

ameliyat operation

Amerikalı amereekal**uh** American

amfiteatr amphitheatre

amortisör amortees**ur** shock-absorber

amper(lik) amp

ampul light bulb

an moment

ana mother

Anadolu Anatolia, Asia Minor

anahtar anaнtar key

anahtarlık anaнtarl**uh**k keyring

anavatan home, homeland

anayol main road

anayol ilerde main road ahead

anayurt home, homeland

ancak an**j**ak only; hardly; but

anıt an**uh**t monument

ani sudden

aniden suddenly

anlam meaning

anlamadım –mad**uh**m I don't understand

anlamak to understand

anlamı yok anlam**uh** there's no point

anlamıyorum anlam**uh**– I don't understand

anlatmak to explain

anlıyorum anl**uh**– I understand

anne ann**eh** mother

anne baba parents

Anonim Şirket sheerk**et** joint stock company, corporation

antifriz antifreeze

antik ancient

antika antique(s)

antikacı anteekaj**uh** antique dealer

Travel tip It is an offence to buy, sell, attempt to export or even possess genuine antiquities (which includes fossils). If you're apprehensive about a proposed purchase, ask the dealer for an invoice recording the exact purchase price – also necessary to satisfy customs – and a declaration stating that the item is not an antiquity.

---

antiseptik antiseptic

antrenman training

antrenman ayakkabısı ī-akkabuhs**uh** trainers

apaçık apach**uhk** obvious

apandisit appendicitis

apartman block of flats, apartment block

apartman dairesi da-**ee**resee flat, apartment

aptal idiot; stupid

apteshane aptes-han**eh** toilet

ara interval; gap; space

araba car; cart

    arabamda in my car

araba ön camı urn jam**uh** windscreen

araba vapuru car ferry

arabesk Turkish 'art' music

araç giremez no entry

araç kurtarma ar**ach** breakdown service

ara durak stopover

aralık aral**uh**k December

aramak to search for, to look for

Arap Arab

Arapça ar**a**pcha Arabic

arasında: ...-lerin arasında arasuhn**da** among the…, between the…

arasıra aras**uh**ra now and then

ara sokak sidestreet

ardında arduhn**da** beyond

arı ar**uh** bee

arı su soo distilled water

arıza ar**uh**za breakdown

arızalı aruhzal**uh** faulty; out of order

arıza servisi faults service

arıza yapmak to break down

arka back (part)

arkada at the back; behind

   ...-in arkasında behind the...

arkadan binilir entry at the back

arkadan göndermek gurndermek to forward

arkadan inilir exit at the back

arkadaş arkadash friend; partner, boyfriend, girlfriend

arka lambalar rear lights

arkamdaki behind me

arka sinyal lambaları lambalaruh rear lights

Arnavut Albanian

arnavut kaldırımı cobblestone pavement, cobblestone sidewalk

Arnavutluk Albania

artık artuhk no longer; residue; remnant

   artık... yok no more...

arzu etmek to wish for

asansör asansur lift, elevator

aseton nail polish remover

asıl asuhl original; base; basis; origin

asker soldier

askeri bölge military zone

askı askuh coathanger

asla never

aslan sütü sewtew slang word for raki

aslen basically; originally

asma kilit padlock

astım astuhm asthma

Asya Asia

AŞ a sheh joint stock company, corp.

aşağı asha-uh down

aşağıda asha-uhda down; at the bottom; downstairs; down there

aşçı ash-chuh cook

aşı ashuh vaccination

aşılama ashuhlama vaccination

aşmak ashmak to cross

AT a teh EC

at horse

ata ancestor

ateş atesh fire; temperature, fever

ateşli ateshlee feverish

atınız insert (coin)

Atina Athens

'at' işareti et eesharetee at sign, @

atkı atkuh scarf (for neck)

atlamak to jump

atletizm athletics

atmak to throw (away)

At Meydanı maydanuh Hippodrome

avanak idiot

avcılık avjuhluhk hunting

avlu courtyard

Avrupa avroopa Europe; European (*adj*)

Avrupalı avroopaluh European (person)

avukat lawyer

Avustralya avoostralya Australia; Australian

Avusturya avoostoorya Austria; Austrian

ay ī month; moon

ayak ī-ak foot
ayak bileği beeleh-**ee** ankle
ayakkabı ī-akkabuh shoe(s)
ayakkabı bağı ba-uh shoelaces
ayakkabıcı ī-akkabuhj**uh**
  shoeshop
ayakkabı cilası jeelasuh
  shoe polish
ayak parmağı ī-ak parma-uh toe
ayakta durmak ī-akta to stand
aybaşı ībashuh period
  (menstruation); beginning of the
  month; pay day
aydın īduhn intellectual; well-lit
aydınlık īduhnluhk well-lit
ay hali period (menstruation)
ayı ī-uh bear; jerk; blockhead
ayık ī-uhk sober; conscious
ayılmak ī-uhlmak to come round
ayırma ī-uhrma parting
ayırmak ī-uhrmak to separate
ayırtmak ī-uhrtmak to reserve
ayin ī-een mass; religious
  ceremony, rite
aylık bilet īluhk monthly season
  ticket
aylık taksitler monthly
  instalments
ayna īna mirror
aynı inuh (the) same
ayrı īruh separate
ayrı ayrı separately
ayrıldım īruhlduhm separated
ayrılmak īruhlmak to leave; to
  go away
ayrılmış iruhlmuhsh reserved
az not many; little

azami ağırlık weight limit
azami genişlik maximum width
azami hız maximum speed
azami park 1 saat parking
  limited to 1 hour
azami sürat speed limit
azami yükseklik maximum
  height

B

baba father; dad
bacak bajak leg
bacanak bajanak brother-in-law
bademcik iltihabı bademjeek
  eelteehabuh tonsillitis
badem şekeri shekeree sugared
  almonds
bagaj bagaJ luggage, baggage;
  boot, (US) trunk
bagaj alma yeri baggage claim
bagaj fişi feeshee baggage
  receipt
bagaj kaydı kiduh check-in
bagaj kayıt kī-uht check-in
bagaj kayıt masası masasuh
  check-in desk
bagaj kontrolü kontrolew
  baggage check
bağ ba cord; string; bond; link;
  vineyard
bağımsız ba-uhmsuhz
  independent
bağırmak ba-uhrmak to shout
bağlantı ba-lantuh connection
bağlı: ...-a bağlı ba-luh
  it depends on…

bahçe baʜcheh garden

bahsetmek baʜsetmek to mention

bahşiş baʜsheesh tip

bakabilir miyim? can I see it?

bakar mısınız! muhsuhnuhz excuse me!

bakım bakuhm care, attention

bakımından bakuhmuhndan from the point of view of

bakır bakuhr copper

bakkal grocer's, food store

bakkaliye bakkalee-yeh groceries

bakmak: -a bakmak to look at; to look after

baksana be! beh hey you!

balayı balī-uh honeymoon

baldız balduhz sister-in-law (wife's sister)

bale baleh ballet

balık baluhk fish

balık adamlık adamluhk skindiving

balıkçı baluhkchuh fishmonger's

balıkçı köyü kur-yew fishing village

balıkçılık baluhkchuhluhk fishing

balık lokantası baluhk lokantasuh fish restaurant

balık pazarı pazaruh fish market

balık tutmak yasaktır no fishing

balkon balcony; circle

balkonlu with a balcony

balsam conditioner

balta axe

bambaşka bambashka quite different

bana to me

banka banka bank

banka hesabı hesabuh bank account

bankamatik cash dispenser, ATM, automatic teller

banket hard shoulder

banknot note, (US) bill

banliyö banlee-yur suburbs

banliyö tren şebekesi local railway system

banyo bath; bathroom

banyolu (oda) with a private bathroom

banyo etmek to develop

banyo tuzları toozlaruh bath salts

banyo yapmak to take a bath

bardak glass

barmen kız kuhz barmaid

barsak intestine

basamağa dikkat mind the step

basın(ız) press

basit simple, easy

baş bash head

baş ağrısı a-ruhsuh headache

başarı basharuh success

başarmak basharmak to succeed; to achieve

baş aşağı asha-uh upside down

başbakan bashbakan prime minister

başka bashka different; other(s)

başka bir another

başka bir şey shay something else; anything else

başka bir yer somewhere else

başka bir yerde yerdeh elsewhere

başkent bashkent capital city

başlamak bashlamak to start, to begin

başlangıç bashlanguhch beginning, start

  başlangıçta bashlanguhchta at the beginning

başlıca bashluhja main, principal

başparmak bashparmak thumb

baş üstüne ewstewneh with pleasure

batı batuh west

  batıda in the west

  ...-in batısında west of...

batmak to sink

battaniye battanee-yeh blanket

bavul suitcase

Bay bī Mr

bayağı bī-a-uh ordinary; vulgar, common

Bayan bī-an Mrs; Miss; Ms

bayan lady; ladies

bayan iç çamaşırı eech chamashuhruh ladies' underwear

bayan konfeksiyon ladies' wear

bayanlar bī-anlar ladies (toilets), ladies' room

bayat bī-at stale

baygın bīguhn unconscious

bayılmak bī-uhlmak to faint

baylar bīlar gents (toilet)

baypas bīpas by-pass

bayrak bīrak flag

bazen sometimes

bazı bazuh some

bebek baby; doll

bebek bezi nappy, diaper

bebek iskemlesi highchair

bedava free (of charge)

beden size

bedesten covered market hall for valuable goods

beğendim beh-endeem I like it

beğenmek beh-enmek to like

bej beJ beige

bekar batchelor; single (unmarried)

bekârım bekaruhm I'm single

bekçi bekchee guard; watchman

beklemek: -i beklemek to wait; to expect

bekleme salonu beklemeh waiting room

beklemeyin beklemayeen don't wait

bekleyin! beklayeen wait!

  beni bekleyin wait for me

bekleyiniz! beklayeeneez wait!

bel spade; waist

belediye binası beledee-yeh beenasuh town hall

belediye sarayı sarī-uh town hall

... belediyesi beledee-yesee municipality of...; municipal town hall

belge belgeh document

belki maybe, perhaps

  belki de değil deh deh-eel perhaps not

belli obvious

ben I
> **ben de** deh so am I; so do I;
> nor do I; me too

bence öyle benjeh ur-ileh
> I think so
>
> **bence öyle değil** deh-eel
> I don't think so

bende bendeh on/in me

benden from me

beni me

benim my; it's me; speaking
(phone)
> **benim için** eecheen for me
>
> **o benimdir** it's mine

benim kendi...-m my own...

benimki mine

benzemek to look like

benzer similar

benzin petrol, (US) gas

benzin bidonu petrol can, gas
can

benzin istasyonu petrol station,
gas station

benzin pompası pompasuh
petrol pump

beraber together

berbat terrible, awful,
dreadful

berber men's hairdresser,
barber's

bereket blessing; abundance

bereket versin fortunately

beri here
> **...-den beri** since...

beş besh five

beşinci besheenjee fifth

Bey bay Mr; sir; ruler; chief;
master; gentleman

beyaz bayaz white

beyazlar whites

beyaz zehir drugs (narcotics)

beyefendi gentleman; sir

beyin sarsıntısı bayeen sarsuhn-tuhsuh concussion

bez cloth

bıçak buhchak knife

bırakmak buhrakmak to leave; to abandon; to let; to allow; to let off

bıyık buh-yuhk moustache

biberon baby's bottle

biçim beecheem shape, form; kind; manner

bijuteri beeJooteree jewellery

bile beeleh even

　...-se bile -seh even if...

bile bile deliberately

bilek wrist

bilet ticket

> Travel tip Don't pay entrance fees to archaeological sites unless the wardens can produce a ticket, but once you've got one keep it for the duration of your visit – some sites straddle the route to a good beach and the ticket is valid for a week, sparing you having to pay again if you re-cross the area.

biletçi beeletchee conductor

bilet gişesi geeshesee ticket office; box office

biletsiz girilmez no entry without a ticket

bilezik bracelet

bilgi information

bilgisayar beelgeesi-ar computer

bilim science

bilinmeyen numaralar beeleenmayen directory enquiries

... biliyor musunuz? do you speak...?

bilmek to know

bilmiyordum I didn't know

bilmiyorum I don't know

bin thousand

bina building

binicilik beeneejeeleek horse-riding

binilir get on here

biniş kartı beeneesh kartuh boarding card

binmek to get on; to get in

bir a, an; one

bir... daha another..., one more...

biraz some; a little, a bit

　biraz daha some more; a little bit more

birazcık beerazjuhk a bit, a little bit

birazdan in a minute

bir çift... cheeft a couple of...

birçok beerchok a lot of, many

birey beeray individual

bir gecesi gejesee per night

biricik beereejeek the only, sole, unique

bir iki tane... taneh a couple of..., a few...

biriktirmek to collect

birinci beereenjee first

birinci kat first floor, (US) second floor

birinci sınıf suhnuhf first class

birisi somebody, someone

birkaç beerkach several, a few

birkaç tane taneh a few

bir kere kereh once

Birleşik Amerika beerlesheek the United States

Birleşik Devletler the States

Birleşik Krallık kralluhk the United Kingdom

birlikte beerleekteh together

bir parça parcha a little bit

bir sonraki next

bir şey shay something; anything

bir şey değil deh-eel you're welcome, don't mention it, not at all

başka bir şey? bashka anything else?

bir yerde yerdeh somewhere

bisiklet bicycle

bisikletçi beeseekletchee cyclist

bisiklete binmek beeseekleteh cycling

bisiklet sporu cycling

bitirmek: -i bitirmek to finish, to end

bitişiğinde beeteeshee-eendeh next to

bitişik beeteesheek next to

bitki plant

bitkin exhausted, tired

bitmek to end, to come to an end; to grow

bitti over

biz we

Bizans beezans Byzantine

bizde beezdeh on/in us

bizden from us

bize beezeh (to) us

bizi us

bizim our

bizim için eecheen for us

bizimki ours

bizimle beezeemleh with us

bizler we

bizzat personally, in person

blucin bloojeen jeans

bluz blouse

bodrum basement

bodrum kat basement

boğa bo-a bull

boğaz bo-az throat; straits

boğaz ağrısı a-ruhsuh sore throat

Boğaziçi bo-azeechee the Bosphorus

boğaz pastil(ler)i throat pastille(s)

bol wide; loose; plentiful

bol bol... plenty of...

bol şanslar! good luck!

bomba bomb

bombok shitty

bone boneh bathing cap

boru pipe (for water)

boş bosh vacant; empty

boşanmış boshanmuhsh divorced

boş oda vacancy

boşta (gezer) unemployed

boş yer vacancy

boy size; height
boya paint
boyamak to paint
boyar not colourfast
boyun neck
boyunca boyoonja along; throughout; during
bozmak to change
bozuk damaged; broken; out of order
bozuk para coins; small change
böbrekler burbrekler kidneys (in body)
böcek burjek insect
böcek ilacı eelajuh insect repellent; insecticide
böceklere karşı ilaç burjeklereh karshuh eelach insect repellent
böcek sokması sokmasuh insect bite
Boğaz boh-az the Bosphorus
bölge burlgeh region; district; zone
bölüm burlewm department
böyle buh-ileh so, this way, like this; such
  böyle tamam that'll do nicely
böyle iken anyhow; while this is so
Britanya Britain
bronşit bronsheet bronchitis
bronzlaşmak bronzlashmak to get a tan
bronzlaşmış bronzlashmuhsh suntanned
bronzluk suntan
bronz ten suntan

broş brosh brooch
broşür broshewr brochure; leaflet
bu this (one); these; this is
  bu... mi? is this...?
  bu ne? what's this?
buçuk boochook half; and a half
  ... buçuk half past...
budala idiot
bu gece gejeh tonight
bugün boogewn today
buji booJee spark plug
buji telleri jump leads
bukle bookleh curl
Bul. Blvd, Boulevard
bu ...-lar these...
bulaşıcı boolashuhjuh infectious
bulaşık boolashuhk washing-up
bulaşık bezi dishcloth
bulaşık deterjanı deterJanuh washing-up liquid
bulaşık lavabosu sink
bulaşık yıkamak yuhkamak to do the washing-up
Bulgar Bulgarian
Bulgaristan Bulgaria
bulmak to find, to discover; to reach
buluşmak boolooshmak to meet
buluşma yeri boolooshma meeting place
bulut cloud
bulutlu cloudy
bulvar boulevard
  ... Bulvarı boolvaruh ... Boulevard
bunlar these

bunları boonlar**uh** these

bunun fiyatı ne kadar? fee-yat**uh** neh how much is it?, how much is this?

burada boorada here; over here

burada aşağıda asha-uhda down here

burda here; over here

burası boorasuh here

burun nose

but boot thigh

buyrun boo-iroon, **buyurun** boo-yooroon can I help you?; yes?; this way; please; there you are; go ahead

buz booz ice

buzdolabı boozdolab**uh** fridge

buzluk booz ice

büfe bewf**eh** kiosk selling sandwiches

büro bew**ro** office

büro malzemeleri office supplies

bütün bewt**ewn** whole; all

büyük bew-yew**k** large, big; great

büyükanne bew-yew**k**anneh grandmother

büyükbaba grandfather

Büyük Britanya Great Britain

büyükelçilik bew-yew**k**elcheel**eek** embassy

büyük jeton Jeton large token

büyüklük bew-yewl**ewk** size

büyük mağaza bew-yew**k** ma-**a**za department store

büyültme bew-yewltm**eh** enlargement

Cad. jad St; Ave

cadde jadd**eh** street; avenue

... Caddesi ... Street, ... Avenue

cam jam glass

cami jam**ee** mosque

... Camii/Camisi ... Mosque

Travel tip When visiting a mosque, women must cover their heads, and both sexes must cover their shoulders and upper arms, avoid wearing shorts or miniskirts and remove their shoes. You're welcome to wander around and admire the building, but photography is often forbidden and you should keep quiet so as not to disturb people praying.

---

cam sileceği seelejeh-**ee** windscreen wiper

canım sıkılıyor jahnuhm suh-kuhluh-yor I'm bored

-a canim sıkılıyor I'm worried, I'm concerned

cankurtaran jankoortaran ambulance; lifeguard

canlı janluh alive; lively; bright

can sıkıcı jan suhkuhjuh annoying

can simidi lifebelt

can yeleği yeleh-**ee** life jacket

can yelekleri life jackets

can yelekleri tavandadır life jackets up above

caz jaz jazz

cazibeli jazeebelee sexy

ceket jeket jacket

cemiyet jemee-yet society

cenaze jenazeh funeral

cep jep pocket

cereyanlı jerayanluh draughty

cesur jesoor brave

cevap jevap answer

cevap vermek to answer

ceza jeza fine (punishment)

check-in yaptırmak yaptuhrmak to check in

cımbız juhmbuhz tweezers

ciddi jeeddee serious

cila jeela polish

cilt jeelt skin

cilt temizleyici temeezlayeejee skin cleanser

cins(i) jeens(ee) type; kind

cinsiyet(i) jeensee-yet(ee) sex, gender

civarında jeevaruhnda about

coğrafya joh-rafya geography

cuma jooma Friday

cumartesi joomartesee Saturday

cumhurbaşkanı joomHoor-bashkanuh president

cumhuriyet joomHooree-yet republic

cüzdan jewzdan wallet

Ç

çabuk chabook quick
  çabuk ol! hurry up!

çadır chaduhr tent

çadır bezi tarpaulin

çadır direği deereh-ee tent pole

çadır kazığı kazuh-uh tent peg

çağ cha time; date; age, era

çağdaş sanat cha-dash modern art

çağdaş sanat galerisi modern art gallery

çağırmak cha-uhrmak to call; to invite

çağlayan cha-lî-an waterfall

çakı chakuh penknife

çakmak chakmak cigarette lighter

çalar saat chalar sa-at alarm clock

çalınız ring

çalışkan chaluhshkan hardworking

çalışmak chaluhshmak to try; to work

çalışma saatleri chaluhshma sa-atleree working hours

çalışmıyor chalushmuh-yor it's not working

çalıştırmak chaluhshtuhrmak to switch on

çalkalamak chalkalamak to shake; to stir; to wash out; to rinse

çalmak chalmak to steal; to play; to ring

çamaşır chamashuhr laundry, washing

çamaşırhane –haneh laundry (place)

çamaşır ipi clothes line

çamaşır makinesi washing machine

çamaşır mandalı mandal**uh** clothes peg

çamaşır suyu bleach

çamaşır tozu washing powder

çamaşır yıkamak yuhkamak to do the washing

çamur chamoor mud

çan chan bell

çanak çömlek chanak churmlek pottery

Çanakkale Boğazı chanakkaleh bo-az**uh** the Dardanelles

çanta chanta bag

çapa chapa anchor

çarpışma charpuhshma crash

çarşaf charshaf sheet; long, baggy dress with a hood worn by religious Turkish women

çarşamba charshamba Wednesday

çarşı charsh**uh** market, bazaar

   ... Çarşısı charshuhs**uh** ... Market

çartır (seferi) chartuhr charter flight

çatal chatal fork

çatal bıçak buhchak cutlery

çay chī tea; stream

çay bahçesi baнchesee tea garden

çaydanlık chīdanlu**hk** kettle

çayevi chī-evee tea shop, tea house

çayhane chī-нaneh café (for families)

çay kaşığı chī kashuh-**uh** teaspoon

çek chek cheque, (US) check

çek arabanı! arabanu**h** get lost!

çek defteri cheque book

çeker cheker will shrink

çekici chekeej**ee** attractive

çekiç chekee**ch** hammer

çekil! chekee**l** go away!

çekilip gitmek chekeelee**p** to go away

çek-in chek check-in

çekin pull

çekingen chekeengen shy

çekiniz pull

çek kabul edilir cheques accepted

çek kartı kartu**h** cheque card, (US) check card

çekmece chekmej**eh** drawer

çekmek chekmek to pull, to draw; to suffer

çekmez unshrinkable

çene chen**eh** chin; jaw

çengelli iğne chengell**ee** ee-ne**h** safety pin

çeşit chesh**eet** variety, sort, kind

çeşme cheshm**eh** fountain

   ... Çeşmesi cheshmes**ee** ... Fountain

çeviriniz cheveereene**ez** dial

çevirmek cheveermek to turn; to translate; to dial

çevir sesi chev**eer** dialling tone

çevir sinyali dialling tone

çevir tonu dialling tone

çevre yolu chevr**eh** by-pass; ringroad

çeyizlik chayeezleek
trousseau goods

çeyrek chayrek quarter (fraction)

çığlık atmak chuh-luhk to scream

çık dışarı! chuk dusharuh get out!

çıkılmaz no exit

çıkış chuhkuhsh exit, way out

çıkış kapısı kapuhsuh gate

çıkmak chuhkmak to go out; to go up

çıkmaz chuhkmaz dead-end alley

   ... Çıkmazı chuhkmazuh
   ... Cul-de-sac

çıkmaz sokak cul-de-sac; no through road

çıkmaz yol dead end

çıplak chuhplak bare, naked

çiçek cheechek flower

çiçekçi cheechekchee florist

çiçekevi cheechekevee florist

çift cheeft pair; couple; double

çiftçi cheeftchee farmer

çiftlik cheeftleek farm

çift yataklı oda yatakluh twin room

çiğ chee raw

çiğnemek için chew

çiklet cheeklet chewing gum

çikolata cheekolata chocolate

çimen cheemen grass; lawn

çimenlere basmayınız keep off the grass

çingene cheegeneh gypsy

çini cheenee tiles

çips cheeps crisps, (US) potato chips

çirkin cheerkeen ugly; offensive

çivi cheevee nail (metal)

çizgi cheezgee line

çizik cheezeek scratch

çizim cheezeem drawing

çizme cheezmeh boot (footwear)

çizmek cheezmek to draw

çocuk chojook child

> Travel tip Turks adore children and it's a great country to visit with kids, but there are few play areas or attractions aimed specifically at younger children. In general, restaurants are very welcoming to families – just don't expect highchairs – and disposable nappies, formula and baby goods are widely available.

çocuk arabası arabasuh pram

çocuk bahçesi baнchesee playground

çocuk bakıcısı bakuhjuhsuh baby-sitter, childminder

çocuk bezi nappy-liners, diaper-liners

çocuk doktoru pediatrician

çocuk havuzu children's pool

çocuk konfeksiyon children's wear

çocuklar chojooklar children

çocuk yatağı yata-uh cot

çoğu choh-**oo** many; most (of)

çoğunlukla choh-oonl**oo**kla mostly; most of the time

çok chok many; much; a lot, lots; very; very much

  çok daha fazla a lot more

  çok daha iyi/daha kötü kurt**ew** much better/worse

  çok değil deh-**eel** not much

  çok fazla too much

  o kadar çok değil not a lot; not so much

çok çok very much; at the most

çok doğru! doh-roo exactly!

çok yaşa! yasha bless you!

çorap(lar) chorap(lar) sock(s); stocking(s)

çöp churp rubbish, garbage; litter

çöp atmayınız no litter please

çöp kutusu bin

çöp tenekesi dustbin, trashcan

çöp torbası torbas**uh** bin liners

çünkü chew**n**kew because

çürük chewr**ew**k bruise; rotten

D

D shared taxi stop

da too, also

-da at (the); in (the); on (the)

  İstanbul'da in Istanbul

dağ da mountain

  dağlarda da-larda in the mountains

    ... Dağı da-**uh** ... Mountain

    ... Dağları da-lar**uh** ... Mountains

dağcılık da-juhl**uh**k climbing; mountaineering

dağ köyü kur-y**ew** mountain village

daha more; extra; still; yet

  ... daha fazla more than...

  çok daha fazla chok a lot more

daha az less

daha iyi better

daha iyi olmak to improve

daha kötü kurt**ew** worse

dahi also, too; even

dahil da**н**eel included

dahilen (alınır) to be taken internally

dahil etmek to include

dahili extension

dahiliye da**н**eelee-yeh internal

dahiliyeci da**н**eelee-yej**ee** specialist in internal diseases

dahiliye mütehassısı mewtehassuhs**uh** specialist in internal diseases

daima da-eema always

daire da-**ee**reh circle; flat, apartment; office; department

dakika minute

  beş dakikaya kadar besh dakeek**ī**-a in five minutes

  bir dakika just a minute

dalga wave

dalmak to dive

dalma techizatı tejheezat**uh** skin-diving equipment

dam roof

damat son-in-law

damla drop

damsız girilmez no entry
without women

-dan from

    İstanbul'dan Bodrum'a from
Istanbul to Bodrum

-dan biraz a little bit (of)

-dan daha iyi better than

-dan beri since

dangalak wally

danışma danuhshma
information

danışma masası masasuh
information desk

Danimarka Danish (*adj*);
Denmark

dans dance

dans etmek to dance

dar narrow; tight

darüşşifa darewshsheefa old
hospital

dava trial

davet invitation; reception

davet etmek to invite

dayı dī-**uh** (maternal) uncle

de deh too, also; and; but

-de at (the); in (the); on (the)

debriyaj debree-ya⌐ clutch

dede ded**eh** grandfather

dedi he/she said

defa time; turn

defol! get out!; go away!

defter notebook; exercise book

değer deh-**er** value

değerli deh-erl**ee** valuable

değil deh-ee**l** not; he/she/it is not

    değil mi? isn't it?

değiler deh-ee**ler** they are not

değilim deh-eel**eem** I am not

değiliz deh-eel**eez** we are not

değilsin deh-eels**een** you are not

değilsiniz deh-eelseen**eez** you
are not

değişir deh-eesh**eer** it varies

değişken deh-eeshk**en**
changeable

değişmek deh-eeshm**ek**
to change; to alter

değiştirilmez goods cannot be
exchanged

değiştirmek deh-eeshteerm**ek**
to change; to exchange

değmek deh-m**ek** to be worth;
to touch

deli mad, crazy

delik hole

delikanlı deleekanl**uh** teenager
(male)

demek to mean; to pronounce;
to say

demek istemek to mean

demir iron

demiryolu railway

demiryolu geçidi gecheed**ee**
level crossing

demlik teapot

-den from; than; of

-den az under, less than

-den başka bashk**a** apart from

den beri since (time)

-den daha az less than

denemek to try

denetçi denetch**ee** inspector

deniz sea

deniz kenarında kenaruhnda at the seaside

deniz kıyısı kuh-yuhsuh seashore; by the sea

deniz kıyısında kuh-yuh-suhnda on the seashore, by the sea

denizanası deneezanasuh jellyfish

deniz gezisi cruise

deniz kabuğu kaboo-oo seashell

deniz kestanesi sea urchin

deniz motoru motorboat

deniz yosunu seaweed

depo tank (of car)

depozito deposit

deprem earthquake

dere dereh stream

derece derejeh degree; step

dergi magazine

derhal at once, immediately

deri skin; hide; leather

deri mamulleri leather goods

derin deep

dernek society

ders lesson; class; lecture

dert pain; suffering; disease; illness; sorrow; trouble

deterjan deterJan washing powder

dev enormous, giant

devam etmek to continue

devamlı virajlar series of bends

deve deveh camel

dev gibi enormous

devirmek to knock over, to knock down

devlet state

devre devreh period, term

dezenfektan disinfectant

-dir: o ...-dir it is...

dırlar: onlar ... dırlar duhrlar they are...

dış duhsh exterior, outside

dışarda duhsharda out; outside; he/she's out

dışarı duhsharuh outside; out

dışarı sarkmayınız do not lean out

dış hatlar international flights

dışında duhshuhnda except

-di he/she/it was

dibinde deebeendeh at the bottom of

Dicle deejleh the Tigris

Didim Didyma

diğer dee-er other

dik steep

-dik we were

dikiz aynası inasuh rearview mirror

dikkat! look out!; caution!

   dikkat ediniz! take care!

   dikkat et! be careful!

dikkatli careful

   dikkatli olun! be careful!

dikmek to sew; to plant

dil language; tongue

dilek: en iyi dileklerimle deeleklereemleh best wishes

> Travel tip The meaning of some of the body language displayed by Turks may not be immediately obvious. Clicking the tongue against the roof of the mouth and simultaneously raising the eyebrows and chin means 'no' or 'there isn't any'. By contrast, wagging the head rapidly from side to side means 'Explain, I don't understand', while a single, obliquely inclined nod means 'yes'.

-diler they were

dilim slice

dil kursu language course

dil okulu language school

din deen religion

-diniz you were

dinle! deenleh listen!

dinlemek to listen (to)

dinlenme deenlenmeh rest

dinlenmek to rest

dip bottom

diploma degree

-dir is

direk pole; column

direksiyon steering wheel

direksiyon sistemi steering

direkt direct

dirsek elbow

disket disk, diskette

dispanser out-patients' clinic

diş deesh tooth

diş ağrısı a-ruhsuh toothache

dişçi deesh-chee dentist

dişeti deeshetee gum

diş fırçası fuhrchasuh toothbrush

diş floşu floshoo dental floss

diş hekimi dentist

diş ipi dental floss

diş macunu majoonoo toothpaste

diş tabibi dentist

diya dee-ya, **diyapozitif** dee-yapozeeteef slide

diz knee

dizüstü bilgisayar deezewstew beelgeesi-ar laptop

doğa doh-a nature

doğal doh-a**l** natural

doğmak doh-ma**k** to be born; to rise

doğru doh-r**oo** correct, right; accurate; straight

  -e doğru -e**h** towards

doğrulamak doh-roolama**k** to confirm

doğu doh-**oo** east

  doğuda doh-**oo**da in the east

  ...-nın doğusu -nuhn doh-oos**oo** east of...

doğum günü doh-**oo**m gewn**ew** birthday

  doğum gününüz kutlu olsun! gewnewn**ew**z happy birthday!

doğum tarihi taree**H**ee date of birth

doğum yeri place of birth

doksan ninety

dokumak to weave

dokunmak to touch

dokunmayınız do not touch

dokuz nine

dokuzuncu dokooz**oo**njoo ninth

doküman dokewma**n** document

dolap cupboard

dolayı: -den dolayı dolī-u**h** because of

doldurmak to fill; to fill in; to fill up

doldurunuz fill in; fill up

dolgu filling

dolmak to be filled; become full

dolma kalem pen

dolmuş dolm**oo**sh shared taxi

dolmuş durağı doora-u**h** shared taxi stand

dolmuş indirme-bindirme yeri eendeerme**h**-beendeerme**h** shared taxi pick-up/set-down point

dolu full, no vacancies; engaged; occupied; hail

doluyuz we're full

domuz pig

don underpants, panties; knickers; frost

donatım donatu**h**m equipment

dondurma külahı kewl-a**h**uh ice-cream cone

dondurulmuş yiyecekler dondorool-m**oo**sh yee-yejekl**er** frozen food

donmuş donm**oo**sh frozen

donuk dull

dosdoğru dosdoh-r**oo** straight ahead

dost friend

dosya d**o**s-ya file

dökmek durkme**k** to pour (out); to spill

döndürmek durndewrme**k** to turn

dönel kavşak durnel kavsha**k** roundabout

dönmek durnme**k** to come/ go back, to return; to get back; to turn

  ... dönün durnewn turn...

dönüş durne**w**sh return

dördüncü durdewnjew fourth

dört durt four

dört yol (ağzı) a-z**uh** crossroads, intersection

döşeme durshem**eh** furniture; upholstery; floor; floor covering

döviz durv**ee**z foreign currency

döviz alım belgesi al**uh**m document for purchase of foreign currency

döviz kuru exchange rate

draje dra.l**eh** coated pill

dudak lips

dudak merhemi lip salve

dul widow; widower

duman smoke

dur! stop!

duracak the bus is going to stop

duracak yer standing room

durak stop

durgun calm, still

durmak to stop; to stand; to lie; to remain

durmak yasaktır no stopping

duru clear

durulmaz no stopping

durum situation

duruma göre gur**eh** it depends

duş doosh shower

duş jeli Jel**eh** shower gel

duşlu with shower

duvar wall

duygu doo-ig**oo** feeling

duymak doo-im**a**k to hear; to feel

düğme dewm**eh** button; switch

düğün dew-**ew**n wedding

dükkân dewkk**a**n shop

dümdüz devam edin dewmd**ew**z go straight on

dümdüz ilerde eelerd**eh** straight ahead

dün dewn yesterday

dün gece gej**eh** last night

dün sabah saba**H** yesterday morning

dünya dewn-ya world

dürüst dewr**ew**st honest

düş kırıcı dewsh kuhruhj**uh** disappointing

düşmek dewshm**ek** to fall

düşünmek dewshewnm**ek** to think; to think about

düşürmek dewshewrm**ek** to drop

düz dewz flat; plain (not patterned)

düzenlemek dewzenlem**ek** to organize

düz gidin straight on

düzine dewz**ee**n**eh** dozen

  yarım düzine yar**uh**m half a dozen

düz vitesli manual, with manual gears

E

-e -**eh** to; towards

...-ebilir misiniz? can you...?, could you...?

...-ebilir miyim? can I...?, may I...?

eczane ejzan**eh** chemist's, pharmacy

edebilir: ... edebilir miyim? can I ...?

edebiyat literature

efendi 'gentleman', 'master' – formerly respectful way of addressing social superiors; now used in a derogatory way

efendim sir; madam

  efendim? pardon (me)?, sorry?

Efes Ephesus

eflatun purple

Ege egeh the Aegean

egzos exhaust (pipe)

eğer eh-**er** if

eğlenmek eh-lenm**ek** to enjoy oneself, to have fun

  eğlendik eh-lend**eek** it was fun

eh eH enough; come on; well; all right

ehliyet ehlee-y**et** licence

ekim October

ekip team

ekonomi sınıfı suhnuhf**uh** economy class

eksik missing; lacking

ekspres express (train)

ekspresyol motorway, freeway, highway

ekspresyol kavşağı kavsha-**uh** motorway junction

ekspresyolun sonu end of motorway/freeway/highway

ekşi ekshee sour

ek ücret ewjr**et** supplement, extra charge

el hand

el arabası arabas**uh** trolley; wheelbarrow

el bagajı bagaJ**uh** hand luggage, hand baggage

elbette elbett**eh** of course, certainly

elbezi dishcloth

elbise elbees**eh** clothes

elbiseler clothes

el çantası chantas**uh** handbag, (US) purse

elçilik elcheel**eek** embassy

elden düşme dewshm**eh** second-hand

elde yıkanabilir can be handwashed

eldiven gloves

elektrik electricity

elektrikçi elektreekch**ee** electrician

elektrik düğmesi dewmes**ee** switch

elektrik kesilmesi power cut

elektrikli electric

elektrikli aletler electrical appliances

elektrikli tıraş makinesi tuhrash electric shaver

elektrik sobası sobas**uh** electric fire

elektrik süpürgesi sewpewrges**ee** vacuum cleaner

el feneri torch

el freni handbrake

eline sağlık! eleen**eh** sa-l**uh**k well done!

elle yıkayınız wash by hand

elli fifty

elmas diamond

el sanatları sanatlar**uh** crafts

el sanatları dükkanı dewk-kan**uh** craft shop

elverişsiz elvereesh-s**eez** inconvenient

emanet left luggage office, baggage check

emanet kasası kasas**uh** left luggage locker

emek work

emekli retired; pensioner

-emem I can't

emin safe; sure

    emin misiniz? are you sure?

emniyet kemeri seatbelt

emniyet kemerlerinizi bağlayınız fasten seat belts

emniyetli safe (not dangerous)

emniyette emnee-yett**eh** safe (not in danger)

emzik dummy

en most; width

enayi en**ī**-ee idiot, fool

en azından azuhndan at least

en çok chok mostly; at the most

ender rare

endişe etmek endeesh**eh** to worry about

enfeksiyon infection

enformasyon information

enişte eneesht**eh** brother-in-law (sister's husband); aunt's husband

en iyi best

enjeksiyon en**J**eksee-y**o**n injection

en kötü kurt**ew** worst

en son latest

en sonunda eventually

epey **e**pay rather; pretty well

e-posta **eh**-posta email

erkek arkadaş arkadash boyfriend

erkek çocuk cho**jo**ok boy

erkek giyim eşyası esh-yas**uh** menswear

erkek gömleği gurmleh-**ee** men's shirts

erkek iç çamaşırı eech chamashuhr**uh** men's underwear

erkek kardeş kard**e**sh brother

erkek konfeksiyon(u) menswear

erkekler men

erkekler tuvaleti gents' toilets, men's room

erkeklik organı organ**uh** penis

erkek tuvaleti gents' toilet

erken(den) early

Ermeni Armenian

Ermenistan Armenia

ertelemek to postpone

ertesi next; following

    ertesi gün g**ew**n the following day, the next day

esas main; basic

eski ancient; old; former

eskimo ice lolly

eski moda old-fashioned

eski şehir sheh-h**ee**r old town

esnasında esnashunda during

esnek elastic

estağfurullah esta-fooroolla**H** don't mention it; don't say so

eş esh wife; husband

eşarp esharp scarf (for head)

eşek eshek donkey

eşek arısı aruhsuh wasp

eşlik etmek eshleek to accompany

eşofman eshofman tracksuit

eşşoğlu eşek eshsholoo eshek ass; lout

eşya esh-ya furniture; things

eşya arabası arabasuh luggage trolley, baggage trolley

eteğinde eteh-eendeh bottom (of hill)

etek skirt

etiket label

etkileyici etkeelay-eejee impressive

etmek to do (used in compounds)

et pazarı pazaruh meat market

etyemez vegetarian

ev house; home

  evde evdeh at home

  evde mi? is he/she in?

eve gitmek eveh to go home

evet yes

evlenmek to get married

evlenme yıldönümü evlenmeh yuhl-durnewm-ew wedding anniversary

evli married

evrak çantası chantasuh briefcase

evvel first; before

  -den evvel before

evvelki the previous; the … before last

  evvelki gün gewn the day before; the day before yesterday

evvelsi the previous; the … before

  evvelsi gün gewn the day before yesterday

evye ev-yeh sink

eyer ay-er saddle

eylemek aylemek to do; to make (used in compounds)

eylül aylewl September

eyvah! ayvaн alas!

eyvallah! ayvallaн cheerio!; thanks!

ezan Muslim call to prayer

F

fabrika factory

Fahrenheit Fahrenheit

faiz fa-eez interest

fakat but

fakir poor

faks çekmek chekmek to send a fax

fakslamak to fax

falan and so on; about

fanila vest (under shirt)

far (head)light; eye shadow

fare fareh mouse; rat

fark difference

farlar headlights

fatura invoice

favori favourite

fayda fida use; advantage

fazla too (excessively); more than

fazla bagaj bagaJ excess baggage

fazla pişmiş peeshmeesh overdone

felaket disaster

fen science

fena nasty, bad

fener lamp

fenni scientific

feribot ferry

fermuar fermoo-ar zip

fes fez

fevkalade fevkaladeh extraordinary, unusual; super

Fırat Fuhrat the Euphrates

fırça fuhrcha brush

fırın fuhruhn oven; bakery

fırtına fuhrtuhna storm

fikir idea

film banyo etmek to develop

film banyosu film processing

film yıldızı yuhlduhzuh film star, movie star

filtre kağıdı feeltreh ka-uhduh filter papers

fincan feenjan cup

fincan tabağı taba-uh saucer

fiş feesh slip of paper; card; plug (electrical)

fiyat price

flaş flash flash

flaster plaster

fondöten fondurten foundation cream

formda fit

formüler formewler form

fotoğraf foto-raf photo

fotoğraf çekmek chekmek to photograph

fotoğrafçı foto-rafchuh photographer; camera shop

fotoğraf makinesi camera

fön furn blow-dry

fönle kurutma furnleh blow dry

Fransa fransa France

Fransız fransuhz French (adj)

Fransızca fransuhzja French (language)

fren brakes

fren yapmak to brake

fuar fwar trade fair

fuaye fwi-eh foyer

futbol football, soccer

futbol maçı machuh football match

G

galeri upper circle

galiba presumably

Galler Wales

Galli Welsh

gar terminus

garaj garaJ garage

garip strange; peculiar; poor; lonely; stranger

garson waiter

garson kız kuhz waitress

gayet gī-et very

gaz gas

gazete gazeteh newspaper

gazete bayii bī-ee-ee newsagent's

gazete satıcısı satuhjuhs**uh**
newspaper kiosk; news vendor

gaz geçirgen lensler
gecheerg**en** gas permeable
lenses

gazi war veteran

gazino open-air restaurant,
nightclub

gaz pedalı pedal**uh** accelerator

gaz tüpü tewp**ew** gas cylinder

gaz vermek to accelerate

gebe geb**eh** pregnant

gebeliği önleyici gebelee-**ee**
urnleh-yeej**ee** contraceptive

gece gej**eh** night; a.m. (from
midnight to 4 a.m.); overnight

   geceleyin gejelay-een at night

gece bekçisi bekchees**ee** night
porter

gecekondu gejekond**oo**
shanty

gecekondu bölgesi burlges**ee**
shanty town

gece kulübü koolewb**ew**
nightclub

gecelik gejel**ee**k nightdress

gece yarısı yaruhs**uh** midnight

gecikme gejeekm**eh** delay

gecikmeli gejeekmel**ee** delayed

geç gech late; cross

geçe gech**eh** past

geçen gech**en** past; last

   geçen hafta last week

   geçen yıl yuhl last year

geçerli gecherl**ee** valid

geçici güzergah gecheej**ee**
gewzerg**ah** diversion, detour

geçin: ...-i geçin gechee**en** go
past the...

geçiş gechee**sh** crossing

geçit gech**eet** pass (in mountains)

geç kalmak to arrive late, to
be late

geçmek gechm**ek** to pass; to
overtake; to go through; to
cross

geçme yasağı no overtaking

geçmiş olsun! gechmee**sh** get
well soon!

geçmişte gechmeesht**eh** in the
past

geldiği ülke country of
departure

gelecek gelej**ek** future

   gelecekte gelejekt**eh** in future

   gelecek hafta next week

   gelecek yıl yuhl next year

gelen bagaj baga**J** baggage claim

gelenek custom; tradition

geleneksel traditional

gel-git tide

gel-git olayı olŕ-**uh** tide

Gelibolu Gallipoli

gelin daughter-in-law; bride

geliş gelee**sh** arrival

geliş nedeni reason for arrival

geliştirmek geleeshteerm**ek**
to improve

gelmek to come; to arrive

gemi boat; ship

   gemiyle gemee-il**eh** by ship

genç gench young; young person

genç kız kuhz teenager (female)

gençler genchl**er** young people

gençlik hosteli genchleek youth hostel

gene geneh again; still

genel general (*adj*)

genellikle genelleekleh usually, generally

genel olarak generally

geniş geneesh wide

gerçek gerchek real, genuine; true

gerçekten gerchekten really

　gerçekten üzgünüm gerchekten ewzgewnewm I'm really sorry

gerçi gerchee although

gerek(li) necessary

gerekmek to be necessary

geri back, rear; backwards; reverse

　geride gereedeh at the back

geri aramak (telefonla) to ring back

geri dönülmez no U-turns

geri gelmek to come back

geri geri gitmek to reverse

geri gidin go back

gerinmek to stretch

geri ödeme urdemeh refund

geri vites reverse gear

germek to stretch

getirmek to get, to fetch; to bring

gevşek malzeme loose chippings

gevşek şev falling rock

gevşemiş gevshemeesh loose

gezi trip

gezinti trip; outing

gezmek to walk about/around; to stroll; to go out; to tour; to look round

gıda zehirlenmesi guhda food poisoning

gibi as; like

gideceği yer geedejeh-ee destination

giden yolcular salonu yoljoolar departure lounge

gidermek to remove

gidilecek yer geedeelejek destination

gidip getirmek: -i gidip getirmek to fetch

gidiş geedeesh single, one-way

gidiş bileti single ticket, one-way ticket

gidiş dönüş bileti durnewsh return ticket, round trip ticket

girilmez no entry

girin enter, come in

giriniz enter, come in

giriş geereesh way in, entrance; admission charge

giriş holü holew foyer

giriş ücreti ewjretee admission fee

giriş ücretledir admission fee charged

giriş ücretsizdir free entrance

Girit Crete

girmek to go in, to enter, to come in

girmek yasaktır no entry, keep out

girmeyiniz do not enter

gişe geesheh counter; ticket window

git! geet go away!

gitar guitar

gitmek to go

gitti he/she's gone

gittikçe geetteekcheh gradually

giydirmek gee-ideermek to dress

giyim eşyası esh-yasuh clothing

giyinmek to get dressed

giyip denemek to try on

giymek gee-imek to wear

gizli secret

golf sahası sahasuh golf course

göğüs gur-ews chest; breast; bust

göğüsleri açık gur-ewsleree achuhk topless

gök gurk sky

gök gürültüsü gewrewltewsew thunder

göl gurl lake

... Gölü gurlew Lake ...

gölge gurlgeh shade; shadow

gölgede gurlgedeh in the shade

gölgede kurutunuz dry away from direct sunlight

gömlek gurmlek shirt

gönderen gurnderen sender

gönderilecek adres gurndereelejek forwarding address

göndermek gurndermek to send

göre: -e göre -eh gureh according to

görevli gurevlee official; officer

görmek gurmek to see

gör(ül)meye değer yerler gur(ewl)mayeh deh-er (the) sights

görümce gurewmjeh sister-in-law (husband's sister)

görünmek gurewnmek to seem; to look

görüşmek üzere gurewshmek ewzereh see you later

görüşürüz! gurewshewrewz see you!

gösteri gursteree show (in theatre)

göstermek gurstermek to show

götürmek gurtewrmek to take (away); to carry

göz gurz eye; drawer

göz boyası boyasuh eye shadow

göz damlası damlasuh eye drops

gözde gurzdeh favourite

göz doktoru optician

gözlük gurzlewk glasses, spectacles, (US) eyeglasses

gözlükçü gurzlewkchew optician

göz makyajı çıkarıcısı
makyaJuh chuhkaruh-juhsuh
eye make-up remover

gramer grammar

gri grey

grip greep flu

grup group; party

gururlu proud

gücendirmek gewjendeermek
to offend

güçlü gewchlew strong

güçsüz gewchsewz weak, feeble

gül gewl rose

güle güle gewleh goodbye (said to
person leaving)

güle güle giy! gee-i literally:
'wear it happily!' – said to
someone who has bought new
clothes

güle güle kullan! literally: 'use
it happily!' – said to someone
who has bought something
new

gülmek gewlmek to laugh

gülümsemek gewlewm-semek
to smile

gülünç gewlewnch
ridiculous

Gümrük gewmrewk Customs

gümrük beyannamesi Customs
declaration

gümrüksüz gewmrewksewz
duty-free

gümüş gewmewsh silver;
silverware

gümüş yaprak silver foil

gün gewn day

gün ağarırken a-aruhrken
at dawn

günaydın gewnīduhn good
morning

günbatımı gewn-batuhmuh sunset

günce gewnjeh diary

günde bir/iki/üç defa once/
twice/three times a day

**günde üç defa ikişer tablet
alınız** take two tablets three
times a day

gündüz gewndewz daytime;
by day

güneş gewnesh sun

güneşte gewneshteh in the sun

güneş banyosu yapmak
to sunbathe

güneş çarpması charpmasuh
sunstroke

güneş gözlüğü gurzlew-**ew** sunglasses

güneş ışığı uhsh**uh**-uh sunshine

güneşli gewnesh**lee** sunny

güneşlik gewnesh**leek** sunshade

güneş losyonu suntan lotion

güneş merhemi sunblock

güneşte yanmak gewnesht**eh** to get a tan

güneşte yanmış yanm**uh**sh sunburnt, tanned

güneş yağı ya-**uh** suntan oil

güneş yanığı yanuh-**uh** sunburn

güney gewn**ay** south

　güneyde gewnayd**eh** in the south

　...-in güneyi gewnay-**ee** south of...

güney batı bat**uh** southwest

güney doğu d**oh**-oo southeast

günlük gewnl**ewk** day; daily

günlük bilet day ticket

günlük gezi day trip

günü gewn**ew** on

Gürcistan gewrjeesta**n** Georgia

Gürcü gewrj**ew** Georgian

gürültü gewrewl-t**ew** noise

gürültülü gewrewl-tewl**ew** loud; noisy

gürültü yapmayın! y**a**pmī-uhn quiet!

güverte gew**v**erteh deck

güzel gewz**e**l beautiful; nice; pretty; fine; attractive

güzergah gewzerga**H** route

H

haber news (on radio, TV etc)

　ne haber? how are things?

hacı haj**uh** literally: 'pilgrim' – respectful way of addressing someone who has made the pilgrimage to Mecca

hafıza çubuğu hafuhz**a** chooboo-**oo** memory stick

hafif light (not heavy); mild

hafif koşu kosh**oo** jogging

hafif müzik mewz**eek** light music

hafif rüzgar rewzg**a**r breeze

hafta week

　haftaya bugün hafti-**a** boog**ew**n a week (from) today

　haftaya yarın yar**uh**n a week (from) tomorrow

　haftada per week

haftalık bilet haftalu**h**k weekly ticket

hafta sonu weekend

　hafta sonunda at the weekend

hakikaten really, truly

hakiki true; real, genuine

hakkında hakkuh**n**da concerning

hakkıyla hakkuh-i**la** properly

haklı hakl**uh** right, justified

hala aunt (paternal)

hâlâ still

halat rope

halı hal**uh** carpet

halıcı haluhj**uh** carpet seller

halı kaplama fitted carpet

halılar haluhlar carpets

Haliç haleech the Golden Horn

haliç inlet; bay

halk people

halka açık achuhk public; open to the public

halk dansları danslaruh folk dancing

halk müziği mewzee-ee folk music

halk oyunları oyoonlaruh folk dances

halletmek: -i halletmek to fix, to arrange

hamal porter

hamam Turkish bath

> Travel tip Turkish baths are well worth visiting – İstanbul boasts many historic *hamams* worth experiencing for their architecture alone – and they make for a relaxing end to a day slogging around the sights. Most towns have at least one set of baths, either for men or women, or sexually segregated on a schedule, with women usually allotted the more restricted hours.

hamamböceği –burjeh-ee cockroach

hamile hameeleh pregnant

han tradesmen's hall; inn; caravanserai; office block

   ... Hanı hanuh ... tradesmen's hall; ... inn; ... office block

hangi? which?

hangisi? which one?

hanım hanuhm lady; wife

   ... hanım Mrs...

hap pill(s); contraceptive pill(s)

hapis(hane) hapees(haneh) prison

hapşırık hapshuhruhk sneeze

hapşırmak hapshuhrmak to sneeze

harabe harabeh ruin

harabeler ruins

harcamak harjamak to spend

hareket etmek to move

hareket saati sa-atee time of departure

hariç hareech except; external; abroad

harika! great!

harikulade hareekooladeh wonderful

harita hareeta map

hasar görmüş gurmewsh damaged

hassas sensitive

hasta sick, ill

hastabakıcı –bakuhjuh nurse

hastalık hastaluhk illness; disease

hastalık sigortası seegortasuh health insurance

hastane hastaneh hospital

   ... Hastanesi ... Hospital

hat route; line

hata mistake; fault

hatıra hatuhra souvenir

hatırlamak hatuhrlamak to remember

hatırlıyorum hatuhrluh-yoroom I remember

hatta even

hava air; weather

hava soğuk soh-**ook** it's cold

havaalanı hava-alan**uh** airport

hava basıncı basuhnj**uh** air pressure

hava cereyanı jereh-yan**uh** draught

havai fişek feesh**ek** fireworks

havale haval**eh** money order

havalimanı havaleeman**uh** airport

havalimanı otobüsü otob**ewsew** airport bus

hava tahmini weather forecast

havayolu havi-ol**oo** airline

havlu bath towel

havuz pond; pool

hay Allah! h**ī** damn!

hayat h**ī**-at life

haydi! h**ī**dee come on!

haydi gidelim! h**ī**dee let's go!

hayhay! h**ī**-h**ī** certainly!, by all means!

hayır h**ī**-uhr no; goodness

hayran h**ī**ran fan; admirer

hayret! h**ī**ret well well!

hayvan h**ī**van animal

hayvanat bahçesi h**ī**vanat ba**H**chesee zoo

hayvanlara yiyecek vermeyiniz do not feed the animals

hazımsızlık hazuhm-suhzl**uh**k indigestion

hazır hazu**h**r ready

hazırlamak hazuhrlamak to prepare

haziran June

hediye hedee-y**eh** present, gift

hediyelik eşya dükkanı esh-ya dewkkan**uh** gift shop

hekim doctor

hela WC, toilet, restroom

hem moreover, besides; both … and …

hemen immediately; almost

hemen hemen almost

hemen hemen hiç heech hardly ever

hemen şimdi sheemdee straight away

hemşire hemsheer**eh** nurse; sister

hemzemin geçit gechet level crossing

henüz hen**ewz** yet; just now; a minute ago

henüz değil deh-**eel** not yet

hep always; the whole

hep birden altogether

hepimiz all of us

hepsi all of it/them, the whole lot

hepsi bu kadar that's all

hepsi o kadar nothing else

her each; every

her gün gewn every day; daily

her defasında defasuhnda every time

herif bloke, guy

her iki … de deh both…

her ikisi de both of them

herkes everyone

her neyse nays**eh** anyway

her şey shay everything**

her şey dahil all-inclusive

her şeyden önce shayden **u**rnjeh first of all

her yer everywhere

her yerde yerd**eh** everywhere

her zaman always

hesap bill, (US) check; account

hesap makinesi calculator

heyecan verici hayejan vereej**ee** exciting

Heyelan! landslides!

heykel hayk**el** statue

hırdavatçı huhrdavatch**uh** hardware store

Hıristiyan huhreestee-yan Christian

hırka huhrka cardigan

hırsız huhrs**uh**z thief

hırsızlık huhrsuhzl**uhk** burglary; theft

hıyar huh-yar lout; cucumber

hız huhz speed

hız kısıtlaması sonu end of speed restriction

hızla huhzla quickly

hızlı huhzl**uh** fast; quickly

hicri heejr**ee** Muslim system of dates

hiç heech none; nothing; never; ever

hiç de değil deh deh-**eel** not in the least

hiç ... iz mi? have you ever...?

hiç ... yok I don't have any...; there isn't any...

hiç bir... no ... at all

hiç biri neither of them

hiç kalmadı kalmad**uh** there's none left

hiçbir şey heechb**ee**r shay nothing

hiçbir yerde yerd**eh** nowhere

hiçbir zaman never

hiç kimse keems**eh** nobody, no-one

hidrofil pamuk cotton wool, absorbent cotton

hikâye heekī-**eh** story

his feeling

hisar fortress, castle

hissetmek to feel

hitap ekmek to call

Hititler the Hittites

hizmet etmek to serve

hoca h**o**ja teacher; teacher in charge of religious instruction

hol entrance hall, lobby

... holü hol**ew** ... hall

horlamak to snore

hostes stewardess

hoş hosh nice, pleasant; fine

hoş bulduk! it's nice to be here! – usual response to 'hoş, geldiniz'

hoşça kal h**o**sh-cha bye (said by person leaving)

hoşça kalın kal**uh**n goodbye

hoş geldiniz! welcome!

hoşlanmak hoshlanm**a**k to like

hükümet hewkewm**e**t government

hür hewr free

hürriyet hewr-ree-y**e**t freedom

-ı -uh his; her; its; accusative noun
 ending
ılıca uhluhja hot spring
ılık uhluhk lukewarm
ılık ütü warm iron
ılımlı uhluhmluh mild; moderate
-ım -uhm my; I am
-ımız -uhmuhz our
-ın -uhn of; your
-ınız -uhnuhz your
 ...-ınız var mı? muh have you
 got...?
Iraklı uhrakluh Iraqi
ırmak uhrmak river
ırza geçme uhrza gechmeh rape
ısırık uhsuhruhk bite, sting
ısırma uhsuhrma bite
ısırmak uhsuhrmak to bite
ısıtma uhsuhtma heating
ıslak uhslak wet
ısmarlamak uhsmarlamak to order
ışık uhshuhk light
-ız -uhz we are
ızdıraplı uhzduhrapluh painful

-i his; her; its; the
iade ee-adeh refund
iade etmek to give back
iç eech interior, inside
iç çamaşırı chamashuhruh
 underwear

içerde eecherdeh indoors,
 inside
içeri eecheree inside
içeride eechereedeh indoors,
 inside
içeri kilitlemek eecheree
 to lock in
içerisi eechereesee inside
içermek eechermek to contain
iç hastalıkları mütehassısı
 hastaluhklaruh mewteHassuhsuh
 specialist in internal
 diseases
iç hatlar eech domestic flights
iç hat seferi domestic flight
içilmez eecheelmez not for
 drinking
için eecheen for; as
içinde eecheendeh in; included
 iki gün içinde gewn in two
 days from now
içinden eecheenden through
içine eecheeneh into
iç kale kaleh citadel
içki eechkee alcoholic drinks
içkili olarak araba sürmek
 sewrmek drunken driving
içkisiz no drinks allowed
iç lastik inner tube
içmek eechmek to drink
içme suyu eechmeh drinking
 water
içten eechten sincere
idi it was
iğne ee-neh needle; injection
iğrenç ee-rench disgusting,
 revolting; obnoxious

... ihtiyacında eeнtee-yajuhnda in need of ...

ihtiyaç eeнtee-yach need

ihtiyaç duymak doo-imak to need

ihtiyar eeнtee-yar old; old person

ikamet stay

ikamet adresi domicile

iken while

iki two

iki hafta fortnight

iki kere kereh twice

iki kişilik oda keesheeleek double room

iki kişilik yatak double bed

iki misli twice as much

ikinci eekeenjee second (*adj*)

ikinci kat second floor, (US) third floor

ikinci sınıf suhnuhf second class

ikisi: ikisi de deh both

  ikisinden biri either of them

iki tane tek kişilik yatak taneh tek keesheeleek twin beds

iki yol ağzı a-zuh fork (in road)

iki yönlü trafik two-way traffic

ikizler twins

iklim climate

il province; county

  ... İli Province of..., County of...

ilaç eelach medicine

ilan yapıştırmak yasaktır stick no bills

ilçe eelcheh administrative district

ile eeleh with; and; by

  otobüs ile otobews by bus

ileri front part; forward

-ileri the

ileride ilereedeh further (on); in future

ilerleyelim lütfen! please move forward!

iletmek to forward; to pass on

ilgilenmek to be interested in; to show interest in; to take care of

ilginç eelgeench interesting

ilim science

ilişki kurmak eeleeshkee to contact

ilişkin: -e ilişkin eeleeshkeen relating to

ilk first

  ilk önce urnjeh at first

  ilk kez the first time

ilkbahar spring (season)

ilk hareket first departure

ilk olarak first

ilk yardım yarduhm first aid

ilk yardım çantası chantasuh first aid kit

iltihap inflammation

-im my; I am

imam prayer leader in a Mosque

imaret soup kitchen and hostel

imdat emergency

imdat! help!

imdat freni emergency brake

-imiz our

imkansız eemkansuhz impossible

imza signature

imza etmek to sign

-in of; your

inanılmaz eenanuhlmaz incredible, amazing

inanmak to believe

ince eenjeh thin

incitmek eenjeetmek to hurt

inç eench inch

indirimli satış satuhsh sale

indirmek eendeermek to download

inek cow

İngiliz eengeeleez English; British; Englishman

İngiliz anahtarı anaHtaruh wrench

İngilizce eengeeleezjeh English (language); in English

İngiliz kadın kaduhn English woman

İngilizler the English

İngiliz sterlini pound sterling

İngiltere eengeeltereh England; the UK

inik lastik flat tyre

inilir get off here

-iniz your

inmek to get off; to get out; to go down; to land; to fly in

insan person; man

insanlar people

inşallah eenshal-lah I hope so; hopefully; God willing

inşallah öyle değildir urleh deh-eeldeer I hope not; God forbid

internet sitesi eenternet seetesee website

ip string; rope

ipek silk

iple çekmek eepleh chekmek to look forward to

iplik thread

iptal edildi cancelled

iptal etmek to cancel

İranlı eeranluh Iranian

iri big

İrlanda eerlanda Ireland; Irish

İrlandalı eerlandaluh Irishman; Irishwoman

İsa eesha Jesus

ishal ees-hal diarrhoea

isilik rash (on skin)

isim name

iskele eeskeleh jetty; quay; ferry terminal

   ... İskelesi ... Jetty; ... Docks; ... Terminal

iskemle eeskemleh chair

İskoç eeskoch Scottish

İskoçya eeskochya Scotland

iskonto discount

İslami eeslamee Islamic

İspanya eespanya Spain

İspanyol eespanyol Spanish (*adj*)

İspanyolca eespanyolja Spanish (language)

israr ediyorum I insist

israr etmek: -de israr etmek to insist on

İstanbul Boğazı eestanbool bo-azuh the Bosphorus

istasyon station

   istasyonda at the station

istemek to want; to wish; to ask for

istemiyorum I don't want

isterim I want

… ister misiniz? do you want…?

istiyor he/she wants

… istiyor musunuz? do you want…?

istiyor(d)um I would like

istiyorsunuz: ne istiyorsunuz? neh what do you want?

istiyorum I want

İsveç eesvech Sweden; Swedish (adj)

İsveççe eesvech-cheh Swedish (language)

İsviçre eesveechreh Switzerland

iş eesh work; job; business; deal

işaret levhası eesharet levhasuh signpost

işe: bu işe yaramaz eesheh it's no good

iş günü eesh gewnew weekdays

işitme cihazı eesheetmeh jeehazuh hearing aid

işitmek eesheetmek to hear

işkembeci eeshkembejee tripe restaurant

işkembe salonu eeshkembeh tripe shop

işlek eeshlek busy

işleme günleri ferry timetable

iş seyahati eesh sayahatee business trip

işsiz eeshseez unemployed

iştah eeshtaH appetite

işte eeshteh here is/are; there is/are; here it is; her; him

İtalya etalya Italy

İtalyan eetalyan Italian (adj)

itfaiye eetfa-ee-yeh fire brigade

itiniz push

itmek to push; push

iyi good; well; kind

iyi misin? are you OK?

iyi akşamlar akshamlar good evening

iyice ee-yeejeh properly

iyi geceler gejeler good night

iyi günler gewnler hello (literally: good day); have a nice day

iyilik sağlık sa-luhk I'm fine

iyimser optimistic

iyi şanslar! shanslar good luck!

iyiyim I'm all right, I'm fine

iyi yolculuklar! yoljoolooklar have a good journey!

-iz we are

izin holiday, vacation; permit

izin belgesi licence

izin vermek to let, to allow

izlemek to follow

J

jaluzi Jaloozee blinds

jant Jant rim; spoke

jarse Jarseh jersey (cloth)

jel Jel jelly; hair gel

jeton Jeton telephone token

jikle Jeekleh choke

jilet Jeelet razor blade

jinekolog Jeenekolog gynaecologist

jogging yapmak to go jogging

jöle Jurleh hair gel

K

kaba rude; rough; vulgar
kabaca kabaja roughly, approximately
kabadayı kabadi-**uh** macho
kabak bald; pumpkin; marrow; courgette, zucchini
kabakulak mumps
kabarcık kabar**juh**k blister
kabız kab**uh**z constipated
kabızlık kabuhz**luh**k constipation
kabin cabin; changing cubicle
kabin memuru steward
kablo lead; wire
kabul etmek to accept
kaburga rib
kaç? kach how many?; how much?

kaç kişilik keesheel**eek** for how many people?
kaç tane? t**a**neh how many?
kaç yaşındasınız? yashuhnda-suhn**uh**z how old are you?
kaç gecelik? kach gejel**eek** for how many nights?
kaçak kach**a**k leak; fugitive; contraband
kaçık kach**uh**k weirdo
kaçırmak kachuhrm**a**k to miss (bus etc)
kadar until; about; as much as; as many as
    kadar ...-e kadar -eh as ... as; until; as much as; as far as
    ne kadar? neh how much?
    ne kadar iyi! how nice!; it's so good!
kadın kad**uh**n woman; lady
kadın bağı ba-**uh** sanitary towel
kadın giyim eşyası esh-y**a**suh ladies' wear
kadınlar kad**uh**nlar women
kadın polis policewoman
kadran dial
kafa head
kafatası kafatas**uh** skull
kafeterya cafeteria
kâğıt ka-**uh**t paper
kâğıt çocuk bezi choj**oo**k disposable nappies/diapers
kâğıt mendil tissues, Kleenex
kâğıt para banknote, (US) bill
kahvaltı ka**h**valt**uh** breakfast
kahvaltı dahil breakfast included

kahve kaнveh coffee; coffee shop (usually for men only)

kahvehane kaнveh-нaneh café (usually for men only)

kahverengi kaнverengee brown

kala: -e … kala -eh to; remaining

  beşe on kala besheh ten to five

kalabalık kalabaluhk crowd; crowded, busy

kalabalık saatler sa-atler rush hour

kalacak yer kalajak accommodation

kalan the rest (of)

kalça kalcha hip

kaldırım kalduhruhm pavement, sidewalk

kaldırınız lift (the receiver)

kaldırmak kalduhrmak to raise; to lift; to remove

kale kaleh castle, fort

  … Kalesi … Castle, Fort…

kalem pencil

kalın kaluhn thick

kalın kafa thickhead

kalite kaleeteh quality

kaliteli high quality

kalkış kalkuhsh departure

kalkmak to stand up; to get up; to take off; to leave

kalmak to stay, to remain

kalorifer (central) heating; heater

kalp heart

kalp krizi heart attack

kamara cabin

kambiyo bureau de change

kamp ateşi ateshee campfire

kamping campsite; caravan site, trailer park

kamp yapmak to camp

kamp yapmak yasaktır no camping

kamp yeri campsite

kamu the public

kamyon lorry

kamyonet van

kan blood

Kanada Canada; Canadian (*adj*)

Kanadalı kanadaluh Canadian (person)

kanamak to bleed

kanat wing

kan grubu blood group

kano canoe

kano kullanmak canoeing

kanun law

kapa çeneni! chenenee shut up!

Kapadokya Cappadocia

kapak cap; lid

kapalı kapaluh closed; off; covered

kapalı çarşı charshuh covered bazaar

kapalı havuz indoor pool

kapalı yüzme havuzu yewzmeh indoor swimming pool

kapamak to switch off; to close; to shut

kapatmak to close, to shut

kapı kapuh door; gate

kapıcı kapuhj**uh** caretaker; doorman; porter

kapı kolu kap**uh** door handle

kap kacak kaj**a**k cooking utensils, pots and pans

kaplıca kapluhj**a** thermal spring

kaporta bonnet (of a car), (US) hood

kapsamak to include

kaptan captain

kaput bonnet (of a car), (US) hood

kar snow

kâr profit, benefit

kara black

karabasan nightmare

karaciğer karajee-e**r** liver (in body)

Karadeniz the Black Sea

karakol police station

karanlık karanl**uh**k dark; darkness

karantina quarantine

karar decision

  (-e) karar vermek -eh to decide (on)

karayolu karí-ol**oo** highway

karayolu haritası hareetas**uh** road map

karbüratör karbewrat**u**r carburettor

kardeş kard**e**sh brother; sister

karı kar**uh** wife

karın ağrısı kar**uh**n a-ruhs**uh** stomachache

karınca karuhnj**a** ant

karışıklık karuhshuhkl**uh**k mess

karıştırmak karuhshtuhrm**a**k to mix

karmaşık karmash**uh**k complicated

karşı: -e karşı -eh karsh**uh** across; against; towards; contrary

karşıda karsh**uh**hda opposite

karşıdan gelen taşıtlara öncelik oncoming traffic has right of way

karşılaşmak karshuhlashm**a**k to meet

karşın: -e karşın -eh karsh**uh**n in spite of

karşısında karshuhsuhnd**a** opposite

karşıt karsh**uh**t opposite; contrary; anti-; counter-

kart card

kartlı telefon kartl**uh** cardphone

karton cardboard; box

kartpostal postcard

kartvizit business card

kas muscle

kasa till, cash desk; cashier

kasaba small town

kasadan fiş alınız please obtain ticket from the till

kasap butcher's

kasap dükkanı dewkkan**uh** butcher's shop

kase kas**eh** bowl

kasetli teyp tayp cassette recorder

kasım kas**uh**m November

kasis uneven road surface

kasiyer cashier

kask helmet

kasket cap

kasten deliberately

kaş kash eyebrow

kaşık kashuhk spoon

kaşıntı kashuhntuh itch

kaş kalemi kash eyebrow
  pencil

kat floor, storey

katakomp catacomb

katedral cathedral

kat görevlisi gurevleesee maid

katiyen olmaz! no way!

Katma Değer Vergisi deh-er
  VAT

Katolik Catholic

kavanoz jar

kavga fight

kavga etmek to fight

kavim people; tribe

kavşak kavshak crossroads,
  intersection; junction

kaya kī-a rock

kayak skiing

kayak pisti ski slope

kayak yapmak to ski

kaybetmek kībetmek to lose

kaybolmak kībolmak to disappear

kaygan kīgan slippery

kaygan yol slippery road

kaygı kiguh worry

kaygılanmak kiguhlanmak to
  worry about

kayık kī-uhk small boat; rowing
  boat

kayınbirader kī-uhn-beerader
  brother-in-law (husband's/wife's
  brother)

kayınpeder kī-uhnpeder
  father-in-law

kayınvalide kī-uhnvaleedeh
  mother-in-law

kayıp eşya kī-uhp esh-ya lost
  property

kayıp eşya bürosu bewrosoo
  lost property office

kayış kī-uhsh strap

kayıt numarası ki-uht
  noomarasuh registration
  number

kaymak kīmak to skid; cream

kaynak kīnak spring, source

kaynana kīnana mother-in-law

kaza accident

kazak jumper, sweater

kazan boiler

kazanmak to earn; to win

kazık kazuhk rip-off; tent peg

KDV ka deh veh VAT

kebapçı kebapchuh meat
  restaurant

keçe uçlu kalem kecheh oochloo
  felt-tip pen

keçi kechee goat

kederli depressed

kedi cat

kel bald

kelebek butterfly

kelime keleemeh word

kemençe kemencheh small violin
  with three strings

kemer belt

kemik bone

-ken while

kenar edge

  deniz kenarında kenaruhnda
    by the sea

kenar mahalle poor quarters near the edge of the town, slum

kenar şeridi shereedee hard shoulder

kendi himself; herself; itself; oneself; his/her/its own

kendileri themselves

kendim myself

kendimiz ourselves

kendin yourself

kendiniz yourselves

kent town

kepenk shutter

kere kereh time; occasion

kerpeten pliers

kervansaray kervansarī inn, caravanserai

kes (artık)! artuhk stop it!

kesici platinler keseejee points

kesik cut

kesinlikle keseenleekleh definitely; certainly

   kesinlikle! absolutely!

   kesinlikle (öyle) değil (urleh) deh-eel definitely not, certainly not

keskin sharp

kesmece kesmejeh word used by street vendors meaning that melons can be cut open and examined before you buy

kesmek to cut

kestirme kesteermeh shortcut

keten cotton

keyif kayeef pleasure; disposition

kez time

Kıbrıs kuhbruhs Cyprus; Cypriot (adj)

Kıbrıslı kuhbruhsluh Cypriot (person)

Kıbrıslı Rum Greek Cypriot (person)

Kıbrıs Rum Greek Cypriot (adj)

Kıbrıs Türk tewrk Turkish Cypriot (adj)

kılavuz kuhlavooz guide; leader

kılık kuhluhk appearance; costume

kına kuhna henna

kır kuhr countryside

kırık kuhruhk broken; fracture

kırk kuhrk forty

kırmak kuhrmak to break; to offend

kırmızı kuhrmuhzuh red

kırsal alanlar kuhrsal countryside

Travel tip In remote areas, black and Asian people may find themselves something of a curiosity, and may receive unsolicited comments, but Turkey is, in fact, one of the least racist countries around the Mediterranean.

kırtasiye kuhrtasee-yeh stationery

kırtasiyeci kuhrtasee-yejee stationer's

kısa kuhsa short; brief

   en kısa zamanda kuhsa as soon as possible

kısa yolculuk yoljoolook short journey

kısım kuhsuhm part, portion

kıskanç kuhskanch jealous

kış kuhsh winter

  kışın kuhshuhn in the winter

kış tatili winter holiday, winter vacation

kıvırcık kuhvuhrjuhk curly; lettuce

kıyafet kuh-yafet dress, attire; general appearance and dress

kıyı kuh-yuh coast

kıymık kuh-imuhk splinter

kız kuhz girl; daughter

kızaklı tekne kuhzakluh tekneh hydrofoil

kızamık kuhzamuhk measles

kızamıkçık kuhzamuhkchuhk German measles

kız arkadaş arkadash girlfriend

kızarmak kuhzarmak to be fried; to be roasted; to be toasted; to blush

kızartmak kuhzartmak to fry; to roast; to toast

kız(evlat) kuhz(evlat) daughter

kızgın kuhzguhn angry; furious

Kızılay kuhzuhlī Red Crescent – Turkish Red Cross

Kızılhaç kuhzuhlhach Red Cross

kızıl saçlı kuhzuhl sachluh red-headed

kız kardeş kardesh sister

kızlık adı kuhzluhk aduh maiden name

kızmak kuhzmak to get angry

ki that; who; which; so that; seeing that

kibrit matches

kilidi açmak achmak to unlock

kilim rug

kilise keeleeseh church

  ... Kilisesi Church of...

kilit lock

kilitlemek to lock

kilitli locked

kilometre kısıtlaması yok keelometreh kuhsuhtlamasuh unlimited mileage

kim? who?

kimi some

kimin? whose?

kimlik identification

kimlik kartı kartuh ID card

kimse keemseh anybody; nobody

kira rent; rental

kiralamak to rent, to hire

kiralık keeraluhk for rent, for hire

kiralık bisiklet bicycle hire

kiralık kayık kī-uhk boat hire

kiralık otomobil keeraluhk car rental; rented car

kira ücreti ewjretee hire charge

kirli dirty; polluted

kişi keeshee person

kitabevi bookshop, bookstore

kitap book

kitapçı keetap-chuh bookshop, bookstore

kitaplık keetapluhk library

KKTC Turkish Republic of Northern Cyprus

klakson horn

Klasik Batı müziği bat**uh**
mewzee-**ee** Western classical
music

klima air-conditioning

klimalı kleemal**uh** air-conditioned

koca koja husband; large; great;
old; huge

kod numarası noomaras**uh**
dialling code

koğuş ko-**oo**sh ward

koklamak to smell

kokmak to smell; to stink

koku smell

kol arm; handle

kolay ko-l**ī** easy

kolej koleJ college

koleksiyon collection

koli kolee parcel(s)

koli gişesi geeshes**ee** parcels
counter

kolonya eau de cologne

kol saati sa-at**ee** watch

koltuk armchair; seat; stalls

kolye k**o**l-yeh necklace

kombinezon slip (garment)

komik funny

kompartıman kompartuhman
compartment

**kompartıman sigara
içmeyenlere mahsus**
eechmayenler**eh** ma**H**s**oo**s
nonsmoking compartment

komple kahvaltı kompl**eh**
ka**H**valt**uh** full breakfast

komşu komsh**oo** neighbour

konak large private residence

konaklamak to stay the night

konfeksiyon off-the-peg clothes

konferans conference

konser concert

konserve açacağı konserveh
achaja-uh can-opener

konserve kutusu tin, can

konsolosluk consulate

kontak ignition

kontak lensleri contact lenses

kontrol check, inspection

kontrol etmek to check

konu subject, topic

konuk guest

konukseverlik kon**oo**kseverl**ee**k
hospitality

Travel tip Hospitality is a
pillar of rural Turkish culture,
and being invited for a meal
in someone's home is both
an honour and an obligation.
Always remove your shoes
at the door, and if the meal
is served at a low table with
cushions on the floor, hide
your feet under the table
or dropcloth provided (feet
are considered unclean and
should never be pointed at
anyone).

---

konuşma konooshma speech,
talk; conversation; call

konuşmak konooshm**a**k to talk;
to speak

konut residence; house

koridor yanı yan**uh** aisle seat

korkmak: ...-den korkmak
to be afraid (of)…

korku fear

korkunç korkoonch appalling; shocking; horrible

korna horn

koruma faktörü fakturew protection factor

korumak to protect

koruma kremi aftersun cream

koruyucu gözlük koroo-yoojoo gurzlewk goggles

koruyucu sıvı suhvuh soaking solution

kostüm kostewm dress; costume

koşmak koshmak to run

koşu koshoo race; jogging

koşu yapmak to race; to go jogging

kova bucket

koy bay

koymak to put

koyu dark

koyun sheep

köpek kurpek dog

köpek var beware of the dog

köprü kurprew bridge

kör kur blind

körfez kurfez gulf; bay

köşe kursheh corner

köşede kurshedeh on the corner; in the corner

köşk kurshk lodge; pavilion, gazebo; villa

kötü kurtew bad; nasty; badly

kötü kalite kaleeteh poor quality

köy kuh-i village

köylü kurlew villager; peasant

köy yolu country road

kral king

kraliçe kraleecheh queen

krank mili crankshaft

kravat tie, necktie

kredi kartı kartuh credit card

kredi kartı kabul edilmez credit cards not accepted

kredi krizi krehdee kreezee credit crunch

krem cream, lotion

krema cream

krem rengi cream (colour)

kreş kresh creche

kriko jack

kuaför kwafur hairdresser's (women's)

kubbe koobbeh dome

kuduz rabies; rabid

kulak ear

kulak, burun ve boğaz veh boh-az ear, nose and throat

kulaklıklar koolakluhklar headphones

kule kooleh tower

kullanım koollanuhm use

kullanmak to use

kulübe koolewbeh kiosk; hut; booth

kulüp koolewp club

kum sand

kumanda tablosu dashboard

kumanya packed lunch

kumaş koomash cloth, fabric, material

kumullar sand dunes

kundura shoes

kunduracı koondoorajuh shoe shop**

kundura tamircisi tameerjees**ee**
shoe repairer's

kupa mug; cup (sporting)

kupür bilet koop**ewr** book of bus
tickets

kur rate

kuron crown

kurşun kalem koorsh**oo**n pencil

kurşunsuz benzin koorshoons**ooz**
unleaded petrol

kuru dry

kurukahveci koorookahvej**ee**
coffee seller

kurulama bezi tea towel

kurum society; institution

kurumak to dry oneself

kuru temizleme temeezlem**eh**
dry clean

kuru temizleyici temeezl**a**yeejee
dry-cleaner's

kurutmak to dry

kuru yemişçi yemeeshch**ee**
seller of dried fruit and nuts

kurye koor-y**eh** courier

kusmak to vomit

kusura bakmayın bakmī-**uh**n
pardon me

kuş koosh bird

kuş beyinli bayeenl**ee** stupid,
bird-brained

kuşet koosh**et** couchette

kutu box; carton

kuyruk koo-ir**oo**k queue; tail

kuyruk olmak to queue

kuytu koo-it**oo** secluded

kuyu well

kuyumcu koo-yoomj**oo** jeweller's

kuzen cousin (male)

kuzey kooz**ay** north; northern

kuzeyi north of

kuzey yönünde yurnewnd**eh**
to the north

kuzeyde koozayd**eh**
in the north

kuzeybatı bat**uh** northwest

kuzeydoğu koozaydoh-**oo**
northeast

Kuzey İrlanda eerlanda Northern
Ireland

**Kuzey Kıbrıs Türk
Cumhuriyeti** kuhbr**uh**s tewrk
joomHooree-yet**ee** Turkish
Republic of Northern Cyrprus

kuzin cousin (female)

küçük kewch**ew**k little; small

küçük jeton Jeton small token

küçük paket small packet

küfür kewf**ew**r swearword

külliye kewllee-y**eh** complex
of buildings attached to a
mosque

külot kewl**o**t pants, briefs, panties

külotlu çorap kewlotl**oo** chorap
tights, pantyhose

kül tablası kewl tablas**uh** ashtray

kültür kewlt**ew**r culture

kültür merkezi cultural centre

küpe kewp**eh** earring(s)

kürek çekmek kewr**e**k chekm**e**k
to row (boat)

kürk kewrk fur

Kürt kewrt Kurdish; Kurd

küsmek: -e küsmek -**eh**
kewsm**e**k to be in a huff with

kütüphane kewtewp-haneh
library

küvet kewvet bathtub

L

lacivert lajeevert navy blue

lağım la-uhm drain; sewer

lamba lamp

-lar they are; -s, -es (plural endings)

-ları -laruh their

lastik rubber; elastic; tyre

lastik bant rubber band

lastik basıncı basuhnjuh tyre
pressure

lastik patlaması patlamasuh
puncture

lavabo washhand basin

lazım lazuhm necessary; must;
should

  bana ... lazım I need...

-le -leh by; with

Lefkoşa lefkosha Nicosia

lehçe leHcheh dialect

leke lekeh spot

-ler they are; -s, -es (plural endings)

-leri their

libre leebreh pound (weight)

liman harbour; port

lira lira, Turkish unit of currency

lisan okulu language school

lise leeseh high school

...-'liyim I am from...

lokanta restaurant

lokum Turkish delight

Londra London

Londra'da in London

losyon lotion

-lu with

Lübnan lewbnan Lebanon

lügat lewgat dictionary; word

lüks lewks luxury; luxurious;
posh

lütfen lewtfen please

**lütfen ayakkabılarınızı
çıkarınız** please take off your
shoes

lütfen bozuk para veriniz small
change please

M

-m my

maalesef ma-alesef
unfortunately

maç mach game, match

madem since, seeing that

madeni para coin

Magosa Famagusta

mağara ma-ara cave

  ... Mağarası ma-arasuh ... Cave

mağaza ma-aza store

mahalle mahalleh quarter; area
of city

mahallesi district;
neighbourhood

mahsus deliberately

mahzen cellar

makas scissors

makbuz receipt

makina/makine makeeneh
machine

makinist mechanic; engine driver

makul reasonable

makyaj makya**J** make-up

makyaj malzemesi cosmetics

Malazgirt Manzikert

...-malı -mal**uh** he/she has to...

...-malıyım maluh-y**uh**m I have to...

mallar goods

mal olmak to cost

mal sahibi owner

manastır manast**uh**r monastery

manav greengrocer's

mandal hook; clothes peg

manifatura drapery; textiles

manivela lever

mankafa thick, stupid

mantar mushroom(s); cork

manto coat (**woman's**)

manzara view; scenery

marka make, brand name

Marmara Denizi the Sea of Marmara

marş marsh starter

mart March

martı mart**uh** seagull

masa table

masaj masa**J** massage

masa örtüsü urtews**ew** tablecloth

masatopu table tennis

masum innocent

maşallah! mashall**ah** wonderful! – used to express admiration and wonder, and to avert the evil eye

matbua printed matter

matine mateen**eh** matinée

mavi blue

Mavi Tren blue train – Ankara-Istanbul train

mayıs mī-**uh**s May

mayo mī-**o** swimming costume; swimming trunks

Travel tip Turkey remains a conservative country concerning dress. Beachwear should be confined to the beach, while strolling shirtless around resort streets is ultra-offensive. Tight clothing, halter tops, skimpy shorts and the like should be avoided away from heavily touristed areas, and nude sunbathing is not acceptable anywhere.

---

mazot diesel

mecburi mejboor**ee** compulsory

mecburi iniş emergency landing

mecburi trafik sigortası seegortas**uh** third party insurance

meç mech highlights

medeni hali marital status

medrese medres**eh** theological school

... Medresesi ... Theological School

mefruşat mefroosh**at** fabrics and furnishings

mektup letter

mektup arkadaşı arkadash**uh** penfriend

mektup kutusu letterbox

...-meli he/she must...

...-meliyim I must...

...-mem I won't...;
I don't...

meme vermek memeh
to breastfeed

memleket (home) country

memnun glad, pleased

memnun oldum I am pleased;
pleased to meet you

memur official

memur bey bay officer

mendil handkerchief

mensup: -e mensup -eh
belonging to, connected with

merak hobby

mercek merjek lens

merdiven ladder; stairs

merhaba! hello!, hi!

merhem ointment

merkez centre

merkezi central

merkez postanesi main post
office

mersi thank you

Meryemana Virgin Mary

mesai saatleri mesa-ee
sa-atleree opening hours

mesaj mesaJ message

mesaj atmak to text

mescit mesjeet small mosque

mesela for example

mesele meseleh question,
problem

mesleği mesleh-ee (applicant's)
occupation

meslek profession; occupation

meşgul meshgool busy; engaged,
occupied

meteliksiz broke, penniless

meteliksizim I'm broke

metro underground (railway),
(US) subway

mevsim season

meydan maydan square

meyhane mayhaneh tavern
serving alcohol and food,
usually frequented by men only

mezar grave, tomb

... mezarı mezaruh ... grave,
...tomb

mezarlık mezarluhk cemetery

mı? muh question particle

... mı? is it...?, is that...?

-mız -muhz our

mi? question particle

... mi? is it...?, is that...?

mide *meedeh* stomach

midem bulanıyor *boolanuh-yor* I feel sick

mide ağrısı *a-ruhsuh* stomachache

mide bozukluğu *bozookloo-oo* upset stomach

mide bulantısı *boolantuhsuh* nausea

midilli pony

mihrap *meeHrap* niche in a mosque indicating the direction of Mecca

mikro dalga microwave (oven)

mikroplu septic

miktar amount

mil mile

milâdi Christian year-numbering system

millet nation

milletlerarası *meelletlerarasuh* international

milli national

milli park national park

milliyet nationality

milyar one thousand million, (US) one billion

milyon million

minare *meenareh* minaret

minibüs *meeneebews* minibus

minik tiny

minnettar grateful

misafir *meesafeer* guest

misiniz: bana … verebilir misiniz? can I have…?

miyim: …-ebilir miyim? can I…?, may I…?

miyop shortsighted

-miz our

mizah humour

mizanpli set

mobilya furniture

mocamp caravan site, trailer park

moda fashion; fashionable, trendy

modaya uygun *modi-a oo-igoon* trendy, fashionable

mola pause; rest

mor purple

motor motorboat; engine

motor kapak contası *jontasuh* cylinder head gasket

motosiklet motorbike

mozaik *moza-eek* mosaic

M.Ö. BC

MP üç formatı *em-peh ewch formatuh* MP3 format

M.S. AD

mu? question particle

… mu? is it…?, is that…?

muavin assistant; driver's assistant on intercity coaches

muayene *moo-i-eneh* examination

muayenehane *moo-i-enehaneh* surgery

muazzam *moo-azzam* tremendous

muhafaza etmek to keep

muhallebici *mooHallebeejee* pudding shop

muhtar *mooHtar* village headman

muhtemelen *mooHtemelen* probably

mum moom candle

musluk tap, faucet

muslukçu mooslookchoo plumber

mutfak kitchen

mutfak eşyası esh-yasuh pots
and pans

mutlu happy

-muz our

mü? mew question
particle

... mü? is it...?, is that...?

mücevherat mew-jevherat
jewellery

müddet mewddet period (of time)

müdür mewdewr manager;
director

müdür muavini assistant
director

müezzin mew-ezzeen muezzin
– man who pronounces call to
prayer from the minaret of a
mosque

mükemmel mewkemmel
excellent; perfect

mükemmel! that's great!

mümkün mewmkewn
possible

mümkün olduğu kadar çabuk
oldoo-oo – chabook as soon as
possible

mürekkepli kalem mewrek-
keplee pen

mürettebat mewrettebat crew

müsaade etmek mewsa-adeh
to allow

müshil mews-heel laxative

Müslüman mewslewman Muslim

müteakip boşaltma mewteh-
akeep boshaltma next collection

mütehassıs mewtehassuhs
specialist

mütevazı mewtevazuh
downmarket; modest, humble

müthiş mewt-heesh terrific

-müz -mewz our

müze mewzeh museum

müzik mewzeek music

müzik aleti musical instrument

müzisyen mewzees-yen musician

N

-n your

nadide nadeedeh rare

nadiren not often

nahoş nahosh unpleasant

nakil transfer; transmission;
transport

nakit: nakit ödemek urdemek
to pay cash

nakit para cash

nalbur hardware shop

namaz Muslim prayer
performed five times a day

nane şekeri naneh shekeree
peppermints

nargile nargeeleh hookah, water
pipe

nasıl? nasuhl how?

nasılsın? nasuhlsuhn how are you?

nasılsınız? nasuhl-suhnuhz how
are you?; how do you do?

naylon torba nilon plastic bag;
carrier bag

naylon yağmurluk ya-moorl**ook** cagoule

nazik polite; nice; kind, generous

ne? neh what?

   ne...! what a...!

   ne var? what is it?; what's the matter?

   ne kadar? how much?

neden cause

   neden? why?

nedeniyle nedenee-il**eh** because of

nedir: o nedir? what's that?

nefes almak to breathe

nefis delicious; lovely

nefret etmek to hate

nehir neh-H**e**er river

   ... Nehri ne**H**ree River...

nemlendirici (krem) –deeree**jee** moisturizer

nemli damp; humid

ne ... ne ... neh neither ... nor ...

ne oldu? what's up?, what's wrong?; what's happened?

ne oluyor? what's happening?

nerede? ne**r**edeh where?; where is it?

neredeyse ne**r**edayseh nearly; almost; soon

ne var ki but; only; however

ney nay reed flute

ne yazık ki unfortunately

ne zaman? when?

-nın -nuhn of

-nız -nuhz your

niçin? nee**cheen** why?; why not?

nihayet nee-H**ī**-et end; at last

-nin of

nisan April

nişanlı neeshanl**uh** engaged (to be married); fiancé; fiancée

niye? nee-y**eh** why?

-niz your

Noel Christmas

Noel Gecesi gejes**ee** Christmas Eve

Noeliniz kutlu olsun! Merry Christmas!

normal norm**ah**l normal; 2/3 star petrol, regular gas

Norveç norv**e**ch Norway; Norwegian (*adj*)

not defteri notebook

nöbet nurb**e**t fit (attack); turn of duty, watch

nöbetçi doktor nurbetch**ee** duty doctor

nöbetçi eczane ejzan**eh** duty chemist's

numara number

-nun of

-nuz your

nüfus newf**oo**s population

-nün -newn of

-nüz -newz your

O

o that; those; he; she; it; it is

   o işte eesht**eh** that's him/her/it

   o ...-dir it is...

   o nedir? what's that?

obdüratör obdewrat**u**r shutter

objektif ob**J**ekteef lens

ocak oj**a**k January; home; cooker; fireplace

oda room

oda hizmetçisi heezmetcheesee maid, chambermaid

oda numarası noomarasuh room number

oda servisi room service

o dö tuvalet dur eau de toilette

ofis office

oğlan oh-l**a**n boy

oğul o-o**o**l son

oje o**J**e**h** nail varnish

okul school

okumak to read; to study

olağan ola-**a**n ordinary; usual

olamaz impossible; impractical

olay event

oldu OK; alright

  ne oldu? neh what's up?, what's wrong?; what's happened?

olduğunca ... oldoo-oonja as ... as possible

oldukça old**oo**kcha fairly, quite, rather

  oldukça çok chok quite a lot

oldu mu? OK?; is it OK?

olgun ripe; mature

olmak to be; to happen; to become

olmaz it won't do; it's not possible

olur all right; I agree

oluyor: ne oluyor? neh what's happening?

omuz shoulder

on ten

ona him; her; it; to him/her/it

on altı alt**uh** sixteen

on beş besh fifteen

on beş gün gewn fortnight

on bir eleven

onda on/in him; on/in her; on/in it

ondan from him/her/it

ondan sonra then, after that

on dokuz nineteen

on dört d**u**rt fourteen

on iki twelve

onlar they; those; them

onlara them; to them

onlarda on/in them

onlardan from them

onları onlar**uh** them

onların onlar**uh**n their; theirs

onlarınki onlaruhnk**ee** theirs

onlarla with them

on sekiz eighteen

onu him; her; it

onun his; her; hers; its

onuncu on**oo**njoo tenth

onun için eech**ee**n for him/her/it; therefore

onunki his; hers

on üç ewch thirteen

on yedi seventeen

ora that place

orada over there

orası or**a**suh there

oraya orï-**a** there

orda over there

ordu army

orijinal oreeJeen**al** original;
unusual; original soundtrack

orman woods, forest

orta middle; medium; mean;
average

ortada in the middle

orta büyüklükte bewyewklewkt**eh**
medium-sized

orta jeton Jet**on** medium token

ortalama olarak on average

ortopedi uzmanı oozman**uh**
orthopaedist

Osmanlı osmanl**uh** Ottoman

ot grass

otel hotel

otel odası od**a**suh hotel room

otobüs otob**ews** bus, coach

otobüs ile eel**eh** by bus

otobüs bileti bus ticket

otobüs durağı doora-**uh**
bus stop

otobüs garajı garaJ**uh**
bus station

otobüsle gezi otob**ews**leh
coach trip

otobüs terminali bus station

otogar bus terminal, bus station

otomat vending machine

otomatik automatic

otomatik arama direct dialling

**otomatik para çekme
makinesi** chekm**eh** cash
dispenser, automatic teller

otomatik vitesli automatic (car)

otomatlı çamaşırhane
otomatl**uh** chamashuh**r**-haneh
launderette

otomobil car

otomobil ile eel**eh** by car

otomobil kiralama (servisi)
car rental (service)

otomobil yıkama yeri yuhkama
carwash

otopark car park, parking lot

otostop hitch-hiking

otostop yapmak to hitch-hike

otoyol motorway, freeway,
highway

oturacak yer otoorajak seat

oturmak to live; to sit down

oturma odası odas**uh** living
room

oturun! sit down!

otuz thirty

ova plain; plateau

... Ovası ovas**uh** ... Plain

oynamak to play; to folkdance

oynatmak to move

oysa but; yet; whereas

oyun play; folkdancing; game

oyuncak oyoonjak toy

oyuncu oyoonj**oo** actor; actress

o zaman then, at that time**

öbür urb**ewr** the other

öbür gün g**ewn** the day after
tomorrow

öbür türlü tewrl**ew** otherwise

öbürü urbewrew the other one
ödemek urdemek to pay
ödemeli urdemelee reverse charge call, collect call
ödemeli konuşma konooshma reverse charge call, collect call
ödeyiniz urdayeeneez pay
ödünç almak urdewnch to borrow
ödünç vermek to lend
öfkeli urfkelee angry
öğle ur-leh midday, noon
öğleden sonra urleden afternoon; p.m.
öğle yemeği urleh yemeh-ee lunch
öğleyin ur-layeen midday, noon
öğrenci ur-renjee student
öğrenci kartı kartuh student card
öğrenci yurdu student hostel
öğrenmek ur-renmek to learn
öğretmek ur-retmek to teach
öğretmen ur-retmen teacher
öksürük urksew-rewk cough
öksürük şurubu shoorooboo cough medicine
ölçek urlchek scale
öldürmek urldewrmek to kill
ölmek urlmek to die
ölü urlew dead
Ölü Deniz the Dead Sea
ölüm urlewm death
ön urn front
  ön tarafta at the front
ön cam jam windscreen, windshield

önce urnjeh before; ago; first; at first
  -den önce before
önceden urnjeden in advance
öncelik urnjeleek priority
öncelikle urnjeleekleh first of all
önce siz (buyrun) urnjeh – (boo-iroon) after you
önde urndeh in front
önden urnden at the front
önden binilir entry at front
önem urnem importance
  önemi yok it doesn't matter
önemli urnemlee important
önermek urnermek to advise; to suggest
önünde: …-in önünde urnewndeh in front of …
öpmek urpmek to kiss
öpücük urpewjewk kiss
ören uren ruin
ören yeri ruins
örgü urgew knitwear
örnek urnek example; pattern
  örneğin urneh-een for example
örümcek urewmjek spider
övgü urvgew compliment
öyle ur-ileh so, thus
öyle yapmayın! yapmī-uhn stop it!
öyleyse ur-ilayseh then, in that case
özel urzel private; special
özel bakım ünitesi bakuhm ewneetesee special care unit
özel fiyat special price

özel hasta private patient
özel indirim special offer
özellikle urzelleekleh especially
özel ulak special delivery; express mail
özür urzewr apology; excuse; defect
özür dilemek to apologize
özür dilerim I'm sorry; excuse me
özürlü urzewrlew disabled; defective
özürlü kişiler handicapped people, the disabled

P

padişah padeeshaH Sultan; ruler
pahalı paHaluh expensive
paket packet, package
paketlemek to pack
paket tur package holiday
paletler flippers
palto coat
pamuk cotton
pamukçuk pamookchook mouth ulcer
panayır panī-uhr fair, funfair
pansiyon guesthouse
pansuman dressing
pantolon trousers, (US) pants
para money
para almak to charge
para cüzdanı jewzdanuh wallet
para çantası chantasuh purse

paraya çevirmek parī-a cheveermek to cash
parayı geri vermek parī-uh to refund
parça parcha part; piece
   bir parça ... a piece of...
   büyük bir parça bew-yewk a big bit
pardon pardon; excuse me
parfüm parfewm perfume
parfümeri parfewmeree perfumes
park edilir parking
park edilmez no parking
park etmek to park
park lambaları lambalaruh sidelights
park yapılmaz no parking
parlak brilliant
parmak finger
parmaklık parmakluhk fence
parti party
pasaport passport
pasaport kontrolü kontrolew passport control
Paskalya Easter
pastane pastaneh cake shop; café
pasta ve şekerlemeler veh shekerlemeler confectionery
pastil pastilles; lozenges
patika path
patiska cambric
patlak burst; punctured
patlak lastik puncture
patron boss
pavyon cheap nightclub, joint; pavilion; stand

paylaşmak pilashmak to share

pazar Sunday; market

pazar çantası chantasuh
shopping bag

pazar günleri dışında except
Sundays

pazarlık pazarluhk bargaining

pazarlık edilmez no bargaining

pazarlık etmek to bargain

pazartesi Monday

pazen brushed cotton

peçete pecheteh napkin

pek very; extremely; a great deal;
firm; strong

  pek (fazla) değil deh-eel not
  too much

pekâlâ all right; very well

pek az few

peki all right

pembe pembeh pink

pencere penjereh window

pencere yanı yanuh window seat

perçem perchem fringe; tuft of
hair

perde perdeh curtain; act

perdeler curtains

perhiz diet

peron platform, (US) track

perşembe pershembeh Thursday

peşin pesheen in advance

pezevenk pimp

piç peech bastard

pijama peeJama pyjamas

pikap record player

piknik yemeği yemeh-ee packed
lunch

pil battery

pipo pipe (for smoking)

pire peereh flea

pis pees filthy

pislik dirt

pişirmek peesheermek to cook

piyes play

PK PO box

plaj plaJ beach

  plajda on the beach

plaj şemsiyesi shemsee-yesee
beach umbrella

plaj yaygısı yiguhsuh beach mat

> Travel tip Except near
> major cities where seawater
> is often polluted, Turkish
> beaches are generally safe
> places to swim. Tar can be
> a problem on south-coast
> beaches facing shipping
> lanes, however, and if you
> get any on your feet, you
> should scrub it off using
> olive oil rather than chemical
> solvents.

plak record

plaka number plate

plaster plaster(s), (US) Bandaid

poliklinik out-patients clinic

polis police; policeman

polis karakolu police station

polis memuru policeman,
officer

pompa pump

pop müzik mewzeek pop music

popo bottom (of person)

pop şarkıcısı sharkuhjuhs**uh** pop singer

porselen china

porsiyon portion

portatif yatak campbed

portbebe portbeb**eh** carry-cot

portre p**o**rtreh portrait

posta post, mail

postacı postaj**uh** postman

posta kartı kart**uh** postcard

posta kodu postcode, zip code

posta kutusu postbox, mailbox

postalamak to post, to mail

postane post**a**neh post office

Posta Telgraf Telefon post and telephone office

pozometre pozometr**eh** light meter

pratik practical

prens prince

prenses princess

prezervatif condom

priz socket, power point

protez dentures

prova etmek to try on

PTT peh teh teh post and telephone office

pul stamp(s)

puro cigar

puset pushchair, buggy

pusula compass

R

radyatör radyat**u**r radiator; heater

radyo radio

radyoda on the radio

raf shelf

rahat comfortable

rahatsız etmek rahatsuhz to disturb

rahip priest

Ramazan Ramadan – the Muslim month of fasting and prayer

Travel tip During the religious festival of Ramadan, half the population fasts from sunrise to sunset. Some restaurants close for the duration or severely curtail their menus, others discreetly hide their salons behind curtains, but most will serve you with surprisingly good grace. Immediately after dark, there's an orgy of eating, and restaurants may sell out of everything within an hour.

---

randevu appointment

ranza bunk; berth; couchette

ray r**i** track; rail

razıyım razuh-y**uh**m I agree; I accept

rebap three-stringed violin

reçete rech**e**teh prescription

reçete ile satılır prescription only

reçete yazmak to prescribe

rehber re**H**ber guide; guidebook

rehberli tur re**H**ber**lee** guided tour

renk colour

renkli colour

renkliler colours

resepsiyon reception
resepsiyonda at reception
resepsiyoncu resepsee-yonjoo receptionist
resepsiyon masası masasuh reception desk
resepsiyon memuru receptionist
resim picture; painting
resmi formal
resmi tatil public holiday
restoran restaurant
reyon rayon department
rezervasyon reservation
rıhtım ruhHtuhm quay
rıhtımda on the quayside
rica ederim reeja my pleasure, don't mention it
rica etmek to request
rimel mascara
rizikolu risky

robdöşambr robdurshambr man's dressing gown
rock müziği mewzee-ee rock (music)
Rodos Rhodes
roman novel
Romanya Rumania
romatizma rheumatism
rondela washer
rota route
römork rurmork trailer
röntgen rurntgen X-ray
ruh durumu mood
ruj rooJ lipstick
Rum room ethnic Greek
Rumca roomja Greek (language)
Rum kadını kaduhnuh ethnic Greek (woman)
Rum Ortodoks Greek Orthodox
Rus Russian
rüya rew-ya dream

rüzgâr rewzgar wind

rüzgârlı rewzgarl**uh** windy

S

saat sa-**at** hour; o'clock; clock; wristwatch

  saat kaç? kach what time is it?

saat kayışı kĭ-uhsh**uh** watch strap

sabah saba**H** morning; a.m. (from 4 a.m. to noon)

  bu sabah this morning

sabahleyin saba**H**layeen in the morning

sabahlık saba**H**l**uh**k woman's dressing gown

sabun soap

sabun tozu soap powder

saç sach hair

saç fırçası fu**H**rchas**uh** hairbrush

saç kesme kesm**eh** haircut

saç kurutma makinesi hairdryer

saçma sachma silly

  saçma! rubbish!, nonsense!

saç spreyi sach spray-**ee** hairspray

saç tıraşı tu**H**rash**uh** haircut

saç tokası tokas**uh** hairgrip(s)

sade sa-d**eh** plain, simple

sadece sa-dej**eh** only, just

sağ sa alive; right **(not left)**

sağa dön sa-**a** d**u**rn turn right

sağa dönülmez no right turn

sağa dönün d**u**rnewn turn right

sağanak sa-anak shower

sağa sapın sap**uh**n turn right

sağa viraj bend to right

sağda sa-da on the right

sağdan direksiyonlu sa-dan right-hand drive

sağdan gidiniz keep to the right

sağında sa-**uh**nda on the right

sağır sa-**uh**r deaf

sağlığınıza! sa-luh-uhnuhza your health!

sağlıklı sa-luhkl**uh** healthy

sağol sa-**ol** bless you; thanks

saha field; area

sahil coast; shore, seafront

  sahilde sa**H**eeld**eh** on the coast

sahil yolu coast road

sahi mi? really?

sahip owner

sahip olmak to have; to own

sahne sa**H**n**eh** stage

sahte sa**H**t**eh** false; counterfeit

sakal beard

sakal tıraşı tu**H**rash**uh** shave

sakın! sak**uh**n beware!; don't!

sakin quiet; peaceful

sakız sak**uh**z chewing gum

saklamak to hide

saklanmak to hide

saldırgan salduhrgan aggressive

saldırı salduhr**uh** attack

salı sal**uh** Tuesday

salık vermek sal**uh**k to recommend

salon lounge; hall

saman nezlesi hay fever

sana you; to you

sanat art

sanatçı sanatchuh artist
sanat galerisi art gallery
sanayi sanī-ee industry
sandal sandal(s); dinghy
sandık sanduhk box; chest; coffer
saniye sanee-yeh second (in time)
   bir saniye! just a second!
sanki as if
sanmak to suppose; to think
santigrat centigrade
santimetre santeemetreh
   centimetre
santral memuru operator
santrifüjlü kurutma makinesi
   santreefewJlew spindryer
sap stem; stalk; handle
sapak turning
saray sarī palace
   ... Sarayı sarī-uh ... Palace
sargı sarguh bandage
sarhoş sarhosh drunk
sarı saruh yellow
sarışın saruh-shuhn blond
sarmak to wrap
satılan mal geri alınmaz
   goods cannot be exchanged
satılık satuhluhk for sale
satın alma satuhn purchase
satın almak to buy
satış satuhsh sale; selling
satış kuru selling rate
satışlarımız peşindir no credit
   allowed
satmak to sell
satranç satranch chess
savaş savash war

sayfa sīfa page
sayı sī-uh number
sayın ... sī-uhn esteemed...
   (formal way of addressing people
   followed by surname)
saymak simak to count; to value;
   to consider
saz oriental music; reed; Turkish
   string instrument
seans seh-ans performance
sebep cause
sebil public drinking fountain
seçmek sechmek to choose
sefer journey; flight; voyage;
   time; occasion
   bu sefer this time
   geçen sefer gechen last time
   gelecek sefer gelejek next
   time
seferden kaldırıldı kalduhruhlduh
   flight/departure cancelled
sefer numarası noomarasuh
   flight number
sefer sayısı sī-uhsuh flight
   number
sekiz eight
sekizinci sekeezeenjee eighth
seks sex
seksen eighty
sel flood
Selçuklular selchookloolar
   Selchuks
sele seleh saddle
seloteyp selotayp Sellotape,
   Scotch tape
sema dervish ceremony
sempatik nice

semt area, district, neighbourhood

sen you

sende sende**h** you; on/in you

senden (from) you

sene sene**h** year

seni you

senin your; yours

seninki yours

sepet basket

serbest vacant; free, independent; allowed

sergi exhibition; trade fair

serin cool; fresh

sersem silly; fool

serseri tramp, vagabond

sert hard; strong; stern

sert dönüş sharp turn

sert lensler hard lenses

sert viraj sharp bend

servis dahildir service charge included

servis istasyonu service station

servis otobüsü otobews**ew** shuttle bus

servis ücreti ewjret**ee** service charge

ses voice

sessizlik silence

sever:... sever misiniz? do you like…?

sevgi love

sevici seveej**ee** lesbian

sevilen popular

sevişmek seveeshmek to make love

sevmek to love

seyahat sayah**at** travel; journey

seyahat acentası ajentas**uh** travel agency

seyahat çeki chek**ee** traveller's cheque

seyahat çekleri chekler**ee** traveller's cheques

seyahat etmek to travel

seyirci sayeerj**ee** audience

seyretmek sayretmek to watch

-sı -s**uh** his; her; its

sıcak suhj**ak** hot; warm

hava sıcak it's hot

sıcaklık suhjaklu**hk** heat; temperature

sıcak su suhj**ak** hot water

sıçan suhch**an** rat

sıfır suhf**uh**r zero

sığ suh shallow

sıhhat suh-h**at** health

sık suh**k** frequent; dense; thick

sıkıcı suhkuh-j**uh** boring

sıkıntılı suhkuhn-tuhl**uh** dull

sıkışmış suhkuhsh-mu**hsh** stuck

sıkmayınız do not wring

sık sık suh**k** often

-sin -s**uh**n you are

sınav suhn**av** exam

sınıf suhn**uh**f class; sort, kind

sınır suhn**uh**r border

-sınız -suhn**uh**z you are

sırasında suhra-s**uh**nda during

sırf suhrf only

sırf gidiş geede**esh** single ticket, one-way ticket

sırt suhrt back (of body)

sırt ağrısı a-ruhs**uh** backache

sırt çantası chantas**uh** rucksack

sıska suhska skinny

sızıntı suhzuhnt**uh** leak

-si his; her; its

sigara cigarette

sigara içenler eechenler smokers

sigara içilen eecheelen smoking

sigara içilmez no smoking

sigara içmek eechmek to smoke

sigara içmek yasaktır no smoking

sigara içmeyenler eechmayenler nonsmokers

sigara içmeyenlere mahsus bölüm/kısım eechmayenlere**h** ma**H**s**oos** burlew**m**/kuhs**uh**m nonsmoking section

sigara içmeyenlere mahsus (kompartıman) kompartuhman nonsmoking (compartment)

sigara içmeyiniz do not smoke

sigorta insurance; fuse

sigorta kutusu fuse box

sigorta teli fuse wire

silah weapon

silecekler seelejekler windscreen wipers

silgi rubber, eraser

-sin you are

sinek fly

sinema cinema, movie theatre

sinir hastası hastas**uh** neurotic

sinirli nervous

-siniz you are

sinyal indicator

sipariş seepare**esh** order

sis fog; mist

sisli foggy

site seete**h** estate

sivil civilian

sivilce seeveelje**h** pimple

sivrisinek mosquito

sivrisinek ilacı eelaj**uh** mosquito repellent

siyah black

siyah beyaz bay**a**z black and white

siz you; one

-siz without

sizde seezde**h** on/in you

sizde kalsın kals**uh**n please keep it

sizden from you

size seeze**h** to you

sizi you

sizin your; yours

sizinki yours

sizinle seeze**e**nleh with you

sizlerin your

ski yapmak skiing

slayt sl**i**t slide

sofa hall

soğuk so-**ook** cold

soğuk aldım ald**uh**m I have a cold

soğuk algınlığı alguhnluh-**uh** cold

soğuk su cold water

Sok. St

sokak street; road

sokma insect bite

sokmak to sting; to bite; to thrust into; to insert

sokulgan friendly

sol left

sola to the left

sola dön durn turn left

sola dönülmez no left turn

sola dönün durnewn turn left

solak left-handed

sola sapın sapuhn turn left

sola viraj bend to left

solda on the left

solgun pale

solunda on the left of

somun nut (for bolt); loaf

somun anahtarı anaнtaruh
    spanner

son end; last; final

  yolun sonunda at the end of
    the street

sona erdi it's over

sonbahar autumn, (US) fall

  sonbaharda in the autumn, in
    the fall

son derece derejeh extremely

son durak terminus

son hareket last train; last bus

son istasyon rail terminus

son kullanma tarihi... use
    before…

son moda trendy

sonra next; after; afterwards;
    later

  -den sonra after

  daha sonra later; later on

sonradan afterwards

sormak to ask

soru question

sorumlu responsible

sorun problem

  hiç sorun değil! heech – deh-
    eel no problem!

  sorun nedir? what's wrong?

sorup öğrenmek ur-renmek to
    find out

soyadı soyad**uh** surname

soyunma odası odas**uh** fitting
    room; changing room

sömestr surmestr term

söndürmek surndewrmek to put
    out, to extinguish

sönük surn**ewk** off; dim;
    lacklustre; extinguished

sörf surf surf

sörf tahtası taнtas**uh** surfboard

sörf yapmak to surf

söylemek sur-ilem**ek** to say;
    to tell

sözcük surzj**ewk** word

sözlük surzl**ewk** dictionary

söz vermek surz to promise

spiral spee-ra**l** IUD; spiral

spor sport

spor malzemeleri sports goods

spor salonu gym

spor tesisleri sporting facilities

stabilize yol macadam road

su water; river; stream

-su his; her; its

suçiçeği soochech**eh**-ee
    chickenpox

sufi dervish; mystic

su geçirmez gecheerm**ez**
    waterproof

su kayağı ki-a-**uh** waterski; water-skiing

Sultan Ahmet Camii aнmet jamee-**ee** Blue Mosque

-sun you are

suni artificial; false; affected

-sunuz you are

Suriye sooree-yeh Syria

Suriyeli Syrian

sus! shut up!

susadım soosad**uhm** I'm thirsty

susamak to be thirsty

su sporları sporlar**uh** water sports

suyla soo-il**a** with water

-suz without

-sü -sew his; her; its

süet sew-**et** suede

sükseli sewksel**ee** fashionable

-sün -sewn you are

sünger sewnger sponge

sünnet sewnnet circumcision

-sünüz -sewne**wz** you are

süper sewper 4-star petrol; premium gas

süpürge sewpewrg**eh** broom

sürahi sewra**hee** jug; carafe

sürat tahdidi speed limit

süre sewr**eh** period (of time)

sürgülemek sewrgewlem**ek** to bolt

sürmek sewrm**ek** to drive; to rub on; to smear; to continue

sürpriz sewrpr**eez** surprise

sürücü sewrewj**ew** driver

sütlü çikolata sewtl**ew** cheekolat**a** milk chocolate

sütsüz çikolata sewts**ewz** plain chocolate

sütun sewt**oon** column

sütyen sewt-y**en** bra

svetşört svet-sh**urt** sweatshirt

Ş

şadırvan shaduhrv**an** fountain attached to mosque for ritual ablutions

şafak shaf**ak** dawn

şahane shaн**aneh** wonderful, amazing, very good

şair sha-**eer** poet

şaka shak**a** joke

şal shal shawl

şalter shal**ter** mains switch

şamandıra buoy

şampuan shampoo-**an** shampoo

şampuan ve mizanpli veh shampoo and set

şans shans luck

şapka shapk**a** hat

şarj aleti sharJ aletee phone charger

şarkı shark**uh** song

şarkıcı sharkuhj**uh** singer

şarkı söylemek shark**uh** sur-ilem**ek** to sing

şarküteri sharkewter**ee** delicatessen

şart shart essential

... şarttır sharttuhr it is essential that...

şaşılacak shashuhlaj**ak** amazing, surprising

şaşırtıcı shashuhr-tuhj**uh**
  surprising, astonishing
şato shat**oh** castle
şayet shi-**et** if
şebeke planı shebek**eh** plan**uh**
  network map
şef shef boss
şehir sheh-h**eer** city
şehirde sheh-heerd**eh** in town
şehiriçi sheh-heereech**ee** local;
  local mail
şehir kodu area code
şehirlerarası konuşma
  sheh-heerler-aras**uh** konooshma
  long-distance call
**şehirlerarası otobüs
  işletmesi** otob**ew**s eeshletmes**ee**
  long-distance coach service
şehir merkezi city centre
şehir planı plan**uh** streetmap
şehir turu city tour
şehzade sheⱧzad**eh** prince; heir
  apparent
şeker shek**er** sugar; sweet, candy
şeker hastası hastas**uh** diabetic
şemsiye shemsee-y**eh** umbrella
şenlik shenl**eek** carnival;
  amusement
şerefe sheref**eh** balcony of
  minaret
şerefe! cheers!
şerit sher**eet** motorway lane
şerit metre metr**eh** tape
  measure
şey shay thing
şeyh shayⱧ sheikh – head of a
  religious order

şezlong shezl**o**ng deckchair; sun
  lounger
şık shuhk trendy
şiddetli sheeddetl**ee** sharp
şifre sheefr**eh** password
şikayet sheeki-**et** complaint
şikayet etmek to complain
şilebezi sheelebez**ee** cheesecloth
şilte sheelt**eh** mattress
şimdi sh**ee**mdee now
  şimdi değil deh-**ee**l not just
  now
şimdi anladım anlad**uh**m I see, I
  understand now
şimdiden sh**ee**mdeeden already
şimşek sheemsh**e**k lightning
şirket sheerk**et** company, firm
şişe sheesh**eh** bottle
şişe açacağı achaja-uh bottle-
  opener
şişlik sheeshl**eek** swelling
şişman sheeshman fat
şişmiş sheeshm**ee**sh swollen
şofben shofben water heater
şoför shof**u**r driver
şoför ehliyeti driver's licence
şok sh**o**k shock
şort short shorts
şöyle shuh-**ee**leh thus, such
şöyle böyle buh-**ee**leh so-so
şu shoo this; that
şubat shoob**a**t February
şube shoob**eh** branch
şu ...-lar those...
şunlar shoonlar those
şura sh**oo**ra that place

şurada shoorada over there

şurda shoorda there

şurup shooroop cough syrup

T

-ta in

taahhütlü ta-ah-hewtlew by registered mail

taahhütlü mektup registered mail

tabak plate; dish

taban floor; base; sole

tabanca tabanja gun, pistol

tabii! tabee-ee sure!; of course!

tabii değil deh-eel of course not

tabla ashtray

tablet çikolata cheekolata bar of chocolate

tahta tahta wood (material)

takıldı takuhlduh jammed

takım takuhm set; team

takım elbise elbeeseh suit (man's)

takıp denemek takuhp to try on

takip etmek to follow

taklit imitation, fake

takma ad nickname

takma diş deesh dentures

taksi taxi

taksi durağı doora-uh taxi rank

taksimetre takseemetreh taximeter

taksi şoförü shofurew taxi-driver

taksitler instalments

takunya pattens, clogs – worn in Turkish baths

takvim calendar

talep etmek to demand

tali secondary

talihin açık olsun! achuhk good luck!

tali yol kavşağı secondary junction

talk pudrası tahlk poodrasuh talcum powder

tam quite; exact; complete, entire; perfect

tamam OK, all right; complete, finished; perfect

tamam! right!

(böyle) tamam buh-ileh that'll do nicely

...-in tamamı tamamuh the whole of ...

tamamen completely

tamamlamak to finish

tam bilet full-price ticket

tamirci tameerjee mechanic

tamir etmek to mend, to repair

tamirhane tameerhaneh garage (for repairs)

tam pansiyon full board

tampon bumper, fender; tampon

tam ücret ewjret exact fare

tam zamanında zamanuhnda on time

tanbur long-necked stringed instrument like a lute

tane taneh item; piece

tanık tanuhk witness

tanım tanuhm description

tanımak tanuhmak to know; to recognize

tanıştığımıza memnun oldum!
tanuhshtuh-uhmuhza pleased to
meet you!

tanıştırmak tanuhshtuhrmak to
introduce

tanıtmak tanuhtmak to introduce

Tanrı tanruh God

tanrıça tanruhcha goddess

tanrılar tanruhlar gods

tansiyon blood pressure

tapınak tapuhnak temple

taraf side; part

... tarafından yazılan
tarafuhndan yazuhlan written
by...

tarafta: bu tarafta this way

o tarafta that way

taraftar fan (sports etc)

tarak comb

taramak to comb

tarife tareefeh charges, price list;
timetable, (US) schedule

tarifeli sefer scheduled
flight

tarih tareeH date (time); history

tarihi yerler tareeHee historical
places

tarla field

tas bowl

taş tash stone, rock

taşımak tashuhmak to carry

taşıma ücreti tashuhma ewjretee fare

taşıt tashuht vehicle

taşıt giremez no entry for
vehicles

taşıt trafiğine kapalı yol closed
to all vehicles

tat taste; flavour

tatil holiday, vacation

tatilde tateeldeh on holiday, on vacation

tatil köyü kur-yew holiday village

tatil sitesi holiday village

tatmak to taste

tava frying pan

tavan ceiling

tavla backgammon

tavsiye etmek tavsee-yeh to recommend

tayyör ti-ur suit (woman's)

taze tazeh fresh

taze boya wet paint

TC teh jeh Republic of Turkey

TCDD teh jeh deh deh Turkish State Railways

-te teh in

tebrikler! congratulations!

tecrübeli tejrewbelee experienced

tedavi treatment

tedavi etmek to cure

tedricen tedreejen gradually

tehlike tehleekeh danger

tehlike çıkışı chuhkuhshuh emergency exit

tehlikeli dangerous

tehlikeli akıntı dangerous current

tehlikeli eğim steep gradient

tek one, sole, single

tekel government monopoly on alcohol and tobacco

Tekel bayii bī-ee-ee off-licence, liquor store

tekerlek wheel

tekerlekli araba trolley

tekerlekli sandalye sandalyeh wheelchair

tek gidiş bilet geedeesh single ticket, one-way ticket

tekke tekkeh dervish convent; lodge

tek kişilik (bir) oda keesheeleek single room

tek kişilik yatak single bed

teklif etmek to offer; to propose

tekrar again

tekrar gelmek to come back

tekrarlamak to repeat

tek yön yurn one-way street

tek yönlü yol yurnlew one-way street

tel wire

teleferik cable car

telefon phone

telefon etmek to phone, to call

telefon kabini telephone box/cubicle

telefon kartı kartuh phonecard

telefon kodu dialling code

telefon konuşması konooshmasuh phone call; phone conversation

telefon kulübesi koolewbesee phone box

telefonla uyandırma oo-yanduhrma wake-up call

telefon numarası noomarasuh phone number

telefon rehberi reHberee phone book

telesiyej telesee-yeJ chairlift

televizyon television

tembel lazy

temiz clean

temizlemek to clean

temizleme kremi temeezlemeh cleansing lotion

temizleme losyonu cleansing lotion

temizleme sıvısı suhvuhsuh cleaning solution

temizleyici krem temeezlayeejee cleansing lotion

temmuz July

temsilci temseeljee agent; representative

tencere tenjereh pan, saucepan

teneke kutu tenekeh can, tin

tenis kortu tennis court

tepe tepeh hill

tepsi tray

terbiyesiz rude, ill-mannered

tercih etmek to prefer

tercüman terjewman translator; interpreter

tercüme terjewmeh translation

tercüme etmek to translate; to interpret

terlemek to sweat

terlik slipper(s)

termometre termometreh thermometer

termos vacuum flask

tersane tersaneh shipyard

... Tersanesi ... Shipyard

terzi tailor's

tesadüfen tesadewfen by chance

tesisatçı teseesatchuh plumber

teslim delivery

teslim etmek to deliver

teşekkür (ederim) teshekkewr thanks, thank you

   çok teşekkür ederim chok thank you very much

teşekkür etmek to thank

teyp tayp tape, cassette; tape recorder

teyze tayzeh aunt (maternal)

THT teh ha teh domestic air service

THY teh ha yeh Turkish Airlines

tıkaç tuhkach plug (in sink)

tıkalı tuhkaluh blocked

TIR tuhr international road haulage

tıraş fırçası tuhrash fuhrchasuh shaving brush

tıraş köpüğü kurpew-ew shaving foam

tıraş losyonu aftershave

tıraş makinesi electric shaver

tıraş makinesi prizi shaving point

tıraş olmak to shave

tıraş sabunu shaving soap

tırnak tuhrnak fingernail

tırnak cilası jeelasuh nail polish

tırnak fırçası fuhrchasuh nailbrush

tırnak makası makasuh nail clippers

tırnak törpüsü turpewsew nailfile

tiksindirici –reejee disgusting

tip teep sort, type

tipi blizzard
tipik typical
tirbuşon teerbooshon corkscrew
tişört tee-shurt T-shirt
tiyatro theatre
TL teh leh Turkish Lira
tok full; thick
ton vermek tint
top ball
toplam total
toplamak to collect
toplantı toplantuh meeting
toplu iğne ee-neh pin
toprak earth
toprak eşya esh-ya pottery
topuk heel
tornavida screwdriver
Toros Taurus
torun grandchild
toz dust; powder
tozlu dusty
trafik ışıkları uhshuhk-laruh traffic lights
trafik kanunu traffic laws
trafik kazası kazasuh road accident
Trafik Kuralları Highway Code
trafik lambaları –laruh traffic lights
trafik tıkanıklığı tuhkanuhkluh-uh traffic jam
Trakya Thrace
tramplen diving board
tramvay tramvī tram
tren train
trenle trenleh by train

tren bileti train ticket
tren istasyonu railway station
tren yolu geçidi gecheedee level crossing
triko knitwear
troleybüs trolaybews trolleybus
TRT teh reh teh Turkish Radio and Television
Truva Troy
tuğla too-la brick
tuhaf weird
tuhafiyeci toohafee-yejee haberdasher's
tur tour
turist tourist
turistik otel tourist hotel
turizm tourism
turizm bürosu bewrosoo tourist office
turnike toorneekeh turnstile
tur operatörü operaturew tour operator
turuncu tooroonjoo orange (colour)
tutar amount
tutmak to take, to accept; to hold; to hire, to rent; to support
tutuklamak to arrest
tutuşmak tootooshmak to catch fire
tutuşturmak tootooshtoormak to set on fire, to ignite
tuvalet toilet
tuvalet kağıdı ka-uhduh toilet paper
tuvalet temizleyicisi temeezlay-eejeesee bleach
tuzlu salty

tüfek tewfek rifle

tüh! tewH oh no!

tükendi tewkendee sold out

tükenmez (kalem) tewkenmez ballpoint (pen)

tüm tewm whole

tümüyle tewmewyle altogether

Tünel tewnel Istanbul underground/subway

tünel tunnel

tüpgaz tewpgaz camping gas

tür tewr kind, sort, type

   ne tür …? neh what sort of…?

türbe tewrbeh tomb

   … Türbesi tewrbesee Tomb of…

Türk tewrk Turk; Turkish (*adj*)

Türkçe tewrkcheh Turkish (language); in Turkish

Türk Hava Yolları yollaruh Turkish Airlines

Türkiye tewrkee-yeh Turkey

Türkiye Cumhuriyeti tewrkee-yeh joomHooree-yetee Republic of Turkey

Türkiye Cumhuriyeti Devlet Demiryolları Turkish State Railways

Türkiye Radyo Televizyon Kurumu Turkish Radio and Television Corporation

Türkiye'ye giriş tarihi date of entry to Turkey

Türk Lirası leerasuh Turkish Lira

Türk sanat müziği mewzee-ee Turkish classical music

türkü tewrkew folk song

türlü tewrlew sort, kind, variety

tütün tewtewn tobacco

U

-u his; her; its; accusative noun ending

ucuz oojooz cheap, inexpensive

uçak oochak aeroplane

uçakla by air; airmail

uçak postası postasuh airmail

uçak postasıyla postasuh-ila by airmail

uçak seferi flight

uçak zarfı zarfuh airmail envelope

uçmak oochmak to fly

uçuk oochook pale

uğramak: -e uğramak -eh oo-ramak to drop by, to drop in, to stop by

ulus nation

uluslararası oolooslararasuh international

-um my; I am

ummak to hope

umumi general; common; public

umumi hela public convenience

umumi tatil public holiday

umumi telefon payphone

umut hope; expectation

-umuz our

-un of; your

unutmak to forget

unuttum I forget, I've forgotten

-unuz your

unvanı oonvan**uh** title

usta skilful; clever; foreman; master craftsman – often used respectfully/ironically to address master craftsman

ustura razor

utanç ootanch shame

utanç içinde eecheend**eh** ashamed

utandırıcı ootanduhruhj**uh** embarrassing; disgraceful

utangaç ootang**a**ch shy

uyandırmak oo-yanduhrmak to wake

uyanık oo-yan**uh**k awake; vigilant; sharp; smart

uyanmak to wake up

uydurma şeyler oo-idoorma shayl**e**r rubbish

uygun oo-ig**oo**n convenient; appropriate; reasonable; just right

uykuda oo-ik**oo**da asleep

uyku ilacı oo-ik**oo** eelaj**uh** sleeping pill

uykulu oo-ik**oo**l**oo** sleepy

uykusu gelmiş oo-ik**oo**soo gelm**ee**sh sleepy

uykusuzluk oo-ik**oo**sooz**oo**k insomnia

uyku tulumu oo-ik**oo** sleeping bag

uyluk oo-il**oo**k thigh

uyruk oo-ir**oo**k nationality

… uyruğu oo-ir**oo**-**oo** … nationality

uyudunuz: iyi uyudunuz mu? oo-yoodoon**oo**z did you sleep well?

uyumak oo-yoomak to sleep

uyuşturucu oo-yooshtooroojoo drug, narcotics

-uz we are

uzak far

  uzakta in the distance

uzak dur keep out; keep away

uzaklık oozakluhk distance

uzanmak to lie down

uzatma kablosu extension lead

uzun long

uzun boylu tall

uzunluk length

uzun süre sewreh a long time

Ü

-ü -ew accusative noun ending

ücret ewjret cost; pay; fee; wage

ücretler ewjretler charges; wages

ücretsiz giriş admission free

üç ewch three

üçüncü ewchewnjew third

üçüncü kat third floor, (US) fourth floor

ülke ewlkeh country, nation

ülser ewlser ulcer

-üm -ewm my; I am

-ümüz -ewmewz our

-ün -ewn of; your

üniversite ewnee-verseeteh university

ünlü ewnlew famous

-ünüz -ewnewz your

üst ewst top

üst bagaj yeri bagaJ roof rack

üst kat upper floor; upstairs; top floor

üstte ewstteh at the top

üstünde ewstewndeh on; above; over

  ...-in üstünde on top of...

üstünü değiştirmek ewstewnew deh-eeshteermek to get changed

üşümek ewshewmek to feel cold

üşütmek ewsewtmek to catch cold

ütü ewtew iron

ütülemek ewtewlemek to iron

üvey anne ewvay anneh stepmother

üvey baba stepfather

-üz -ewz we are

üzere ewzereh in order to; just about to

üzerinden ewzereenden via; from the top of

üzgün ewzgewn sad

üzgünüm ewzgewnewm I'm sorry

V

vadi valley

vagon carriage, coach

vagon restoran dining car

vajina vaJeena vagina

vakıf vakuhf Islamic religious foundation

vakit time

vali governor

valide sultan valeedeh sultan's mother

valiz suitcase

vana valve

Van Gölü gurlew Lake Van

vantilatör vanteelatur fan

(electrical)

vantilatör kayışı ki-uhsh**uh** fanbelt

vapur steamer; passenger ferry

vapur gezisi cruise

var there is, there are

... var mı? muh is there/are there...?; do you have...?

ne var? neh what is it?; what's the matter?

varış var**uh**sh arrival

varış istasyonu destination

varış saati sa-a**tee** time of arrival

varmak: -e varmak -eh to arrive

varyete var-yet**eh** floor show, variety show

vatan motherland

vay anasını! vī anasuhn**uh** I'll be damned!

vay canına! vī jan**uh**na I'll be damned!

vazo vase

ve veh and

vejetaryen ve**J**etar-y**en** vegetarian

veresiye verilmez no credit allowed

vergi tax

vermek to give

vestiyer cloakroom

veteriner vet

veya vay-a or

vezne vezn**eh** cash desk, till; cashier

veznedar cashier

vida screw

video (aleti) video recorder

video kamera camcorder

vilayet veelí-**et** province

... Vilayeti Province of...

vilayet konağı kona-**uh** provincial headquarters building

viraj veera**J** bend

vites gears

vites kolu gear lever

vites kutusu gearbox

vitrin shop window

vitrinde veetreend**eh** in the window

vize vee**z**eh visa

vizör veez**u**r viewfinder

voltaj volta**J** voltage

vurmak to knock; to hit; to shoot

vurunuz knock

vücut vew**j**oot body

Y

ya or

ya! oh!; really?

-ya to

-'ya to

yabanarısı yaba**n**aruhsuh wasp

yabancı yabanj**uh** foreign; foreigner; stranger

yabancı dil kılavuzu kuhlavooz**oo** phrasebook

yabani wild

yafta placard; label; poster

yağ ya fat; oil

yağlı ya-l**uh** greasy

yağlı güreş gewr**e**sh Turkish

wrestling

yağmak ya-mak to rain

yağmur ya-moor rain

  yağmurda in the rain

  yağmur yağıyor ya-uh-yor
it's raining

yağmurluk ya-moorlook raincoat

yağ seviyesi oil level

Yahudi Jew; Jewish

yaka collar

yakalamak to catch; to arrest

yakın yakuhn near

  ...-e yakın -eh near to...

  en yakın... the nearest...

yakında yakuhnda soon; nearby;
recently

yakınında yakuhnuhnda near

yakışıklı yakuh-shuhkluh
handsome

yakıt deposu yakuht tank

yaklaşık yaklashuhk about,
approximately

yaklaşmak: -e yaklaşmak -eh
yaklashmak to approach

yakmak to burn

yalanlamak to deny

yalan söylemek suh-ilemek to
lie, to tell a lie

yalı yaluh waterside residence

yalnız yalnuhz just, only; alone

  yalnız biraz just a little

  yalnız burada just here

  yalnız başıma bashuhma by
myself

  yalnız başına bashuhna
by yourself

yalnız gidiş geedeesh single

journey

yan side

yanak cheek

yangın yanguhn fire

  yangın var! fire!

yangın alarmı alarmuh fire alarm

yangın çıkışı chuhkuhshuh
emergency exit; fire exit

yangın merdiveni fire escape

yangın söndürme cihazı
surndewrmeh jeehazuh
fire extinguisher

yanık yanuhk (switched) on; burn

yanında yanuhnda beside

yanıt yanuht answer

yanıtlamak yanuhtlamak
to answer

yanıyor yanuh-yor it's on fire

yani that is to say

yankesici yankeseejee pickpocket

yanlış yanluhsh wrong; mistake

yanlış anlama
misunderstanding

yanlış numara wrong number

yanmak to burn

yanmış yanmuhsh burnt

yapı yapuh building

yapma artificial

  yapma! don't!

  yapma be!? beh really?

yapmak to do; to make

yaprak leaf

yar cliff

yara wound

yaralı yaraluh injured

yararlı yararluh useful; helpful

yardım yard**uh**m help
yardım etmek to help
yarı yar**uh** half
yarı fiyat half-price
yarım yar**uh**m half
   yarım düzine dewzeen**eh** half a
   dozen
   yarım saat sa-at half an hour
yarım pansiyon half board
yarım tarife tareef**eh** half fare
yarın yar**uh**n tomorrow
   yarın sabah saba**H** tomorrow
   morning
   yarın görüşürüz
   gurewshewr**ew**z see you
   tomorrow
yarış yar**uh**sh race (competition)
yasa law
yasak forbidden
yasak bölge restricted zone
yasaktır not allowed
yastık yast**uh**k pillow; cushion
yastık kılıfı kuhluh**fuh** pillow
   case
yaş yash age
yaşamak yashama**k** to live
yaşlı yashl**uh** old
yaşlılar yashl**uh**la**r** old people
yat yacht
yatak bed
yatakhane yatakhan**eh** dormitory
yataklı vagon yatakl**uh**
   sleeping car
yatak odası odas**uh** bedroom
yatak takımı takuhm**uh** bed linen
yatmak to lie down; to go to bed
yavaş yav**a**sh slow; quiet

yavaş! slow down!
çok yavaş chok very slowly
yavaşça yav**a**sh-cha slowly
yavaş git go slow
yavaş vasıta şeridi crawler lane
yay y**ī** spring
ya ... ya ... either ... or ...
yaya y**ī**-a pedestrian; on foot
yaya geçidi gechede**e**
   pedestrian crossing
yaya giremez no entry for
   pedestrians
yayalar pedestrians
yayalara mahsus bölge y**ī**-alara
   – burlg**eh** pedestrian precinct
yayan y**ī**-an on foot
yaz summer
yazın yaz**uh**n in the summer
yazık yaz**uh**k pity; it's a pity
   ne yazık! neh what a shame!
yazı kâğıdı yaz**uh** ka-uhdu**h**
   writing paper
yazı makinesi typewriter
yazmak to write
-ye -yeh to
-'ye to
yedek spare; reserve; standby
yedek depo spare tank
yedek lastik spare tyre
yedek parça parch**a** spare part
yedi seven
yedinci yede**e**njee seventh
yeğen yeh-en nephew; niece
yelek waistcoat
yelken sail
yelkencilik yelkenjeele**e**k sailing

yelkenli sailing boat

yelkenli sörf surf windsurfing; sailboard

yelkenliyle gezmek yelkenlee-ileh to sail

yelpaze yelpazeh fan (handheld)

yemek to eat; meal; dish; food

yemeklerden önce urnjeh before meals

yemeklerden sonra after meals

yemekli vagon buffet car, restaurant car

yemek salonu dining room

yemek takımları takuhmlaruh crockery

yemek tarifi recipe

yen sleeve

yenge yengeh sister-in-law (brother's wife); uncle's wife

yeni new

Yeni Yıl yuhl New Year

Yeni Yılınız Kutlu Olsun! yuhluhnuhz Happy New Year!

Yeni Zelanda New Zealand

Yeni Zelandalı zelandaluh New Zealander

yepyeni brand new

yer place; seat; ground; floor

yerde yerdeh on the floor; on the ground

yeraltı şehri shehree underground city

yer ayırtmak i-uhrtmak to book, to reserve

yerel local

yerel konuşma konooshma local call

yerfıstığı yerfuhstuh-**uh** peanuts

yerine yereeneh instead of

yerleşmek yerleshmek to check in; to settle

yesaltı mezarı yesaltuh mezaruh catacomb

yeşil yesheel green

yeşil kart yesheel green card

yeter enough, sufficient

bu kadar yeter that's enough

yeterince yetereenjeh enough; sufficiently

yetişkin yeteesh-keen adult

yetişkinler yeteeshkeenler adults

yetmez insufficient

yetmiş yetmeesh seventy

-yı -yuh accusative noun ending

yıkamak yuhkamak to wash

yıkama ve mizanpli yuhkama veh wash and set

yıkanmak yuhkanmak to have a wash, to get washed

yıl yuhl year

yılan yuhlan snake

Yılbaşı (Gecesi) yuhlbashuh (gejesee) New Year's Eve

yıldırım telgraf yuhlduhruhm express telegram

yıldız yuhlduhz star

yıldönümü yuhldurnewmew anniversary

-yım -yuhm I am

-yız -yuhz we are

-yi accusative noun ending

-yim I am

yine yeeneh (once) again; still

yirmi twenty

yitirmek to lose

yiyecek yee-yejek food

-yiz we are

yoğun bakım ünitesi yo-**oo**n bak**uh**m ewneetes**ee** intensive care unit

yok no; there isn't; there's none (left)

   ... yok there isn't any...

yok be! beh really!

yok canım? jan**uh**m really?

yoksa otherwise

yol road; route; path; way

yolcu yolj**oo** passenger

yolcular passengers

yolculuk yoljool**oo**k trip; journey

yolcu otobüsü yolj**oo** otobews**ew** coach

yolcu salonu passenger lounge

yolda çalışma roadworks

yol hakkı right of way

yol inşaatı roadworks

yol kapalı road closed

yollamak to send

yol ver give way

yorgan duvet; quilt

yorgun tired

yorgunluktan bitmiş beetm**ee**sh very tired, shattered

yosun seaweed

yön yurn direction

yönetici yurneteej**ee** manager

yönetici bayan bī-an manageress

-yu accusative noun ending

yukarı yookar**uh** up

yukarıda yookar**uh**da at the top; above; upstairs; up there

-yum I am

yumuşak yoomoosh**a**k soft

yumuşak kontak lensleri soft lenses

Yunan Greek (adj)

Yunanistan Greece

Yunanca yoon**a**nja Ancient Greek

Yunanlı yoonanl**uh** Greek (man)

Yunanlı kadın kad**uh**n Greek (woman)

yurdumda at home (in my country)

yurt home; homeland; student housing; hostel

yurtdışı yoortduhsh**uh** abroad

yurt dışında duh-sh**uh**nda abroad

yurtdışı posta ücretleri yoortduhsh**uh** – ewjretler**ee** overseas postage rates

yurtiçi yoorteech**ee** inland

yurtiçi posta ücretleri ewjretler**ee** inland postal rates

yutmak to swallow

yuvarlak round

-yuz we are

-yü -yew accusative noun ending

yüksek yewks**e**k tall, high

yükseklik yewksekl**ee**k height

yüksek sesle sesl**e**h loud

yüksek tansiyon high blood pressure

-yüm -yewm I am

yün yewn wool

yünlü yewnl**e**w woollen

yürümek yewrewm**e**k to walk

yürüyüş yewrew-ye**w**sh walk; walking

   yürüyüşe çıkmak yewrew-yewsh**eh** chuhm**a**k to go for a walk

yüz yewz face; surface; hundred

-yüz -yewz we are

yüzde yewzd**eh** per cent

   yüzde yüz 100 per cent

yüz kremi cold cream

yüz losyonu toner

yüzme yewzm**eh** swimming

   yüzmeye gitmek yewzmay**eh** to go swimming

yüzme havuzu swimming pool

yüzmek yewzm**e**k to swim

yüzmek yasaktır no swimming

yüz numara toilet

yüzük yewz**ew**k ring

yüzyıl yewz-y**uh**l century

Z

zam increase

zaman time; when

   zaman? when?

   o zaman then, at that time

   zaman zaman from time to time

zamk glue

zarar damage

zararı yok zarar**uh** never mind

zarar vermek to damage

zarf envelope

zarif elegant

zaruri essential, necessary

zaten anyway

zatürree zatewrr**eh** pneumonia

zaviye zavee-y**eh** lodge for dervishes

zayıf zi-**uh**f slim; thin; weak

zehir poison

zehirli poisonous

zeki intelligent

zemin kat ground floor, (US) first floor

zengin rich

zevkli enjoyable; pleasant; amusing

zil bell

zincir zeenj**ee**r chain

ziyan loss; damage; harm

ziyaret visit

ziyaret etmek to visit

zor hard, difficult

zorluk difficulty

zurna reed instrument like an oboe

zücaciye zewjajee-y**eh** glassware

MENU READER

Food

Essential terms

appetizers meze mez**eh**

cup fincan feenjan

dessert tatlı tatl**uh**

fork çatal chatal

glass (tumbler) bard**a**k
(wine glass) kad**eh**

knife bıçak buhch**a**k

meat dishes et yemekler**i**

menu yem**e**k listes**i**

pepper bib**e**r

plate tab**a**k

salad salat**a**

salt tuz

set menu tabldot tabld**o**t

soup çorba chorb**a**

spoon kaşık kash**uh**k

starter (food) ordövr ord**u**rvr,
meze mez**eh**

table mas**a**

another... başka bir... bashk**a**

excuse me! (to call waiter/
waitress) bak**a**r mısınız!
muhsuhn**uh**z

could I have the bill, please?
hes**a**p, lütfen l**e**wtfen

A–Z

acı biber ajuh hot chillies

Adana kebabı kebabuh spicy meatballs

ahtapot aнtapot octopus

ahtapot salatası salatasuh octopus salad

ahududu aнoodoodoo raspberries

akıtma akuhtma pancake

akşam yemeği aksham yemeh-ee evening meal

alabalık alabaluhk trout

ananas pineapple

ançüez anchew-ez anchovies

armut pear

Arnavut ciğeri jee-eree spicy fried liver with onions

aşure ashooreh 'Noah's pudding' – a dessert made from wheat grains, nuts and dried fruit

av eti game

ayşekadın fasulyesi ishekaduhn French beans

ayva iva quince

ayva laabı la-abuh quince jelly

ayva reçeli rechelee quince jam

az pişmiş peeshmeesh rare; underdone

badem almond(s)

badem kurabiyesi macaroons; giant almond biscuits/cookies

badempare –pareh almond cakes in syrup

badem tatlısı tatluhsuh almond cakes

baharat spice

baharatlı baharatluh spicy

bakla broad beans

baklava pastry filled with nuts and syrup

bal honey

balık baluhk fish

balık buğulaması boo-oolamasuh fish baked with tomatoes

balık çorbası chorbasuh fish and lemon soup

balık köftesi kurftesee fish balls

balık pane paneh fish coated in breadcrumbs and fried

balık plaki fish baked with potatoes, carrots, celery and onions

bamya okra, ladies' fingers

barbunya red mullet; a type of red bean

barbunya pilakisi beans cooked in olive oil and served hot or cold

barbunya tava fried red mullet

bazlama flat bread cooked on a hotplate

beyaz peynir bayaz payneer white sheep's cheese, similar to Greek feta

beyaz peynirli makarna noodles with sheep's cheese

beyin salatası bayeen salatasuh brain salad

beyin tava brain slices in batter

beykın baykuhn bacon

bezelye bezelyeh peas

bıldırcın ızgara buhlduhrjuhn uhzgara grilled quail

bıldırcın yahni quail stew with onions

biber pepper(s), capsicum(s)

biber dolması dolmasuh stuffed green peppers/capsicums

biftek steak

bir buçuk boochook a portion and a half

bisküvi beeskew-vee biscuits, cookies

bonfile bonfeeleh fillet steak

böbrek burbrek kidneys

böbrek ızgara uhzgara grilled kidneys

böbrek sote soteh sautéed kidneys

böğürtlen bur-ewrtlen blackberries

börek bur-rek layered pastry with cheese, meat or spinach filling

börülce burewljeh black-eyed beans

Brüksel lahanası brewksel laHanasuh Brussels sprouts

buğulama boo-oolama steamed; poached

bulgur bulgur wheat, cracked wheat

bulgur pilavı peelavuh bulgur wheat cooked with tomatoes

Bursa kebabı kebabuh grilled lamb kebab on pitta bread with tomato sauce and yoghurt

bülbül yuvası bewlbewl yoovasuh dessert with nuts and syrup

cacık jajuhk cucumber, garlic and yoghurt dip

caneriği janeree-ee greengage

ceviz jeveez walnuts

cezeriye jezeree-yeh carrot, honey and nut bar

ciğer jee-er liver

ciğer sarması sarmasuh minced liver wrapped in lamb's fat

ciğer tava fried liver

çam fıstığı cham fuhstuh-uh pine nuts

çavdar ekmeği chavdar ekmeh-ee rye bread

çerez cherez pumpkin seeds, chickpeas, almonds etc served in bars

Çerkez peyniri cherkez payneeree cheese similar to Edam

Çerkez tavuğu tavoo-oo cold chicken in walnut sauce with garlic

çeşni veren otlar cheshnee herbs

çevirme cheveermeh spit-roasted

çılbır chuhlbuhr poached eggs with yoghurt

çift porsiyon cheeft double portion

çiğ köfte chee kurfteh raw meatballs made from minced meat, bulgur wheat and chilli powder

çikolata cheekolata chocolate

çikolatalı cheekolataluh with chocolate

çikolatalı dondurma chocolate ice cream

çikolatalı pasta chocolate cake

çilek cheelek strawberry

çilekli dondurma cheeleklee strawberry ice cream

çilek reçeli rechelee strawberry jam

çips cheeps crisps, (US) potato chips

çipura cheepoora gilt-headed bream

çiroz cheeroz salted dried mackerel

çoban salatası choban salatasuh mixed tomatoes, peppers/capsicums, cucumbers and onion salad

çocuk porsiyonu chojook children's portion

çorba chorba soup

çöp kebabı churp kebabuh small pieces of lamb or offal grilled on wooden skewers

çörek chur-rek sweet or savoury bun

çulluk choollook woodcock

dana eti veal

dana rozbif roast veal

deniz ürünleri ewrewnleree seafood

dereotu dereh-otoo dill

dil tongue

dil balığı baluh-uh sole

dilber dudağı dooda-uh sweet pastry with nut filling

dil peyniri payneeree cheese similar to mozzarella

dolma stuffed vegetables

domates tomato(es)

domatesli with tomatoes

domatesli pilav rice cooked with tomatoes

domatesli pirinç çorbası peereench chorbasuh rice and tomato soup

domates salatası salatasuh tomato salad

domates salçalı patlıcan kızartması salchaluh patluhjan kuhzartmasuh fried aubergines/eggplants with tomato and garlic sauce

domates salçası salchasuh tomato purée

domuz eti pork

dondurma ice cream

döner kebap durner lamb grilled on a spit and served in thin slices, usually served with rice and salad

dövme dondurma durvmeh special type of sticky ice cream

dut doot mulberries

düğün çorbası dew-ewn chorbasuh 'wedding soup' made from meat stock, yoghurt and egg

ekmek bread

ekmek kadayıfı kadϊ-uhfuh sweet pastry

ekşi ekshee sour

elma apple(s)

elmalı tart elmaluh apple pie

elma tatlısı tatluhsuh dessert made with apples

enginar engeenar artichoke(s)

erik plum(s)

> **Travel tip** During the hot summer months in particular, serious food poisoning is a possibility – even in the biggest cities and resorts. In restaurants, avoid dishes that look as if they have been standing around and make sure meat and fish are well grilled. Don't, whatever you do, eat stuffed mussels in summer.

erişte ereeshteh homemade noodles

et meat

etli with meat

etli ayşekadın īshehkaduhn meat with green beans

etli bezelye bezelyeh pea and meat stew

etli biber dolması dolmasuh peppers/capsicums stuffed with rice and meat

etli börek bur-rek meat pie

etli bulgur pilavı peelavuh bulgur wheat with meat

etli domates dolması dolmasuh tomatoes stuffed with meat and rice

etli kabak dolması marrows stuffed with meat and rice

etli kapuska cabbage and meat stew

etli kuru fasulye fasoolyeh lamb and haricot beans in tomato sauce

etli lahana dolması lahana dolmasuh cabbage leaves stuffed with meat and rice

etli nohut chickpea and meat stew

etli taze fasulye tazeh fasoolyeh stew of meat, runner beans, tomatoes and onions

etli yaprak dolması dolmasuh vine leaves stuffed with rice and meat

et sote soteh sautéed meat

et suyu meat stock

ezme ezmeh purée

ezo gelin çorbası chorbasuh lentil and rice soup

fasulye fasoolyeh haricot beans

fasulye pilaki(si) haricot beans cooked in olive oil

fasulye piyazı pee-yazuh haricot bean and onion salad

fava broad bean purée

fındık fuhnduhk nuts; hazelnuts

fındık fıstık fuhstuhk nuts

fırın fuhruhn baked; oven-roasted

fırında fuhruhnda baked; oven-roasted

fırın sütlaç sewtlach baked rice pudding

fıstık fuhstuhk peanuts; pine nuts

fıstıklı fuhstuhkluh with pistachio nuts

fıstıklı dondurma fuhstuhkluh pistachio ice cream

fıstıklı muhallebi rice flour and roewater pudding with pistachio nuts

fileto fillet

füme fewmeh smoked

garnitür salata garneetewr
side salad

gözleme gurzlemeh crêpe-like
bread with various toppings;
pancake

greyfrut grapefruit

güllaç gewllach rice wafers filled
with nuts, cooked in rose-
flavoured milky syrup

gümüş balığı gew-mewsh baluh-
uh silverfish

güveç gew-vech meat and
vegetable casserole

güvercin gew-verjeen pigeon

hamsi anchovy

hanım parmağı hanuhm parma-
uh 'Lady's Fingers' – finger-
shaped pastry sticks in syrup

hardal mustard

has ekmek white bread

haşlama hashlama boiled; stewed

haşlanmış yumurta
hashlanmuhsh boiled egg

havuç havooch carrot(s)

havuç salatası salatasuh grated
carrot salad

havyar caviar

haydari hidaree thick garlic dip
with parsley or spinach

hazır yemek hazuhr ready-to-
eat food

helva baked flour, butter, sugar
and flavoured water with
various fillings like tahini paste

hesap bill, (US) check

hıyar huh-yar cucumber

hindi turkey

hindiba wild chicory

hindi dolması dolmasuh stuffed
turkey

hindistan cevizi jeveezee
coconut

hoşaf hoshaf stewed fruit

höşmerim hurshmereem
cheese helva

hurma dates

hünkar beğendi hewnkar beh-
endee 'Sultan's Delight' – lamb
served with aubergine/eggplant
purée

ıspanak uhspanak spinach

ıspanaklı börek uhspanakluh bur-
rek pastry filled with spinach

ıspanaklı yumurta eggs with
spinach

ıstakoz uhstakoz lobster; crayfish

ızgara uhzgara grilled

ızgara balık baluhk grilled fish

ızgarada grilled

ızgara köfte kurfteh grilled meatballs

… ızgarası uhzgarasuh grilled…

ızgara tavuk uhzgara grilled chicken

ızgara yemek meat dishes grilled to order

iç eech filling

içecek eechejek beverage

içli köfte eechlee kurfteh meatballs stuffed with bulgur wheat

iç pilav eech rice with currants, pine nuts and onions

imam bayıldı bī-uhlduh 'Imam Swoons' – aubergine/ eggplant with tomatoes and onions, cooked with olive oil and eaten cold

incir eenjeer figs

irmik helvası helvasuh semolina helva – sweet made from semolina, nuts, butter and sugar

islim kebabı kebabuh steamed kebab

istavrit horse mackerel

istiridye eesteereed-yeh oyster(s)

işkembe çorbası eeshkembeh chorbasuh tripe soup

İskender kebabı eeshkender kebabuh döner kebab on pitta bread with tomato sauce and yoghurt

iyi pişmiş peeshmeesh well-done; well-cooked

jambon Jambon ham

jelatin Jelateen gelatin

kabak courgette, zucchini; pumpkin; marrow

kabak dolması dolmasuh stuffed courgettes/zucchini

kabak kızartması kuhzartmasuh fried marrows

kabak reçeli rechelee marrow jam

kabak tatlısı tatluhsuh pumpkin with syrup and walnuts

kabuklu deniz ürünleri ewrewnleree shellfish

kadayıf kada-yuhf shredded wheat-type dessert in syrup

kadın budu köfte kaduhn – kurfteh 'Lady's Thighs' – meat and rice croquettes

kadın göbeği gurbeh-ee 'Lady's Navel' – a ring-shaped pastry with syrup

kağıt kebabı ka-uht kebabuh lamb and vegetables baked in paper

kağıtta barbunya ka-uhtta red mullet baked in paper

kağıtta pişmiş peeshmeesh baked in paper

kahvaltı kahvaltuh breakfast

kalamar squid

kalamar tava fried squid

kalkan turbot

kara biber black pepper

karadut black mulberries

kara ekmek brown bread

karagöz karagurz black bream

kara turp horseradish

kara zeytin zayteen black olives

karışık karuhshuhk mixed

karışık dondurma karuhshuhk
mixed ice cream

karışık ızgara uhzgara
mixed grill

karışık salata mixed salad

karides prawns

karides güveç gewvech
prawn stew

karides kokteyl koktayl
prawn cocktail

karides tava prawns in batter

karides tavası tavasuh
prawns in batter

karnabahar cauliflower

karnabahar tavası tavasuh
fried cauliflower

karnıyarık karnuh-yaruhk split
aubergine/eggplant with
meat filling

karper peyniri payneeree
processed cheese,
cheese spread

karpuz water melon

kaşar (peyniri) kashar payneeree
mild yellow cheese

kaşar peynirli makarna
noodles with kaşar

kavun honeydew melon

kavunlu dondurma melon
ice cream

kayısı kī-uhsuh apricot(s)

kayısı reçeli rechelee
apricot jam

kaymak kī-mak clotted cream

kaymaklı kīmakluh with clotted
cream

kaymaklı dondurma dairy ice
cream

kaynamış yumurta kīnamuhsh
boiled egg

kaz goose

kazan dibi pudding with a
caramel base

kebap roast meat, kebab

keçi eti kechee goat's meat

keçi peyniri payneeree
goat's cheese

kefal grey mullet

kefal pilakisi mullet cooked in
olive oil with vegetables

kek cake

keklik partridge

Kemalpaşa kemalpasha syrup-
soaked dumpling

kepekli ekmek bread made
from whole bran

kerevit crayfish

kereviz celery

kestane kestaneh chestnut(s)

kestane şekeri shekeree
marrons glacés, candied
chestnuts

keş kesh dry curd cheese

keşkek keshkek lamb with
bulgur wheat

keşkül keshkewl
almond pudding

ketçap ketchap tomato ketchup

kılıç (balığı) kuhl**uh**ch (bal**uh**-uh)
swordfish

kılıç ızgara uhzgara
grilled swordfish

kılıç şiş sheesh swordfish
on skewers

kırmızı biber kuhrmuhz**uh**
paprika; red pepper, capsicum

kırmızı mercimek çorbası
merjeem**e**k chorbas**uh** red lentil
soup

kırmızı turp radish

kısır kuhs**uh**r bulgur wheat salad
with spring onions, green
pepper/capsicum and tomatoes

kış türlüsü kuhsh tewrlews**ew**
stewed winter vegetables

kıvırcık salata kuhvuhrj**uh**k
lettuce

kıyma kuh-im**a** minced meat

kıymalı kuh-imal**uh**
with minced meat

kıymalı bamya okra
with minced meat

kıymalı ıspanak uhspanak
spinach with minced meat

kıymalı karnabahar cauliflower
with minced meat

kıymalı makarna noodles with
minced meat

kıymalı mercimek merjeem**e**k
minced meat and lentils

kıymalı pide peed**eh** flat bread
with minced meat topping

kıymalı yumurta eggs with
minced meat

kızarmış kuhzarm**uh**sh fried;
toasted; grilled

kızarmış ekmek kuhzarm**uh**sh
toast

kızartma kuhzartma fried; broiled

kiraz cherries

kiremitte balık keeremeett**eh**
bal**uh**k fish baked on a tile

koç yumurtası koch yoomoortasuh ram's testicles

kokoreç kokorech lamb's intestines grilled on a spit

kolyoz chub mackerel

komposto fruit compote

koyun (eti) mutton

köfte kurfteh meat balls or patties

köpek balığı kurpek baluh-**uh** shark

krema cream

kremalı mantar kremaluh mushrooms with cream

kremalı pasta cream cake

krem karamel crème caramel

krem şantiye shantee-yeh whipped cream

krik krak cracker

kupes type of sea bream

kurabiye koorabee-yeh cake with almonds or nuts

kuru dried

kuru fasulye fasoolyeh haricot beans in tomato sauce

kuru köfte kurfteh fried meatballs

kuru üzüm ewzewm raisins

kuru yemiş yemeesh dried fruit and nuts

kuskus pilavı peelavuh couscous – semolina grains with a meat stew

kuşbaşı et koosh-bashuh small pieces of meat

kuşkonmaz kooshkonmaz asparagus

kuzu (eti) lamb

kuzu fırında fuhruhnda roast leg of lamb

kuzu kapama lamb stew with lettuce and carrots

kuzu pirzolası peerzolasuh lamb chops

külbastı grilled cutlet

kümes hayvanları kewmes hïvanlaruh poultry

lahana laнana cabbage

lahana dolması dolmasuh stuffed cabbage leaves

lahana turşusu toorshoosoo pickled cabbage

lahmacun laнmajoon kind of pizza with spicy meat topping

lakerda pickled tuna fish

leblebi roasted chickpeas

levrek sea bass

limon lemon

limonlu dondurma lemon ice cream

lokum Turkish Delight

lop yumurta hard-boiled egg

lüfer lewfer bluefish

makarna macaroni; noodles; pasta

mama baby food

mandalina tangerine

mantar mushroom(s)

mantarlı omlet mantarluh mushroom omelette

mantı mantuh similar to ravioli

Maraş dondurması marash dondurmasuh type of ice cream

margarin margarine
marmelat jam
marul cos lettuce
maydanoz midanoz parsley
mayonez mī-onez mayonnaise
mayonezli balık baluhk fish with
mayonnaise
menemen omelette with
tomatoes and peppers/
capsicums
mercan merjan bream
mercimek merjeemek lentils
mercimek çorbası chorbasuh
lentil soup
mersin balığı baluh-uh sturgeon
mevsim salatası salatasuh
seasonal salad
meyve mayveh fruit
meyveli pay mayvelee pī
fruit pie
meze mezeh hors d'œuvres,
appetizers

> **Travel tip** At restaurants
> without menus, ascertain
> prices beforehand and review
> bills carefully when finished.
> Waiting staff are adept at
> bringing you small items and
> side dishes (pickles, garlic
> bread, mini-meze, bottled
> water, etc.) that you haven't
> specifically ordered, but for
> which you will be charged.

mezgit whitebait
mısır muhsuhr corn
midye meed-yeh mussels
midye dolması dolmasuh stuffed
mussels

midyeli pilav rice with mussels
midye pilakisi mussels cooked
in oil with vegetables
midye tava/tavası tavasuh
deep-fried mussels
misket limonu lime
muhallebi pudding made from
rice flour and rosewater
musakka moussaka
muska böreği bur-reh-ee
triangular pastries filled with
cheese and parsley
Mustafakemalpaşa –pasha
syrup-soaked dumpling
muz banana
mücver mewjver vegetable
patties

nane naneh mint
nar pomegranate
nemse böreği nemseh bur-reh-ee
meat pie made with puff pastry
nohut chickpeas
nohutlu paça pacha lamb's
trotters with chickpeas
nohutlu yahni lamb stew
with chickpeas

omlet omelette
ordövr ordurvr starter, hors
d'œuvre
orfoz giant grouper
orman kebabı kebabuh veal or
lamb, fried then cooked with
vegetables
orta pişmiş peeshmeesh
medium-rare

otlu peynir payneer herb-flavoured cheese from around Lake Van

öğle yemeği urleh yemeh-ee lunch

ördek urdek duck

paça pacha lamb's trotters

paça çorbası chorbasuh lamb's trotter soup

palamut tunny fish

pancar panjar beetroot

pancar turşusu toorshoosoo pickled beetroot

pandispanya sponge cake

pane paneh coated in breadcrumbs and fried

papaz eriği eree-ee green plum

parça parcha piece, slice

paskalya çöreği chureh-ee 'Easter bread' – slightly sweet plait-shaped bread

pasta cake

pastırma pastuhrma beef cured with cumin and garlic

pastırmalı yumurta pastuhrmaluh fried eggs with 'pastırma'

patates potato(es)

patates kızartması kuhzartmasuh chips, French fries

patates köftesi kurftesee potato and cheese balls

patatesli with potatoes

patates püresi pewresee mashed potatoes

patates salatası salatasuh potato salad

patlıcan patluhjan aubergine(s), eggplant(s)

patlıcan dolma turşusu toorshoosoo pickled stuffed aubergines/eggplants

patlıcan ezmesi aubergine/eggplant pâté

patlıcan kebabı kebabuh pieces of meat wrapped in aubergine/eggplant and roasted or baked

patlıcan kızartması kuhzartmasuh fried aubergines/eggplants with garlic sauce

patlıcanlı pilav patluhjanluh rice with aubergines/eggplants

patlıcan salatası salatasuh aubergine/eggplant purée

pavurya crab

pestil pressed dried fruit

peynir payneer cheese

peynirli with cheese

peynirli omlet cheese omelette

peynirli pide peedeh flat bread with cheese topping

peynirli tepsi böreği bureh-ee cheese pie

peynir tatlısı tatluhsuh small cheesecakes in syrup

pırasa puhrasa leek(s)

pide peedeh leavened flat bread

pilaki haricot bean vinaigrette

pilav cooked rice

pilavlı tavuk peelavluh chicken and rice

pil füme fewmeh smoked tongue

piliç peel**ee**ch young chicken

piliç ızgara(sı) uhzgara(suh) grilled chicken

pirinç peer**ee**nch rice (uncooked)

pirzola chop

pisi plaice

pişkin peeshk**ee**n well-cooked, well-done

pişmemiş peeshmemeesh underdone; not cooked

poğaça po-**a**cha pastries filled with meat or cheese

portakal orange(s)

portakallı ördek portakall**uh** urdek duck with orange

portakal reçeli rechelee marmalade, orange jam

puf böreği bur-r**eh**-ee cheese or meat pasties

püre pewr**eh** purée

rafadan (yumurta) soft-boiled egg

reçel rech**e**l jam

revani sweet semolina pastry

roka rocket

rosto roasted

rozbif roast beef

rus salatası sal**a**tasuh Russian salad – potatoes, peas, salami and gherkins with mayonnaise

saç kavurma sach Anatolian speciality made from meat, vegetables, spices and oil, fried in a Turkish wok

sade omlet sa-d**eh** plain omelette

sade pilav plain rice pilav

sahanda yumurta fried eggs

salam salami

salata salad

salatalık salatal**uh**k cucumber

salata sosu salad dressing

salça sal**c**ha tomato sauce or paste

salçalı salchal**uh** with tomato sauce

salçalı köfte kurft**eh** meatballs in tomato sauce

salyongoz snails

sandviç sandv**ee**ch sandwich

sandviç ekmeği ekmeh-**ee** roll(s)

sap kerevizi celery

saray lokması sar**ī** lokmas**uh** fried batter in syrup

sardalye sardal-yeh sardines

sarıgöz saruhg**u**rz black bream

sarığıburma saruh-**uh**-boorma 'Twisted Turban' – turban-shaped baklava

sarmısak sarmuhsak garlic

sazan carp

sazan güveç gewv**e**ch carp casserole

sazan kiremit carp baked on a tile

sebze sebz**eh** vegetables

sebze çorbası chorbas**uh** vegetable soup

semizotu purslane – a herb used in salads and stews

semizotu salatası salatasuh
  purslane salad

servis course

servis ücreti service charge

sıcak suhjak hot; warm

sığır (eti) suh-uhr beef

sigara böreği burreh-ee
  cigarette-shaped filo pastry
  filled with cheese and parsley

simit ring-shaped bread covered
  with sesame seeds

sirke seerkeh vinegar

sivribiber long, thin hot or mild
  peppers

siyah zeytin seeyaH zayteen black
  olives

soğan soh-an onion(s)

soğan dolması dolmasuh stuffed
  onions

soğuk soh-ook cold

soğuk antreler so-ook cold hors
  d'œuvres

soğuk büfe bewfeh cold food

som balığı sohm baluh-uh salmon

somun loaf

sos sauce; gravy; salad dressing

sosis sausage

soslu with sauce

sote soteh sautéed

söğüş et so-ewsh cold meat

söğüş salata salad served
  without dressing

su böreği bur-reh-ee layered
  pastry filled with cheese,
  parsley and dill

sucuk soojook spicy Turkish
  sausage with garlic

sucuklu with sausage

sucuklu pide peedeh flat bread
  with sausage

sumak sumach – herb eaten with
  kebabs

su muhallebisi rice flour
  pudding with rosewater

supanglez chocolate pudding

sülün sewlewn pheasant

süt sewt milk

sütlaç sewtlach rice pudding

sütlü tatlılar sewtlew tatluhlar
  milk puddings

süzme yoğurt sewzmeh yoh-oort
  strained yoghurt

şalgam shalgam turnip

şamfıstığı shamfuhstuh-uh
  pistachio nuts

şam tatlısı sham tatluhsuh dessert
  with syrup

şeftali sheftalee peach(es)

şeftali reçeli rechelee peach
  jam

şehriye sheHree-yeh vermicelli

şehriye çorbası chorbasuh
  vermicelli soup with lemon

şehriyeli with vermicelli

şehriyeli pilav rice with
  vermicelli

şeker sheker sugar; sweets,
  candies

şekerpare shekerpareh small
  cakes with syrup

şinitzel sheeneetzel cutlet, thin
  slice of meat

şiş sheesh cooked on a skewer

şiş kebabı kebabuh small pieces
of lamb grilled on skewers

şiş köfte kurfteh grilled meatballs
on skewers

şöbiyet surbee-yet sweet pastry

şurup shooroop syrup

tabldot set menu

tahin helvası helvasuh sesame
seed paste helva

talaşkebabı talashkebabuh lamb
baked in pastry

tam ekmek wholemeal
bread

tarama roe pâté

tarator nut and garlic sauce

taratorlu karnabahar
cauliflower with nut and garlic
sauce

tarhana çorbası chorbasuh soup
made with dried yoghurt,
tomato and pimento

taskebabı taskebabuh diced lamb
with rice

tatar böreği bur-reh-ee ravioli

tatlı tatluh sweet, dessert

tatlı sucuk soojook fruit, nut and
molasses roll

tava(da) fried

tavşan tavshan rabbit

tavuk chicken

tavuk çorbası chorbasuh chicken
soup

tavuk göğsü gur-sew chicken
breast pudding – creamy
dessert made with rice flour
and finely shredded chicken

tavuk ızgara(sı) uhzgara(suh)
grilled chicken

tavuklu pilav chicken and rice

tavuk söğüş sur-ewsh cold
chicken

tavuk suyu chicken consommé

taze tazeh fresh

taze beyaz peynir bayaz payneer
fresh sheep's cheese

taze soğan soh-an spring
onions

tekir striped mullet

tel kadayıf kadī-uhf shredded
wheat-type dessert with nuts
and syrup

terbiye terbee-yeh egg and lemon
sauce

terbiyeli with egg and lemon
sauce

terbiyeli haşlama hashlama boiled lamb with egg and lemon sauce

terbiyeli köfte kurfteh meatballs with egg and lemon sauce

tere tereh cress

tereyağı tereh-ya-uh butter

ton balığı baluh-uh tuna

torik large tunny fish

tost toast; toasted sandwich

tulumba tatlısı tatluhsuh semolina doughnut in syrup

tulum peyniri payneeree dry, crumbly, parmesan-like cheese made from goat's milk in a goatskin

turna pike

turp radish

turşu toorshoo pickled vegetables

turşu suyu juice from pickled vegetables

turta fruit pie

turunç tooroonch Seville oranges

tuz salt

tuzlama salted; pickled

tükenmez tewkenmez eggs fried with tomatoes and peppers/ capsicums

türlü (sebze) tewrlew (sebzeh) meat and vegetable stew

un flour

un helvası helvasuh helva made from flour, sugar, milk, butter, and sometimes with nuts

Urfa kebabı kebabuh very spicy kebab

uskumru mackerel

uskumru dolması dolmasuh stuffed mackerel

üzüm ewzewm grapes

vanilya vanilla

vanilyalı dondurma vaneel-yaluh vanilla ice cream

vişne veeshneh black cherries, morello cherries

yağ ya oil; fat

yağda yumurta ya-da fried egg

yahni meat stew with onions

yalancı dolma yalanjuh stuffed vine leaves

yaprak dolması dolmasuh stuffed vine leaves

yayın sheatfish

yayla çorbası yīla chorbasuh yoghurt soup

yaz türlüsü tewrlewsew stewed summer vegetables

yemek meal; dish

yemek listesi menu

yengeç yengech crab

yerfıstığı yerfuhstuh-uh peanuts

yeşil biber yesheel green pepper, capsicum

yeşil mercimek çorbası merjeemek chorbasuh green lentil soup

yeşil salata green salad

yeşil zeytin zayteen green olives

yiyecek yee-yejek food

yoğurt yoh-oort yoghurt

yoğurtlu with yoghurt

yoğurtlu kebap kebab with pitta bread and yoghurt

yoğurtlu paça pacha lamb's trotters with yoghurt and garlic

yoğurt tatlısı tatluhsuh yoghurt cake with syrup

yufka filo pastry

yufka ekmek thin sheets of unleavened bread

yumurta egg

yumurtalı yoomoortaluh with egg

yumurtalı pide peedeh flat bread with egg

yürek yewrek heart

zerde zerdeh saffron rice dessert

zeytin zayteen olive(s)

zeytinyağı zayteenya-uh olive oil.

zeytinyağlı zayteenya-luh vegetable dish in olive oil, served cold

zeytinyağlı biber dolması dolmasuh stuffed peppers/capsicums cooked with olive oil

zeytinyağlı enginar artichokes cooked with olive oil

zeytinyağlı kereviz celery cooked with olive oil

zeytinyağlı patlıcan pilavı patluhjan peelavuh rice with aubergines/eggplants cooked in olive oil

zeytinyağlı pırasa puhrasa leeks cooked with olive oil

zeytinyağlı pilaki red haricot beans cooked with olive oil

zeytinyağlı taze bakla tazeh fresh broad beans cooked with olive oil

zeytinyağlı taze fasulye fasoolyeh runner beans cooked with tomatoes and olive oil

zeytinyağlı yaprak dolması dolmasuh vine leaves stuffed with rice, pine nuts and raisins

Drink

Essential terms

beer bira
bottle şişe sheesheh
brandy konyak
coffee kahve kaнveh
cup fincan feenjan
alcoholic drinks içkiler
   eechkeeleer
gin cin jeen
glass (tumbler) bardak
   (wine glass) kadeh
milk süt sewt
mineral water maden suyu
red wine kırmızı şarap
   kuhrmuhzuh sharap
soda (water) maden sodası
   sodasuh

soft drinks meşrubat meshroobat
sugar şeker sheker
tea çay chï
tonic (water) tonik
vodka votka
water su
whisky viski
white wine beyaz şarap bayaz
   sharap
wine şarap
wine list şarap listesi

another... başka bir... bashka
a glass of tea bir bardak çay
a gin and tonic bir cintonik
   jeentoneek

A–Z

acıbadem likörü ajuhbadem leekur**ew** almond liqueur

açık achu**h**k weak

ada çayı chī-**uh** type of sage infusion

alkol alcohol

alkollü alkoll**ew** alcoholic

alkolsüz –**sew**z non-alcoholic

alkolsüz içki eechk**ee** soft drink

ananas suyu pineapple juice

ayran iran yoghurt drink

az şekerli kahve shekerl**ee** ka**h**veh slightly sweetened Turkish coffee

bardak glass

beyaz şarap bayaz shara**p** white wine

bira beer; lager

bitkisel çay chī herbal tea

boza thick fermented grain drink

buz boo**z** ice

buzlu with ice

buzlu kahve ka**h**ve**h** iced coffee

cin jeen gin

cintonik gin and tonic

Çankaya chankī-**a** dry, white wine from Cappadocia

çay chī tea

çok şekerli kahve chok shekerl**ee** ka**h**ve**h** very sweet Turkish coffee

demli steeped

Travel tip Tea is the national drink and an essential social lubricant – you'll most likely be offered some within twenty minutes of arrival. It's prepared in a double-boiler apparatus, decanted into tiny tulip-shaped glasses and diluted with water to taste. Sugar comes as cubes on the side; milk is never added.

domates suyu tomato juice

dömi sek durm**ee** medium-dry

Efes Pilsen type of lager

elma çayı chī-**uh** apple tea

elma suyu apple juice

elma şırası shuhrasu**h** cider

fıçı birası fuhchu**h** beerasu**h** draught beer

fincan feenjan cup

gazlı gazlu**h** fizzy

gazoz fizzy drink

greyfrut suyu grapefruit juice

ıhlamur uh-**H**lam**oo**r lime blossom tea

içecek eechej**ek** beverage

içki eechk**ee** alcoholic drinks

içkiler eechk**ee**le**e**r alcoholic drinks

içkili eechk**ee**le**e** alcoholic drinks served

ithal imported

kafeinsiz kahve kafeh-eenseez kaHveh decaffeinated coffee

kahve kaHveh coffee; coffee shop (usually for men only)

kakao kaka-o hot chocolate; cocoa

kanyak kanyak French brandy

kayısı suyu ka-yuhsuh apricot juice

kırmızı şarap kuhrmuhzuh sharap red wine

konyak brandy

koyu steeped

köpüklü şarap kurpewklew sharap sparkling wine

Lâl dry, rosé wine from Denizli

likör leekur liqueur

limonata still lemon drink

limonlu çay chī lemon tea

maden sodası sodasuh soda (water)

maden suyu mineral water

Marmara type of lager

menba suyu spring water

meşrubat meshroobat soft drinks

meyve suyu mayveh fruit juice

Travel tip Turkish tap water is heavily chlorinated and usually drinkable, though not exactly delectable (some restaurants may serve it chilled and minimally filtered). In İstanbul, however, it is absolutely to be avoided in favour of bottled water.

---

milkşeyk meelkshayk milkshake

Mocca almond liqueur

Narbağ narba white, medium-dry wine from Central Anatolia

neskafe neskafeh general word for any instant coffee

orta şekerli kahve shekerlee kaHveh medium sweet Turkish coffee

papatya çayı chī-uh camomile tea

pembe şarap pembeh sharap rosé

portakal suyu orange juice

porto şarabı sharabuh port

rakı rakuh spirit distilled from grape juice and flavoured with aniseed, similar to Greek ouzo

rom rum

roze rozeh rosé

sade kahve sadeh kaHveh Turkish coffee without sugar

sahlep drink made from sahlep root infused in hot milk and cinnamon

sek dry; straight (no ice)

sek şarap sharap dry wine

sıcak süt suhjak sewt hot milk

su water

suyla soo-ila with water

suyu juice

süt sewt milk

sütlü sewtlew with milk

sütlü kahve kaHveh coffee with milk

süzme kahve sewzmeh filter coffee

şampanya shampanya champagne

şarap sharap wine

şarap listesi wine list

şaraplar wines

şeftali suyu sheftalee peach juice

şeker sheker sugar

şekerli shekerlee with sugar

şerbet sherbet sweetened and iced fruit juice

şeri sheree sherry

şıra shuhra grape juice

şişe sheesheh bottle

tatlı şarap tatluh sharap sweet wine

taze portakal suyu tazeh fresh orange juice

tonik tonic (water)

torba çay chī teabags

Tuborg type of lager

Turasan dry red or white wine from Central Anatolia

Türk kahvesi tewrk kaHvesee Turkish coffee

Venus type of lager

viski whisky, scotch

vişne suyu veeshneh black cherry juice

votka vodka

Yakut dry, red wine

yarım şişe yaruhm sheesheh half-bottle

Yeni Rakı rakuh brand of raki

yerli Turkish brand

Picture credits

All maps and photos © Rough Guides unless otherwise stated.

Photography by: Kate Clow, Terry Richardson, Dominic Whiting/ DK Images (pp. 114, 137, 171, 215); Roger d'Olivere Mapp (front & back cover; pp. 5, 6–7, 16–17, 30, 31, 45, 46–7, 53, 60, 68, 73, 80, 100, 127, 140–1, 150, 160, 180, 191, 201, 210, 219, 222, 224–5, 226, 231, 234, 240, 243); Christopher and Sally Gable/DK Images (p. 90); Tony Souter/DK Images (pp. 20, 43).